Philosophy of Man
at Recreation and Leisure

PETER LANG
New York • Washington, D.C./Baltimore • Bern
Frankfurt am Main • Berlin • Brussels • Vienna • Oxford

Christopher Berry Gray

Philosophy of Man
at Recreation and Leisure

PETER LANG
New York • Washington, D.C./Baltimore • Bern
Frankfurt am Main • Berlin • Brussels • Vienna • Oxford

Library of Congress Cataloging-in-Publication Data
Gray, Christopher B.
Philosophy of man at recreation and leisure / Christopher Berry Gray.
p. cm.
Includes bibliographical references.
1. Leisure. 2. Philosophical anthropology. I. Title.
BJ1498.G68   128—dc22   2006101460
ISBN 978-0-8204-9512-5

Bibliographic information published by **Die Deutsche Bibliothek**.
Die Deutsche Bibliothek lists this publication in the "Deutsche
Nationalbibliografie"; detailed bibliographic data is available
on the Internet at http://dnb.ddb.de/.

Cover design by Lisa Barfield

The paper in this book meets the guidelines for permanence and durability
of the Committee on Production Guidelines for Book Longevity
of the Council of Library Resources.

Printed in Germany

This book is dedicated to my wife Kathleen who, with
our children and grandchildren, has led me to reflect
on the experience of recreation and leisure that
they have opened for me

CONTENTS

PART V. HUMAN SPIRITUALITY

           Notes   227
           Appendix 1. Paideia, Schole, Paidia, Then and Now   237
           Appendix 2. Immortal Philosophy: What does
                       a Philosopher do Forever After?   243

PREFACE

Purpose and Method

In this text we seek for philosophical knowledge of human existence. We identify and test insights into human worth, human nature and the human condition. We conclude to not all that is true of human existence as a matter of fact, but rather to some of what must, cannot and might justifiably be claimed of human existence. We approach this knowledge through studying the activity of humans. Every human activity shows all the features and faculties of its agent, but each commonly recognized sort of activity (e.g., recreation and leisure) makes some features available more forcefully than others. To know human existence and not just the single sort of human activity, we must ask why we come at all to recognize that activity and from what we commonly distinguish it (e.g., work and labor).

INTRODUCTION

When I designed my university's first courses in leisure studies some thirty years ago, it was a foregone conclusion that we were entering a leisure society, characterized by reduction of busyness. Now it is clear that this conclusion has been foregone. Increased business, leaner and fueled by communications, has brought "24/7" work weeks and "freedom 75" work lives to the "9/11" era.[1] Union membership is at a lower ebb than before great-grandfather won the workforce liberties we've now relinquished anew, along with their facilitation of leisure.[2]

Tragic as this is, it does relieve leisure thought from its false dependency upon free time. If leisure is a human reality, it must be found in human being busy or idle, and not in economic fashions. It is the task of this book to suggest how leisure penetrates human being and so can continue to be a blessing.[3] I have tried to do this by associating with a taxonomy of our specially human features some of the leisure topics consistent with each of these dimensions, indeed bound up with them, even if not inferred from them. The inherent incompleteness of these selections is a call for readers to participate by carrying my few starts further into their own humanity.

As I hope the studies here on gender and sexuality show, the prominence of pronouns and nouns gendered masculine is meant to illuminate generic human reality, and not to make it invisible behind one genital part.

· 1 ·

HUMAN BEING

Philosophy

Philosophy is an activity with a history behind it, peculiarly suited to investigating leisure and recreation,[4] for persons have been carrying on an activity with a name akin to "philosophy" for two and a half millennia in both East and West. While they have disagreed what it is, they have agreed that they were doing it. Because we would not know what to look at without taking into account this history and tradition, it has to serve as our commencement; otherwise we might as well use the term to refer to drapery rods.

Among the less disputed statements about philosophy has been that it is an activity, and an activity performed by human beings; it is not an object, not even when in books, nor is it the deed of plants or brutes, gods or spirits. In general, philosophy has been a highly regarded activity, whether as beneficial or as dangerous, with the ups and downs of fashion. It has served to mark men out for contempt or for admiration.

Whether men have to do it or are just capable of doing it, whether all men are able to do it or just some, and which some, where and when, how it is able to be begun and how it is able to be stopped, whether it is done in the course of doing other things or is done all by itself—all these have been disputed. So also has been the question of whether philosophy is a kind of knowing or is an activity of some other sort.

Events current to the time of its practice have been thought important for the most part, but in vastly different ways, whether as mere examples or as making up its substance, as vile rejects from it or as threats to it.

It is also the case that philosophy has been done in pieces. That is, it is an activity with various parts which are done one at a time and which most often are taken as fitting together in some way to make it up. Different portions at different times have been taken as the key activity, while other portions become trivial or even outlawed. Even without some agreement on what sorts of realities populate the universe (ontology), there has been some agreement on how the activity dealing with the existence of realities (known overall as metaphysics) breaks up: into the search for godhead (theodicy, philosophical theology), for manhood (philosophy of man, philosophical psychology, rational psychology or philosophical anthropology, and special philosophies of one or another human activity: philosophy of knowledge, mind or action, of science, social science, biology, logic or mathematics, of history, culture or future, of love, language or communication, of religion, art, literature, law or sexuality, just to sample some of the more frequent titles of books and courses), and for worldliness (cosmology), as well as for the proper ways of acting (logic, ethics, aesthetics), and the history of philosophy added to each as well as sometimes carved off separately.

The sketch gives us the impression that whatever else philosophy has been, it certainly has covered everything. That would not be an incorrect impression. But many other activities lay the same claim from specified stand points: law over the laws covering the use of everything, science over the experience of everything insofar as it is . . . (here fill in the missing word: bodily, living, behaving, social . . .), theology over god over-and-in-all, literature over all in the individual, etc.[5] It appears that if philosophers looked to all, they must have had their standpoint, too; and what is that?

The question is embarrassing to philosophers, for it requires that they make the arrogant rejoinder, "From the standpoint of being," the existence of everything; or, that is to say, the standpoint of having no standpoint at all, or else one penetrating all others, and so beyond and governing them, and thus not comprehensible to or in them. Any inquirer who has not by then left philosophy to cultivate its own cloud might be soothed by the next line: . . . or any standpoint you choose to give, it is up to you. For every standpoint is as equally existent as any other, and its object is also, and thus is just as sure to yield up what being is. The story of the various studious activities is recapitulated by this; for as each of them arose by hurling off from philosophy a limited focus, philosophy now accepts both that focus and the fact of its separation off as really existing and as philosophical bait.

This has distinguished philosophers' standpoints from the ordinary attitude to life, whether found in daily occupations, in artistic endeavor or in scientific enterprise. The natural attitude arises from activities which we find lying there in front of us; people are performing them, there are certain things to be done, so we do them. We do not bring into question the propriety of doing them. As a result, there is fastened onto the world a set of purposes which comes from persons, not from the world; the reverse side of this is that, once people have exercised their purposes and finished their job, the result is looked upon as being merely there in front of us, instead of being seen as filled with human purposefulness and having no meaning but what has been given it. The object is taken to have simply the features ascribed to it; and so when one begins to work at knowing it, he is knowing it with all the baggage of distinctions, based upon theories, which history has placed upon it. Taking then this starting point, one can carry on a fairly straightforward activity, however difficult it is; he can conform himself to the canons of inquiry, performance or creation which he comes upon.

Most persons intuitively know this, especially of activities they are criticizing, although few do so in a reflective manner. So most persons perform activities without it crossing our minds that the activity is not limited; we accept that it is, so we take it up and put it down again and go on to something else. But without the limits being clearly seen, there comes a point in any activity when it threatens to become unlimited and to overrun the whole of experience. Usually this happens with a dashing new insight which, at least for the followers if not for the inventor, seems to sweep away the clutter of disconnected reality and to replace it with a unified view whose cry is "This is all there is!" or, negatively put, "Reality is nothing but . . .." Besides simply the error of this, it cripples human possibilities and puts directive power in the hands of the specialist.

This technocracy (or mythology, dogma, urbanity, craftsmanship, nobility—however the unquestionable is named) is where we begin to do philosophy. The philosopher must look like a fool in all this, for he does not pretend to anyone's cleverness but admires theirs. Nor does he know what he is doing himself: he has no given starting point nor materials peculiar to himself; he has no particular goal to set alongside others'; he has no set of methods for carrying out his activity; he has no shiny new experience to offer, only a return upon the old;

he has no service or comfort for mankind to perform that gives him respect in their eyes nor confidence in his own. "Philosophy is not a hospital," said one tormented soul. Philosophy comes to serve each and all only in making possible the insights of each by puncturing the pretensions of all. The philosopher is driven by the unhealthiness he experiences along with his fellows' drive to be all that exists. He is not whole, but he will not substitute some unholy idol as security for it; his devotion to being makes him stand idle in the swirl of beautiful and self-assured people.[6]

With nowhere to go for a privileged standpoint, the philosopher can only stay where he is, not passively but by turning back upon his spot. This argument is an examination of what seems to be, in order to see whether it permits of itself. Since the problem, however, is that things do not speak for themselves but are spoken for, this "retrorsive" argument is carried on by asking whether what is said of reality describes a reality such that the words should be able to be spoken. Do they make themselves impossible? His argument is circular, and works upon and with whatever experience we have, of any object and of any amount. It can start with any starting point because that point will eventually involve the entirety.

If these positions are correct, then they say that they cannot be defended now, but require waiting upon the conclusions to determine whether you and I are such persons as could do this, could question our way of existing and look to existence as a whole. If it is possible, philosophy is here something self-contained and not a means to anything else, exemplarily so, which will be what we also might suspect that leisure is.

Worldviews for Leisure

Some philosophical efforts have described being in such a way that it would permit play, leisure and recreation, and even demand them. The basic ploys would be to describe the wholeness of being in such a way that either it provides the needed conditions of these activities or else it is itself involved in them.

External Impossibilities

The universe, and the principles of its existence, are free from any constraint upon its operations. Because there is no being outside of itself, outside of the totality of being, by definition, there is nothing to bound it or set limits upon it. Everything is within, nothing is without. Existence can only be limited by its inability to enter or become what is beyond it, nothing; it cannot become nothing because that would have to be conceived as passing into a darkness beyond, but that darkness is not there to be passed into, and so being must continue to exist. Changes of form may be drastic, obliterating everything we might recognize; but this would not be to become nothing. This sole limit, then, is no limit, nothing; and so being is unlimited, free from any constraints upon its activity. Without further ado, we may presume this to be something more akin to leisure and recreation than it would be to any other activities set against these latter.

Internal Impossibilities

This may seem to be enough. However, it is possible to go on to inquire what sort of existence would there have to be for leisure and recreation to be possible. For even if any and all approaches would have to admit the absence of external impossibilities, since it is true by definition, yet there might seem to arise conditions within existence which would make leisure and recreation impossible. The most prominent suggestion is that the internal structure of being might be such that it was imagined as having no free space, nowhere into and out of which being might move in its exercise of play. Even if there is room for movement and change, still on the other hand everything which does move about might be conceived as moving about only under the pulling of some objects and the pushing of others, like the pocket puzzle of numbered squares to be arranged by moving one piece in and another out. Or the mobile realities may not be pushed and pulled, there may be play among the alternatives; but only one alternative may suffice to maintain the mobile being, while all others contribute to its destruction, so that the play is only illusory insofar as beings are intent upon their own continued existence. Or, again, the alternatives may be there in existence absolutely, but the sort of existence we have is one in which domination of one by another is inescapable, and neither the dominant nor the submissive can be at play within a narrowed set of alternatives permitted the dominant by his commanding and the subject by the dominant's commands. Or the absolutely unlimited and the relationally uncommanded alternatives may be such that only involved in some can a person find the contentment needed to give leisure categories any contact with how we usually employ them, whatever may turn out to be the specific content which we give them.

Existence seems to have no free space for movement on the doctrine of the Greek philosopher, Parmenides, and in different ways in the theories of some idealist philosophers, recent and not so recent, of both East and West.[7] Since no one can deny the senses' claim that both change and multiplicity abound, one can recognize that claim as only an illusion and proceed to make it unreal in a time also unreal. In the oriental version, the reality of this compelling illusion is to be dealt with without any seriousness and is to have therapy given to it; the only game to be played here is that of being in its entirety jesting with itself by presenting itself with illusion.

What Parmenides overlooked is that what he says seriously of being as a whole can only be said at all if he acknowledges being in the particular, i.e., individually multiple and changing being. For in order to operate with the categories of negativity and externality upon the whole of being, in denying anything outside and not being, he must be dependent upon the individual beings he denies. These categories are unavailable to someone operating with unique being. Surely Parmenides might refuse as illusion these categories of changing, multiple being; but he does not, using them instead of the unique totality of being. In order for us to know what he says, we must know that it is wrong. The change indispensable for play, leisure and recreation is also undeniable.

The idealist alternative is to grant that there is multiplicity but to refuse change; the multiplicity is confined to an order of unchanging realities, ideas as they are frequently called, which spreads out in advance all the possible turns of the changes. The idea is the pool of possibilities determined in advance, since the individual being's reality consists in a further and further approximation to the idea; there is no real movement among them, for the reality is the idea more and more manifested rather than the approximations to it. So every stage is set, all positions have been mapped out in advance, as well as when they are to be filled. Perhaps the best example of this is Henri Bergson, because he seems otherwise to be so full of the playful spirit, with the unrestricted operation of *élan vital* being self-directive over all changes: life rules time and alone gives it persistence, duration, and life is the universal whose tempestuousness rules the earth. But within it arise no new possibilities. All are given from the start. Because life develops itself, there is no further room for it to go when it has exhausted its possibilities. All the surprises it contains are a function of our ignorance rather than of being. Already they are within life seminally, as seeds are, and in fact as the seed of the female ova which are all present from the beginning of life rather than as the seed of male sperm which is developed as needed.

The key to opening up this perspective lies in the final remark above. Of course, the restrictions here may not be problematic to some views of leisure and recreation; but to others they appear too restrictive. If it is possible so to conceive of existence that new possibilities arise only upon the further development of life forms, then we may go beyond this view. What is requisite is a view of existence upon these lines: each development is not just the switching onto one track of a branching among many tracks laid down in advance of the selection among them by organism. This replacement view would have to establish those possibilities, as well, or in metaphysical terms establish out of itself the matter as well as the form. Whether such a metaphysics is forthcoming depends upon the subsequent investigation; here this is taken as simply the sketch of a possibility.

The same hesitation regards the image of a limited number of spaces, as on the pocket puzzle. If the possibilities are aligned in advance, then there are a limited number of them; one can be realized only by pushing out another, and by being pushed in by a third. The first dimension is not the problem, for under whatever model one approaches leisure and recreation it is true that two contradictory possibilities cannot be realized at the same time. But to insist that this parallels the spatially confined pocket puzzle overlooks how a mover or a motive can bring into place the new possibility. For the pocket puzzle can move only because there is one space on the face left open, whereas the universe has no such openings. The model, then, cannot apply; if there are openings, they have to be part of each of the realities which occupy the space to satiety. The movement of each can be only a movement to not be, relatively. Again, if it is possible to introduce into each existent man the ability to create new possibilities which were not present prior to his action which completes them, then the problem of where the room is for his exercise dissipates.

The self-destructive model for the exercise, and the consequent disintegration, of leisure-like activities, cannot be fully discounted. But the only way the model would present a problem would come from separating the exercise and the disintegration. If there were not a way of exercising such that among its potentialities lay the possibility of destroying those potentialities or the faculties for exercising them, then that would be the true restriction upon leisure-like activities, such that no matter what a man did he could not do it wrong, could not misuse his abilities. Thus would fall any chance of failure, and so any interest in the activity performed. One would be assured of success, of some kind or another, and would thenceforth find it boring; no enthusiasm can be found in anything assured of success. All one need do is start it; from there it carries itself. So only if self-destruction is possible is leisure possible.

Whether the dominating and the submissive elements in the next model are principles of the universe or are social classes, the only threat to leisure would arise if leisure is impossible in a condition of submission, first; or if secondly

leisure is alien to competitiveness and combativeness entirely. Various expla-
nations of leisure would make this so; and so would nearly any popular conception of leisure. However, it will be suggested that under a concept of leisure
enforced by the development of this study, that conclusion does not follow.

The final possibility, of activities not necessary themselves but only necessary for happiness, changes gears from the possibility at all to the possibility
for me. In respect of these, then we become the whole of being; for the problem
of activities in a worldview of existence becomes a problem of activities only
in each one's own existence. The presumption underlying the problem is that
human existence is achieved only with satisfaction, and in turn that satisfaction
is to be explicated in terms of pleasure. Such is an appealing image, but no assurance of it is given. The performance of some activities may not be able to be estimated on the axis of pleasure or, at least, on pleasure unconfirmed by any other
input.

Universes for Leisure

Besides worldviews which would threaten the status of leisure, there are some
others which permit and yet others which enforce it. Like saying that there is
play in a rope, and meaning by this that there is room for it to move, taughten
and slacken, a universe with movement may permit leisure.

A universe without any fixed design, for example, would be one where nothing was bound to happen and where everything is a surprise. The only meaning
which is found in such a world is that which is put there by human beings. Not
that this is a very noble deed; every species makes the world centre around itself
in its myopia, as thinkers representative of this viewpoint characteristically note
(Zenophanes, Bacon, Nietzsche). But a universe in which nothing is predecided
is surely a universe allowing of play; one would surely talk, in fact, of the play
of the universe.

This is not the universe we experience, which is frequently an obstacle to
us, where indeed much happens which we would not have happen; so the sense
of this universe is rather that any *meaning* even to the imperatives of the universe are derivative from us. We make the rules, even though what we make them
about happens anyway, ruled or not by us. Like the Cloud King in *The Little
Prince*, when we cannot make the world come out to our rules, then we rule the
world the way it is going to come out, lest it escape our control. It has been suggested that we overthrow the way we have ruled it thus far, as dull and restrictive of our potentialities. But there is no suggestion that we not replace these

rules with other ones; the world's sun still appears in the morning, whether we refuse to acknowledge it as a matter of course or not. That we can stand in wonder at what we must acknowledge is affirmed by Heraclitus and Nietzsche; perhaps this is what has made theirs such a popular was of seeing the world, from existentialist viewpoints to pragmatist and Marxian, all today in reaction to the idealism their predecessor Hegel is thought to have propounded in making all events the labor of existence achieving itself.[8]

Other ways in which leisure can be introduced into the world are stated by ancient Greek philosophy. Wonder is only the start of human activity, and wonder as the finish as well, are the respective positions of Aristotle and Plato. For Aristotle the regenerative patterns and cycles of biological life are only the halting approach to the regularity of the heavenly bodies, and this in turn to the retrorsive perfection of self-thinking thought which rules the cosmos by the centripetal motion it solicits. Once man had exercised that dimension of his own mind which is a sharing in this cosmic mind, he can end the ignorant wonder of not knowing the causes for all he sees around him; he can see the universe whole. In this self-identification by mind with the whole of being, man escapes the necessity of repeating his activities, of running as fast as he can just to stay put. This escape from necessity is what Aristotle terms leisure, *scholia*.[9]

Plato, however, uses the same term in a considerably different way, with not a widely different view of being; we shall stress the difference rather than the similarity with Aristotle in order both to develop an alternative worldview to his and to give it some historical footing. Here again the universe is constructed along the exemplary lines which Aristotle later stresses. The universe has consistency through its incessant change only by reason of striving to realize ever more the perfection of the idea glimpsed through the change, making it at all intelligible. Plato is doubtful, however, that human individuality can be laid aside either in life or in death in order to join to the perfection of idea; this was the price Aristotle was willing to pay. As a result the philosophical search for principles is successful when one recognizes that his variable experience is governed or regulated by the invariable. But since he never simply joins to the idea "in the flesh," as it were, he retains the learned wonder at unknown causes even when he knows the idea; the continual perfection of wonder and the resultant attitude toward particulars makes up his *scholia*.[10]

Philosophy coordinated with revealed traditions mediates the classical positions in presenting its worldview such that leisure is a real possibility. Herein the universe of being is the creation after nothing by a deity whose own existence is so altogether and thus so full that it stands in no need of creating.

The creation is pictured as an overflowing of the being of this deity, whose own existence is not under any constraints and is unlimited in fullness and perfection. The overflowing imagery, however, needs to be modified since it is not his own existence which is shared; rather, completely new and autonomous existence is created, as autonomous as deity except that it is created and not self-existent. The oneness of Allah, the fullness of Yahweh, is a source whence workaday ecstasy can be found in the community communing with him.[11]

Man

If we take as our own entry point the philosophy of man, one almost seems to need all the conclusions before beginning. For the answer to such questions as the following are both the directives for investigation and the conclusions of the study: do we speak of all men, of all times, of all stages and varieties of development? Is there anything like a human essence or human nature to go after, or are there only the conditions in which human being appears, or are there only individual men making for themselves something singular and peculiar as a nature? Should we look to man as a species or men as individuals? Is it man as a fact, or the ideal man whom we should be concerned with? Should we begin with others, or with ourselves; and can we even get at both—or either?

Even in the limited confines of Western man, the total variations in frameworks for investigation are overwhelming. Depending on the context of activity found most relevant, we are *homo politicus, homo faber, homo ludens*. Depending on the position given him in the cosmos among other species, he is the "man-machine," an "imperial animal," a "naked ape"; he is the amphibian swimming in the watershed among the whole gamut of species, or the useless passion continually trying to become what he cannot, something of one single species. In the social critique of who man is forced to be by our current society, we see ourselves called "economic man," "technological man," "one-dimensional man" and "fabricated man." We are not left entirely hopeful by what is said among recent geniuses of human being: we are said to have been wrong about our species by Darwin, wrong about our society by Marx, wrong about our self by Freud—and by Einstein not even to know what time it is! Each of these would determine a whole methodological context for investigation, or rather would pre-decide everything within it.

Although we shall not succumb to the temptation of taking up any of these contemporary perspectives, a few words about our ignoring of some of the more popular should be inserted. The fact that human existence shares or does not share (whatever "share" can mean here) some features with other forms of existence is eminently unimportant. It has value if at all only in a polemic context. Beasts or machines which have features sufficiently similar to us may have to be treated in a sufficiently similar way; but nothing that they do makes any contribution to knowing who we the clear instances of humans are, we self-claimants distinct from those others whom we still might deign to recognize as pretenders.

Furthermore, the fact that some men and their products dominate others has no more initial claim to be a privileged perspective; it certainly does not speak for itself. It may be advisable, in fact, not to light upon this datum, for methodological reasons: the data we shall consider are so commonplace that they allow wonder, openness and receptivity, whereas domination is encountered in such a disillusioned and cynical frame of mind that one cannot be amazed but only protective and sophisticated. Our thrust at every level here is that man is wellfitted; our nature is not made up of being alienated although the possibility is open to us. Negativity and distance will be seen as essential to us, but they cure themselves. When we permit the exercise of our faculties for displacement, we must be wary not to be so displaced that we have lost any sense of what we are displaced from.

Our approach shall be to consider directly those dimensions of human activity manifest even under any of the foregoing models—bodily, mental, moral, social, spiritual activity. We shall examine them separately. They do not exist as separate, except in enlighteningly negative failures of our activity. Because each involves an overlap of description, one feels dishonest describing any of them thoroughly and overextending the description. This is remedied by in turn describing the overlap.

These dimensions do not form an ordered set in that they build to a hierarchically most important peak. All are of equal importance; but although this means that one could start anywhere among them, the order we shall pursue will manifest a peculiar dynamism. Although we start with those nearest in awareness, we shall find that the dimensions become more and more concretely real the further through the initially more "abstract" dimensions we advance. Bodiliness is not a different thing in man than spirituality; but the very patency of the former misleads us to think that it is more real than the latter.

We see ourselves in a fragmentary way. At each stage we see that the earlier fragments were not separated off, in fact. Rather they had been separated, out of the whole. But we do not know it is a fragment until we go on to see progressively larger wholes wherein we see the fragment not separated but at most distinct, and more accurately subsumed or *aufgehoben*—negated, preserved and raised. The limitations upon this technique is that we *do* in fact see fragmentarily, and that something real is happening at the time we do; everything is not one. Even the final "one"[12] is not self but makes itself other, a community which we enter. We shall interpret the alleged splits of human existence as the presence of a variety of possible objects to a faculty, not as the separateness of the faculty and its object from some other and its object opposing the first.

Man is to be seen whole; this brings to point the earlier description of philosophy as research into totality. But the wholeness of man is not the wholeness of being, nor is it the wholeness of other sorts of beings, whose unity we shall mention here without prejudging the mode of human unity, to be concluded later.

The *handful of sand* is one existent insofar as it has been separated, "ascertained" in legal terminology, out of a whole from which it differs in no other way. The unity is spatial, one of a contained juxtaposition; it is completely due to the exercise of a particular external force for beginning and continuing, and would collapse without the continued exercise of it. The *rock*, or one of the grains of the sand, on the other hand, needs no particular external force to keep its unity, although of course the general forces of the universe are required for this end. Its unity depends upon an internal set of relationships: the chemical bonds, the crystalline formation, the molecular energy. No functional unity is present; while it can be done with as a whole, it cannot do as a whole. One part of it may be moved into causing an effect without the other parts needing to be brought into force. When the unity is broken, the rock remains what it was, but smaller, while the splinter becomes one of the same, another rock, with its own unity or wholeness of the very same sort. The *machine*, including artificial intelligence machines, has in addition a unity of function: the activity of the whole is more than the sum of the activity of its parts, while the same is not true of a stone. Its parts are differentiated, and the functional wholeness depends upon this differentiation. Parts are specialized in role, and so is the machine whole. The parts, however, exist in an independent state prior to their assembly into the machine; they are assembled when fully formed, and the machine becomes a unity only when the final part needed for functioning is added. From this wholeness there is no change during its "life." The *plant* is a whole from its first generation; its pieces are formed simultaneously, and the plant exists whole even before they are fully formed, as in fact they never are since they continue changing throughout life. "Functional" unity is present, although the plant "does" nothing but what it is, it leaves no effects but itself.

As for the machine, broken pieces are not new plants but remain only parts separated from the whole unless a plant recommences; the plant stands more separate from its environment than does the stone. Activities are focused upon individual or species' continuance, and do not emerge into the world beyond. But the *animal's* wholeness adds the fact that the world is relevant and is centered by one response after another upon the organism. It has functions, but no function. Its function is manifold, but concentrated upon the whole; the concentration of functions brings the concentration of its world by environment.

What we have seen is a progressive centering of the whole. We may expect this to continue with human wholeness, but do not anticipate just how at this moment. Other types of unity, e.g., logical and systematic unity, artistic unity, associative unity, cannot be introduced until after the study of their agent. Each whole manifests the totality of being in a specialized manner. None duplicate the totality of being, of course, or they would be the whole of existence; in each, the fact that the being becomes one, or exists, depends upon what sort of being it is. Given the relevant sort of unity, that being exists, can be known to exist as such, and can respond to our desires and its own demands. True also of man, we may presume that our unity (our wholeness) will both make possible or be the same as the fact of our continuing existence (our health) and be the same as the perfection of our existence (our holiness), as the word *Heil* means both at once, heartiness and salvation, as well as salute to the individual.

Philosophy, of Man, at Recreation and Leisure

We shall approach philosophy through man, and we shall approach man through our recreative and leisure activities. No further apology for this specialized viewpoint will be attempted now. Suffice it to say that the spread of issues related to these terms, while currently of fashionable interest, are of classical origin and answer a pressing need in the philosophy of man.

Today it is difficult to go beyond the sociological study of recreation and leisure, because such is the primary study taking them seriously. The categories and terms are jumbled together in the existing studies under a natural attitude, however; recreation and leisure as synonymous or as distinct; as absolute end carrying their own meaning, or as relative and defined only over against something else—be that sport, game and play or be it work, labor and seriousness. They are each and jointly taken as states or as acts, as dispositions or as causes or as consequences.[13] Nor is there any good reason why they should not be jumbled, since no exploration of the philosophical foundation has been done. We shall not look on recreation and leisure as the prime categories of this philosophy of man, but will permit them to sustain that role when they seem sufficiently powerful to do so. Otherwise, we shall see them as: examples of categories in the philosophy of man; or sometimes the determinants of categories in philosophy of man, or a symbol and model of total man; one activity over against other activities, one facet of all activities which also include complementary activities, a describable set of activities, or a structure among activities.

That is, at first we shall view man as a model for recreation and leisure. Whether the outcome will indicate that recreation and leisure are better seen as the model or at least a model for man will have to be seen later. We could not tell in advance whether or not they are the essential feature of man until we examine how we operate with our faculties.

PART I
HUMAN BODILINESS

· 2 ·

PHYSICAL BODILINESS

Spatiality

Even if the first contract with human bodiliness we have now does not take place in terms of a category of "spatiality," these first contacts quickly return to it. We shall take spatiality as a starting point which will rapidly return us to the actual contacts that we do sustain.

Spatiality is not just an observation limited to a single human dimension. It is a metaphor for language, mind and society; one speaks of the space of each of these, extending spatiality through unsuspected dimensions. A favorite metaphor was a reference to being "spaced out" for a detached mental condition, and later of one's "head space" as one's range of interests and presuppositions. Spatiality has probably been no better described than by the ancients, as extension, as having parts outside of parts. This would bring within spatiality, and so bodiliness, any parts which are not identified with other parts, i.e., it gives bodily standing to many parts we might not ordinarily think of as spatial. But this indefinitely open horizon would require us now to do the whole following study under this head.

Surface

Instead, we return to the more commonplace setting of our bodiliness by recognizing, first, that extension means that there is a surface to the being. The being does not extend beyond its last part; this part forms a boundary up against the boundaries of other things. This surface appears to the other things; it responds to others' contact and attracts them, but it also reflects and so repels contacts. We initiate the contact with a surface, even when it does not; but it responds somehow.

It is essential to a surface that it have a set of the following characteristics; it cannot be surface and extended without doing so. It must be flat or curved, reflective or absorbent, friable or impermeable, smooth or irregular, these clearly can be expanded. The point of relevance, however, is that these characteristics of spatial surface make possible containment and release, visibility and audibility, ability to be tasted and smelled, and tangibility respectively. That is, the human body has the same characteristics which make possible human doing and knowing. Not only is there a kinship which makes only another body, exercising its own spatiality, able to contact a body; it also means that our human body with these same features is able to be manifested, that it cannot help being manifested. There is an affinity between being bodily and being known, rather than a root alienation of knowledge from being able to grasp the human person. While surface is also a covering, it is a covering which manifests the person; it is how the person turns outward and is invariably turned outward. The only way to hide this publicity is to cover this in turn, to place over it another surface within which the human surface becomes invisible. However, unlike this covering, the human surface is a living organ, the skin, and is not something extra added to withdraw humanity from the public.

One noteworthy feature of human bodily surface is that it cannot help but be colored. There is a remarkable penchant for the Caucasian to consider his skin surface as white, as neutral in color, uncolored, and thus a starting point and norm for human normality. Every other skin coloring seems a deviation from the norm, no matter how much more numerous those deviations may be. Aside from the evident observation that no skin is uncolored and that it would be invisible if it were—a hint at the Caucasian preference for privacy?—it is also true that in principle no surface could be uncolored and that, while variations in color are more systematic than mere happenstance, in principle there is no starting point or privileged norm or even expectation for one rather than another.

Surface is the appearance, but it cannot support itself; it is not self-sufficient. It is supported by and is in fact no different from the volume, only its outermost boundary, where it meets up against other things. Yet hardly can it just meet others without developing a specialized organ of meeting: a film, layer, at least a surface tension. The volume is bounded by surface which is part of our volume, and our volume needs also to be bounded from without by something to hold the volume together, to push up against it for my volume to push up against. This outside goes on when and whence our volume ends.

This means that the spatiality of which human bodiliness is a part, this part outside of part, cannot cease and leave nothing beyond itself, cannot be the only bodily existent—nor even seem to be that. It can only return upon itself through intermediary bodily others, in a roundabout fashion. If nothing lay outside the last part of the continuum we partake in as an essential intermediary, this last part would be outside of only the previous parts; it would not be outside of parts on its other side, and that other side would be no face. It would not face upon anything. For our body to be the facing front that it is, there must be something there; again, we are able to be what we are only by insertion into reality other than us. The solipsist body would explode. Its last part would be everything else there is; there would be no bounds to it, nothing locating it, and so it could not locate either what it is the last part of.

Volume

But surface cannot be pure surface. Any part must be a part all around, not just in a flat plane; that is, a surface demands volume and exists only as the uppermost part of the volume. In fact, our experience is not of surface, for we abstract from volume to surface; surface carries the announcement of volume with it. That is the remarkable feature of the mirror image and the design, which portray volume only in perspective; the mirrored image has no depth of its own, although the design does, and this is the source for representing illusion as a matter of mirrors.

Although this dimension is embraced by the mathematical principle of three planes, there are never just three but multiple planes to the human figure, which never becomes merely in—out—up except on a mathematical set of coordinates. The human existence is angular, diagonal, sliced under and curved across what the perpendicularity of the three axes would suggest. It is this which is meant by human form, not the measurement of it on a scale.

Each of our forms is peculiar to ourselves, but also falls within certain boundaries common to the species of man. Surely the fact that we stand at a particular stature and shape in existence contributed remarkably if obscurely to our life activities, to our being. It cannot be of no importance at all that we are longer than we are wide, instead of spreading flatly over the earth's surface like a sports car, aerodynamically designed, or being ball-like. There is some importance to the fact that we are smaller than most trees, larger than most plants, have insects much tinier and mountains much larger than us, are comparable in stature to most animals, wild and domestic, though they exceed us in each direction. Pascal found this a sign of human being as both everything and nothing, grandeur and misery; but few people so experience their statute. It has been argued at length that human erectness is humanness, so that the first man is whoever is *homo erectus*—his mandibles freed from walking for carrying, the massive carrying muscles of his jaw diminish; room is freed for increased head and torso resonance, and for his forebrain to grow; his control of small organs such as tongue, lips and fingers becomes refined; his thumb grows opposable; his pelvic bones narrow for balance; birth must occur earlier in gestation; longer postnatal care, differentiated sex roles, pair bonding and increased sensuality ensue. True and important as this is, it does not attain the point of telling how I experience the world by reason of being erect and not hunched.

The human form is mostly curved, with appendages that move with relative independence; there are few rigid lines. The form we have is an elongated doughnut: hollow inside although the two skinned sides of the doughnut hole—our intestines—press upon each other and obscure this form. There are no clearly separated areas, no sharp breaks in our dimensions; but there are many areas distinguished off—the head area by the neck, with such a peculiar concentration of sensory organs in the front of the head, the torso by the waist, the legs by the hips, the neck seemingly more part of the head and the waist and hips meeting each other. It is uncertain where in this the beauty of proportion arises: from the bilateral symmetry of our bodies, from the gradation of part to part, area to area. We seem able to pinpoint our perfection of form only in the light of deformations of our bodies, which are not just statistical variations but cripplings of function as well. Our taken-for-granted sense of our beauty is validated by these examples.

A feature about a form with depth is that the form has a front and back. Body is not fully within my line of vision, with eyes located in front, and in fact may not be fully within my range of touch if I am stiff or muscle bound. Only in a reflection, a bending back upon by body am I fully present bodily to myself. We anticipate the rest of the body we see, and others too anticipate the rest of us, our back sides.

Thus far what we have is largely an outline, a silhouette in three dimensions. There is also the shape, the contours which mold this framework more concretely. The boney joints, the muscular swells, the protrusion of sexual organs and sensory organs—these are too evident to describe; but we feel compelled to do it, to dwell upon them until their meaning unlocks—not just what function their formations allow, but what positioning in existence and upon existence they give us by being so.

More clearly than color, the surface quality of texture is a function of our volume. Texture is the surface descending into the volume and rising out from there, instead of just wrapping the innards glassily. We are not exceedingly bumpy, but are soft covering hard, and the soft moves over the hard, pouches out and depresses, sags and tightens, wrinkles and effaces, pimples and cuts. A large part of the body surface is relatively ineffectual, doing nothing, just covering organs which are effectual, and receiving only tactile sensations.

These are maddeningly suggestive of hidden meaning, but do not reveal it to us, this color, form and texture. The notice of them stirs us, because it is unimaginable for us to be persons without them, whereas we could prune off even some operations imaginatively and still recognize ourselves. These features seem mute, and that is perhaps their human reality: to do nothing but to make possible everything else. We might ask of each further operation, could we experience this the same ways with a different shape or texture, and perhaps by penetrating the negative answer gain more insight than we seem to be able to do directly.[14]

Volume and surface of our bodies are inseparably related. If volume is cut into, it is not destroyed or disemboweled, but only divided; it develops new faces, new surfaces, as jewelry cutting brings to light the potential faces of the gem. That in the course of doing so, the human body is destroyed tells us something important about the peculiarity of the human body.

While surface is the possibility for appearance, volume in the dimensional sense of depth is that which so appears. When it is recognized that the depth is hidden under the surface, the double entendre of appearance comes to light, and thus of the human existence based on his bodiliness. Surface may be the appearance of reality, or it may be mere appearance, i.e., appearance of some other reality; depth is that which appears in surface, but it may also be hidden by surface. It is the mediatory character of surface which is both the precondition for publicity and the possibility for hiddenness and privacy being retained. But the privacy of our depth is not a pure privacy; there cannot fail to be surface, appearance, and so there is either accurate publicity or deceptive publicity, not pure privacy. What is hidden, is public as something—hidden, and present by its very absence. One cannot hide anything without surface, and one would not have anything to hide without depth.

Depth is the domain of what privacy we shall achieve. It remains hidden until revealed, where things happen secretively and secretedly. But it cries for publicity as well, since it remains private only by being announced as private, that is, by the imposition of yet a further covering and surface over its appearing surface, if we put aside the possibility for privacy by deception.

Depth is a symbol of seriousness; associated with it are the symbols of gravity and weightiness. All are opposed to the surface and the shallow. There are several dimensions of this that need consideration. From one point of view, all of these have in common that the serious is the unchanging, while the surface keeps shifting and playing in the light. Things in the depths move slowly, because under greater weight they are less moveable. Instead they are reliable, predictable, dependable; they remain the same, and by reason of this they can be known to be lacking less.

From another viewpoint, the serious is what does not jump right out at you; it is hidden, and has to be dug out, brought to light. Perhaps that is the reason for letdown, disillusionment and anti-climax upon completion of the search for the serious; it has been brought to the surface and thus deprived of the only thing that made it serious to begin with. Furthermore, the serious cannot be adequately expressed; it is usually in garbled and clumsy discourse or obtuse jargon when it is expressed, and there is a tradition of learned ignorance which says it should not be expressed at all. All one would end with by expressing it would be a substitute for the real thing, an idol that attracted to itself the devotion which belongs to the reality.

Something more than just the fact of surface—depth juxtaposition is involved, for some things can only exist as depth, not surface; thus human innards are destroyed by exposure, and we shall later further the same argument for various activities of humans. But, on the other hand, the presumption of seriousness and the added presumption of importance can be granted to the mere fact of depth, difficulty, inaccessibility or intransigence. In such a case, the depth needs to be brought to light to make sure it is not really the surface of something itself masquerading as a depth underneath some foreign substance as its surface.

A feature of this depth is that it may be empty; this must be why emptiness often is thought profound. By reason of the surface being something in its own right as well as just the externality of body, body may act also as a container whose emptiness is able to be filled. We can go into depth as emptiness, and let it surround us. We can be where we have never been before. We can then at least raise the possibility of us being either in our body or out of our body, but not independent of our body. In effect it changes the notion of body to that of being more a marker than a container, since body is one place among others by reason of spatiality. The possibility arises for body being the rough location for myself, instead of myself being identified with and therefore contained within body. This does not seem literally possible, insofar as the surface appearance would not be able to manifest what lay outside of it, which would then rather be an unmanifested observer of itself manifested. The inherent contradiction of the last clause excludes this possibility in the gross sense.

Bodily emptiness is possible, however—a relative emptiness consisting in distance from what is needed or wanted. There are no spaces in body architecturally unfilled, but there may be emptiness relevant to the sort of body we are when the filling is inappropriate.

The spatial isolation by surface makes a platform for human individuality. By being bounded off from the world, I am located into myself and not confused with any other. Bodily features are what permit of something, which allows something to be done to or done by body. This seems to be the sole sense in which it makes sense to talk of body as matter; only in the sense that materiality means potentiality is my body material. Beyond this sense, it is as spiritualized as anything about me; indeed, from the foregoing one would be ill put to find any other location for his spirituality.

Suntanning

Suntanning is an interesting phenomenon in the light of racial prejudice. Surely this must be among the most leisurely of activities, done with no other movement or preoccupation at all. It is an attempt to make skin color richer and deeper. Although it does change the appearance, the color inseparable from surface, it is not a drastic change such as the wearing of a mask; it is seen as the improvement of the given skin color, letting out the potentialities for beauty it has.

Why enriching the color of the skin should be found desirable and beautiful might be looked at in terms of surface and depth. The deepness of coloring when it appears seems to be something which is not induced from without by ultraviolet rays but to be a condition which comes from within. It is a bringing to light what is latent and, by reason of its latency, backs up and gives quality to whatever it is that does appear on the surface; the more substantial the underlying support, the less vapid seems the however well-built surface. The tanned skin has a look which anticipates a feel which is much softer and yielding than light-colored skin. The tanned skin takes on an oily appearance, too, which shows more prominently the muscles and contours of the physique. What tanning does is to make them look more sleek and sensual, by reason of increased contrasts of light and shadows as well as by contrast with the light-colored clothing suited to the season when tanning usually occurs.

Throwing oneself into tanning requires the relaxation to remain still and to permit the skin surface sensations to run their course uninterrupted. The expression "soaking up sun" is not inapt: the activity is one of submission and exposure to whatever comes, and even the usual postures carry out this direction.

Dressing

Where does the joy of dressing up come from? The more cynical answer is that it is an invidious comparison with the poor who could not afford to do what the fancy dresser does. Aside from this being untrue (the comparable poor get themselves up remarkably when the occasion warrants, although at much greater sacrifice) and inappropriate (the poor take as much pleasure in dressing, either up or down, as anyone), this does not get to the heart: why should dressing be so invidious to those who cannot dress up, unless there were something desirable about it? That what is desirable is the expense is inadequate as an answer; for the expense only follows the demand. The rapid shift of fashion is another question, perhaps designed for nothing other than oppression; but we shall look to that in the next part of the book.

Dressing covers the surface of the body, and hides it from direct view. Unlike the mask, however, the purpose is not to have the viewer ignore the personage nor the body underneath; rather, the clothing is similar to the skin, rather than to the mask, because like the skin it is meant to reveal by means of hiding. The clothing takes one dimension of the wearer and highlights it; even the clothing which is enjoyed simply because it is "good clothes," which is nearly the sole description masculine formal clothing can be given as an expression of anything about males, highlights that dimension of a person's fitting into social proprieties, which certainly is one of his dimensions and one from which he derives great comfort, although again for most males it is nearly the sole expression of who they are that they can make.

The expressible dimensions—gay, provocative, elegant, sober, profound, stable, wild, dangerous, tough, pussycat, etc. without end—are not substituted for the entire person. One interacting with a person so dressed is willing to interact within the perspective announced by the clothing as the one on which the greatest vibrancy will be exhibited; this is presuming that one is living the clothes and not embarrassed by what they say. But interacting in this way is not taken as completely displacing the broad spectrum of the personality. What is given is the privileged access, but it is access to all of the dimensions not just the vehicle. There is always one or a few privileged accesses, although not always the same one or few; but that access always leads beyond it. The wearer sometimes is unable to be present in other than the way the clothes present him; but he can always be found out by another.

This discussion does not go on to the use of uniforms, which is a matter to be taken up later. Nor does it consider the use of ornamentation or coloring, taken separately. One attempt to build up a worldview around the leisure of self—clothing is Thomas Carlyle's *Sartor Resartus*.

Ornamentation

The inability not to present some exterior, and to present it actively, means that ornamentation even more than clothing will be a matter of presenting who we are rather than of hiding it.[15] Rings and bracelets, beads and earrings, chains and necklaces, belts and bags, tiaras and barrettes and pins, watches and anklets, pens and pencils, tie clasps and cufflinks, neckerchief slides and wallets—all this "hardware" is objects suspended from our bodies. It decorates us by being shiny or noisy, however subdued it is. This is somewhat less true of males' decoration, which is frequently to appear as crude and leathery as possible.

In every case the object is meant to draw attention, seldom to itself but instead to the decorated part of the body. The attention paid to the object itself will be taken as a slight if it becomes too pronounced; usually the attention is simply a vehicle for prolonging the attention to the body without embarrassing either wearer or viewer.

Why does the object attract beyond itself to the body? And what does this do to the bodily appearance? Like clothing, a piece of hardware does not have to be attached to the wearer before it will carry any import; on the contrary, it is selected and either bought or made because it already is anticipated to give a specific effect. Worn, it allows the wearer to interpret himself in diverse ways, again to present one aspect of himself above other ones. Here, however, the recognition is left much more to the viewer; the object provides less cover and so there is more of the person to be read into the object. The object breaks the body's continuity and rivets attention upon the break. The most global effects are of delicacy and of muscularity, respective to the sexes wearing the hardware. As with clothing, the possibility of declaring oneself in a coherent and focused way, instead of the dispersed and multi-faceted way in which we exist, is a relief and a simplification not to be disregarded despite the need to express all sides of the person now sequentially through changes of gear.

Ornamentation of oneself is indeed superficial, in the most literal sense, because it keeps one on the surface of the body. Whether this implies superficiality in some moral sense is not decided by this observation. There is no attempt to keep others out of my depths, only to present to them one limited access into there. The aspect they perceive is as much part of my person as is any other they might prefer. If surface is the way of my being, access without it being mediated by surface is out of the question; so in that case even the appearance of openness, which may or may not be achieved by absence of ornamentation, is also but a single way of presenting oneself, and no more comprehensive than the person shown by decoration.

Mime

Surface, and the inseparable possibility of appearing in some fashion other than that of our reality, provides the preliminary possibility for drama and role-playing. This is a separate and distinct feature of human activity, as well as a component or dimension within each and every human activity. The dynamism needs to be described: the human person exists; he exists with a surface to his body; this surface is an expression of what is hidden about him; it may also cover that, and manifest something else.

Why should it be considered a leisure or recreative activity so to cover one's reality and substitute for it an appearance? Firstly, it is not an activity which one is compelled to do. The only pressure upon activity would have to come from what is real, rather than from what is not real and so not present as a cause in any sense. The actor's reality, however, is real within the confines of the acting and he seeks to make it so also for the spectator. If one were simply to present the reality of himself, he would not have to act. When he acts he presents the reality of another, which could not be shown in his own person. While not losing the reality of himself, he has expanded his own reality because now he adds the reality of another person, time and circumstance.

The actor does not have to hide himself in order to do this. Simply hiding would not be acting but retreat. This is instead the use of surface for the purpose first of hiding, then of substituting and ultimately of revealing—no longer oneself but the other which does not stand behind the appearance. One may very well know the identity of the actor or, even if one does not, he may be known to be an actor and so a presenter of false appearances. It is not beyond possibility that the actor could play for himself alone, with no audience; surely that is what he does when he practices movements or speeches. And even if this is not considered as really acting but only a mechanical and narrow perfecting of a set of movements, still other circumstances in which he is no doubt truly acting for himself could be presented. Indeed, even his practicing is practiced for the very purpose of finding what is the best mode of representation.

Simultaneous with acting being perhaps a hiding of the actor's person and the substitution of another, acting may also be a great enrichment of his personhood. Attending first simply to the pleasure he derives, the acting frees him from the limitations and particularly the failing of his own personhood. He may be lazy, whereas the character played may be industrious. Even if the character bears the same faults, they no longer are the actor's faults; it is in fact a source of pleasure to him that he can better play the character because he comprehends his faults. He can flaunt the faults in his played character without having the finger of scorn pointed at himself; although the audience reaction is toward the point in space where he is active representing the character, it is focused only upon the surface and not upon himself.

The incomplete and contradictory way in which the actor is whatever he is in himself is gone beyond in the role. He is now the character through and through, but calculating in a way the character himself could not calculate how to bring alive that character. The surface, if it were a surface of some reality, i.e., if this were not a play but the presence of this other human being, would be hesitant at how fully he could behave in the fashion the actor does; he is perhaps aware of his own mannerisms, but could not even carry them off successfully while aware of them. The actor is aware of them, they are very much on his mind; but because of his removal from the reality, his standing behind the appearance as himself and not the character, he both calculates and convinces.[16]

Mask

One need not go this far in order to have the perspective upon how surface contributes to leisure. For the same functions are active in the more simple circumstance of someone wearing a mask. He is not engaged in making the movements of face, presenting his face, as someone else's; this is a possibility, but a more complex one. Nor is it necessary that the mask itself be representative of someone; it may simply be a mask which blanks off the face of the wearer, or else a mask which is so outrageous that no one is taking it seriously that the wearer does really intend to represent the character.

In this more simplified situation, the wearer is still experiencing a delight. Whether child or adult, he is freed of his need to bear the responsibility of his own personhood, even though he may not be taking on the personhood of another. What occurs is a lifting from the wearer of the weight that being one individual person involves. He does not now have to restrict himself to the behavior expected of him properly as himself. Behind the blank mask, there is no person he needs to represent, either, and he is abandoned to behavior which has nothing to do with himself. He is indeed hiding, and enters into the covering fully; no embarrassment nor guilt accrues to him while he wears the mask, although the moment it is snatched off he feels the full weight of himself. Should the mask fall without him noticing its fall, he is not flustered; but when he notes it, then he is chagrined not just at the deeds he was about to perform but also those performed unmasked. If on the other hand he should complete a set of deeds masked and then remove it, no stigma remains upon him in his own estimate from those deeds. Good or bad, they were not his for he was covered.

The person wearing a representative mask is seldom found outside a ritual. However, wherever found he is midway between the two possibilities presented thus far. No one believes he is the figure on the mask, nor does he; but the response he expects and that which in ritual is given to him is the response the figure itself would expect, not that due to his unmasked self. Again, no one is fooled and no one is expected to be fooled; if they were, the figure would be expected to perform all that it would in the flesh. What its masked presence permits, however, is the response that the presence of the real figure would elicit. The masked figure allows, in fact, what perhaps would not be able to be done in the presence of the real figure. Instead of real flight or real attack, a mere cringing is possible so that all are able to express their fear without experiencing its intensity; they undergo fear, but it is fear which is directed toward the mask precisely as a mask. The obsequiousness shown the mask of a respected figure is excessive; it would be a patent insult to treat that way the real figure. But to the mask the gestures are as extravagant as the stereotyped gesture is. The movements are made by a mask conscious of itself as mask, a mask which reveals more than the very presence of the represented figure could, since now the absence of the figure is brought vividly alive by his being a mere surface, an appearance with nothing which appears behind it, nothing "backing it up." In person, the represented figure would be all too accessible; whereas here, it keeps all the distance which its reality deserves but does not allow in its presence. The person behind the mask as well is as responsive to the figure he wears as are those viewing it. His own distance from his surface is a s great as anyone else's; for though he bears it, he is not it. Although it is a surface, it is not his surface but one laid over his own. So surface is not just surface; it is as much part of the real human being as is that of which it is the surface. Parting from the response to it temporarily may reinforce this recognition.

Charade

Form is able to take on form. One is not confined to the single shape he has, but can use this shape into other shapes. When I remodel it, I am confident that it will return to itself later; there is a difference between the momentary form and its persistent form, with the former being the ways in which the latter is used. The latter can never be without some of the former. One molds another form than his own, while using his own to do it. Inherent in his are all the possibilities for the others. The impossibility of having no such molded form makes even the characteristic personal visage and bearing a mime, the habitual attempt to become the person we would want to be, a habitual leisure-like activity.

Mirroring

Because surfaces are able to be returned by surfaces, giving rise to the persistent metaphor of appearance as a mirroring, it is possible for the mirroring to be distorted. In distorting the form, as in the fat-and-skinny mirrors at a carnival sideshow, one works out the precariousness of his own conformity, his own possession of coherence in form. For it is not a different form which is imaged but the same form drawn out to extremities before it breaks off and ceases to the same form at all. I have not changed, but I can see how I could change or how it might have been for me. Further possibilities of my existence are opened up and I can see my being expanded, perhaps in ways I deplore. Because it is possibility and not actuality, I can laugh at it in ways I would not do about others who did in fact have such forms, certainly not as I would feel about myself with the form. Because, however, it remains in possibility it is a pleasure to me to open up my potentialities.

Surfing

Surfing is one of a very few sports activities in which the whole objective is to remain upon the surface. The movement can only come about if the surface is skinned; boating of any kind may partake of this character, although there is some change by reason of the greater dominance of the equipment and in the unimportance of trying to stay afloat; perhaps skiing has an affinity, although there is no danger of leaving the surface and there is no problem of keeping up the speed by remaining on the surface.

One might be tempted to say that thence stems the superficiality of surfing enthusiasts, but that would be an easy temptation to resist. The surface is being cultivated as a unique environment, the features which make it a distinctive environment are exploited for activity. Only if one keeps moving on the surface can he remain upon it; and, if we exclude artificial sources of power, one can keep moving only because the surface itself is moving. Unlike the water itself, which only moves in part and for the other part communicates its wave energy from one portion of relatively stable water to another, the surfer as an object is moved with the rate of movement of the energy in the waves rather than with the rate of movement of the water itself. It points up the separability of surface and depth, their distinctness; he would not be moved so rapidly if he were underwater, indeed not if he falls off the surfboard. Exploiting the features of this environment with his tools, he perfects that one feature. It does not occur automatically; besides the perfection of tools he also needs to perfect a way of using them. But the new environment yields only to tools, since of himself he does not and cannot live there. He does not know what it would be like to exercise there, and so he transforms that environment itself into a human environment from a natural one by his application to it of tools.[17]

Contain and Release

If the possibilities for leisure are dependent upon our way of being, surely our bodiliness is highly important. Only a being with surface and depth can and must be active in the way our sports activate us. For no sport has absent from it the use of body in such ways as containing and releasing of projectiles or handles, striking objects, resisting their push and pushing in turn, and being moved by their push or by other forces. Sports which seem to have none of this, such as skiing, are dependent at least upon the friction with surfaces, with pushing in a gravitational manner. Without this neither skating nor skiing, neither sky diving nor water diving would be possible, although these seem at first to be the very denial of such frictional contact. Their activity consists in a reduction of these forces to a minimum, a minimum which cannot be superseded without losing the ability to control the activity, and then proceeding to use this altered state of bodiliness for a further exploration of human possibilities.[18]

Deformity and Handicapping

In various forms of leisure, the physical and emotional and mental handicaps which people carry each his own, have an impact on how well activities can be performed. One way of including this fact is to design levels of capacity and to keep persons within the range of others at their own capability. An alternative method is to permit open contact in the performance between the handicapped and those not handicapped, which alleviates the ghetto of the handicapped, but to give the handicapped some kind of advantage such that no longer just they but also the non-handicapped individual are required to reach the limits of their tolerance, of their potentialities, in order to win over the other. Either one may win, and this equalizes the competition.

The handicapped are identified relatively to some other group; they are those who consistently and roundly are beaten by some other persons. That is to say, their handicap is relative to the persons and the activity; since everyone is in this position vis-à-vis some others regarding at least some activities, everyone is handicapped in some respect. It is not merely that some are all around better qualified persons, but do less well in some things than in others simply because they cannot turn their attention to everything equally. In addition to this, the strengths of anyone serve as vulnerabilities in his person, since they tempt one towards unwarranted seriousness about the activities he is engaged in.

Seriousness

The association of depth with seriousness can be used to pry open the relationship, if not the exclusion, of seriousness from play and games. Play and game are taken as non-serious because of their unimportance; the reverse is also true, when one judges that what is not serious cannot be important. Whatever is of importance, it would have to be what is associated with depth: whatever else happens, what touches us in our depth is important, and so serious. The reason seems to be that our depth is always with us the same, despite the inaccuracy of this biologically, while our exterior is undergoing constant shifts and revisions. What remains the same is a way of coping with what changes, so this we must consider as important; then one can deal with the superficial as it arises.

This model would make game and play unimportant and not serious because they are not continuing conditions of our lives. They come and go with great ease, while the really serious things about life—death and taxes, love and birth, education and work—are things which we can count on always coming around again; they are continuing and unchanging conditions of existence. When it is laid out this way, some pause must be made before it; for clearly these events are not continuing. They come only on occasion, when they do come at all, and to some they never come at all. Once doubt is laid on the exposition, it can also be laid on the exclusions: all that is needed in order to make leisure and play serious is to point out how they persist as continuing and invariant conditions of life while the variety of play and leisure activities may readily change.

The sense of seriousness is something we cherish deeply, and would feel guilty at giving up. It is a refusal to laugh or to use humor about something, or to acknowledge pleasure in it; it is almost a dislike of something. It treats the object that is serious as something which should be made the prime consideration in any decisions; nothing can successfully stand in conflict with it and compete with it. Whether there is any dimension of human life that is like this, or whether human life itself is, is a question hard to pin down. The ultimate point always is reached, as the cry that this is the only life I have, and so I have to use it well-for my own happiness, or for the love of neighbor, or for the service of country or God. . . . Each of these is a human concept, however, and whatever view of knowledge one takes, it is clear that human concepts are sometimes wrong and always inadequate. Therefore, even if the object is a serious object, my approach to it cannot be serious but instead must be sufficiently detached from itself that error can be admitted; it must be non-serious, playful. Even in moral judgment the inability to know the moral condition of any agent must act as a check upon what perhaps might be our certainty regarding some moral principle; moral subjectivity cannot be substituted for by moral objectivity. Nor is there a disintegration of the emotions by this view; just because everything is playful, this does not mean that everything is not also serious and liable for deep emotions of sorrow and joy. Perhaps everything is important and serious in itself, but not for us. On the other hand, perhaps everything for us is not serious, but in our estimate it may be; in fact, we can say that everything must be serious for us, since it is this fact which has indicated that not everything is serious. That is, if we saw wholly, everything might be serious as far as we are concerned; but we do not see wholly, so not everything is serious for us in fact. Yet since we see only partially we cannot help being serious about what seems to be comprehensive just because we see it only in part.

Temporality

Individual Time

To the extent man is a spatial being, he is also inescapably a temporal being. While spatiality consists in having part outside of part so that both parts are available together, simultaneously, temporality is having parts outside of parts in such a way that the parts are not available together, but only consecutively. As spatiality makes our depth unavailable, temporality also makes some portion of our existence unavailable, except by mediation. We have no access to one portion of our existence, but we have available our whole existence which spans and is both parts, as well as whatever mediates the parts to one another in the present.

Because of spatial limitation, only one part of another body can contact one part of my body. If more than one part of other bodies is contacting me, this must occur following removal of the first contact. That is to say, bodily spatial events cannot all happen at once. Instead they must pass in some order of one, then another, just as arrangement in space gives order spatially. Some of the occurrences may endure, while others may pass away; by measuring one occurrence against another, we discover different times.

This means that what does not happen now is able to happen later. What is not possible at one time may be possible at another time, perhaps on the basis of what we do at this time. Thus novelty can arise in our existence; not everything about us is tied up in the here and now.[19]

Body endures throughout the changes which measure time. What it is that endures through change can be seen as either the crystallizing of action, if change is seen to be ultimate and impenetrable, or a stability whence action arises. The latter is the preferable standpoint, since spatial features make possible the temporal ones: there is time only by reason of presence, and there is no presence of us unless it is our bodily spatial presence.

Bodily time does not mean just one thing after another, but an accumulation and replacement. What happens does not just happen upon body, but to body; there is a continuity of events. Because the later event is not possible except on account of the earlier, that later event brings the past, what there was, into the present, what is now, an operational memory. Adding to this the fact that not all event sequences are the same, the result is that further endurance in time makes our bodies ever more and more individual and distinctive. Fewer and fewer other bodies have even approximately the same sequence as this one does, and so older bodies have a uniqueness far greater than even the novelty of young ones. The novelty of our bodies is still dependent upon spatiality; for although the space our volume occupies is new, in that its surface has never before been supplied by the surface of this new body, yet the place it occupies is not new and in fact has never been unoccupied. It would not be necessary for body to begin, for it could simply continue to endure; but ours do not, they begin.

Similarly, then, they can end. By reason of having part outside of part, which makes up what they are as spatial and temporal, the parts can also separate. This ends the time of being distinct from other bodily beings; and so there is no further time at all for this bodily being. For though it cannot decompose into nothingness but only into parts which become parts of other beings, still the relation of surface to volume which identified the enduring sequence of events as this individual one is no more.

Repetition

In every form of activity there is some repetitiveness. Aristotle recognized that since we cannot be doing an activity without parts then we approximate it by doing an activity with parts over and over. One of the differences among various forms of activity is whether they are pure repetition and nothing else or whether there is more to them than repetition. The repeatedness of activity is self-contained, because it comes back upon itself, and this makes it autonomous and independent, the freedom associated with leisure activity.

There is great pleasure in the repetition of play and games. One feels the security of knowing the activity has been completed at all times and that if it needs to be ended it cannot be flawed by this. The activity is a mantra, which by its continued return brings all attention onto itself and so relieves one of the burden of shifting attention from one object to another. The consciousness centers and rests in itself, unwearied by continually going out after new materials. Such is the repetition of sing-songs, even of most folk songs, the catching of objects back and forth and the skipping of rope, the structuring of sports into periods of sharing between two teams—first one has the ball, then the other.

The imitation which other forms of leisure partake of is also a form of repetition. As my very life blood is made up of imitation, with cells formed of RNA replicating on DNA, so my activity includes it. In imitation games, or in dramatic acting, there is not utter freedom and the activity is bound, in the sense of a ball bounding back and forth rather than in the sense of the boundaries within which it does its bounding back and forth. We do not see the importance at one showing but have to keep coming back to it. Nor can we simply stay with something for attention; the only constancy in our knowing is for our activity to keep returning over the same rather than remaining immobile and fixed upon it.

Musical Rhythm

Playing or attending to music is much a matter of rhythm; it is just that it is impossible to have audible rhythms without there being some tone, just as it would for there to be tone without some rhythm. A tone which lacks rhythm of any sort is frequently not heard at all, any more than an excessively rhythmical tone which lulls attention; or else it is heard as noise, not even sound. The rhythm of music is imposed upon the surrounding environment of tonal rhythms, either creating new ones or in some few cases benefiting from their presence for its creation. The listener is as penetrated by the rhythm as the musician, and his purely reflex biological response starts long before he may even be aware of the audibility of some music. His response is usually a rhythmical tapping, i.e., one which is repetitive. The musician, and sometimes the attuned listener as well, may well resist this tendency toward replication physically of the repetitiveness of the musical rhythm; he may "work against the rhythm," in fact, and compose different simultaneous parts of it in different tempos, or at least refrain from tapping it out. In directed groups performers are forbidden visually to reproduce the repetitions, so that they can be more responsive to the sole keeper of rhythm, the conductor, and ready to be swept as quickly or slowly as the conductor leads at a moment's notice. Working against the rhythm, on the other hand, is not in order to make one apt for change but rather to intensify the experience. It becomes more intense when it must press itself upon us, and push up against our resistance, instead of sweeping over and flowing in and back out with total transparency on the receiver's part.

Musical rhythm, then, has already moved beyond the most basis sense of a repetition of sounds, into a repetition of other sounds which can only be identified as following the first ones because somehow the context that they both fall into, the piece of music, is indicated off from the rest of the environment. Even "concrete" music stops and starts at the composer's behest.

Music now includes variety not just in the tones but also in the rate of movement between them. Not only is the structuring of a single rate of movement varied among note and intervals of various values, but even the rates of movement are altered. Yet one continues to demand that there be rhythm in the sequence of tones. The rhythm, then, seems to be defined by the presence of movement throughout the whole: within it, the musical piece, a rhythm cannot help but be set up because there is movement from beginning to end. The presence of ends confines the steps so that there can be nothing haphazard; all movements are seen in terms of their relationship to the whole. Thus the greater demand is made upon a listener or performer by the longer musical piece with less regular rhythms; it is exhausting to keep the whole in view in order to interpret properly parts which bear less regular and evident relationships to one another. These confines make rhythm not only possible but necessary;

there is none of the randomness of tones loosed free into the world at large, whose only coherence comes from the activities of which they are the sounds. Here the artificial universe of an abstracted audible environment, limited in duration, restores meaning to audible reality and so restores the possible meaning of the audible reality at large, of the world at large. A leisure activity has become a vehicle for the meaning of the world.

Leisure-Time

A dispute rages around the difference between leisure and leisure-time. Classically, leisure is looked upon as activity which is not time related; but leisure-time is time related by definition. Leisure is taken to be unrelated to time in this sense, that the activities which constitute leisure are ones which are not measured in temporal terms, and so they take place outside of time, even if performed by temporal beings. As a result, not all activities could constitute leisure activities. Time as the measure of movement will be invoked wherever there is movement; non-temporal activities would be ones in which there is a non-moving object of the activity, and a mode of operation which can attain such non-moving object in an unmoving way. What is supplied for this is the return of thought upon itself, since self-thinking is autonomous or independent, self-reliant, has no lacks and so need engage in no movement to supply those lacks. The thought which attains that object is itself the object, and so clearly need not move in order to obtain it.

On the other side, activities which are time-bound are those of beings which are made up of parts and so must be continually about keeping those parts together, servicing them one part by another, and traversing the parts in order to get anything done. Time, then, is associated with necessity, repetition and incompleteness. An extension of this is that when temporality is measured by machines, i.e., clocks of any sort, then the chunks of time are dissociated and can stand alien to one another; for the machine consists in it being made of parts which existed independently of one another before they were assembled. The machine divides up time because it is itself divided up.[20]

Biological and other natural rhythms, and the duration of human projects, are not peculiar by reason of possessing vast units of measurement, as distinct from the clock's "minutes." The instantaneous speed of half-life decays, metabolic events or synaptic events is difficult to surpass with any clock. Instead these rhythms are distinctive because the whole event does not allow of division into smaller and more exact intervals; the whole event forms the unit, and exactitude is a function only of successful accomplishment and not of minute divisibility—it would be senseless to call a process "exact" if it matched a clock but failed its purpose. Events come to completion in their own time, and the time of something else can at best be matched to them.

But the matching is highly problematic.[21] If two events are mapped onto a clock-event perhaps not causally related to either, the two events can be related only through this filter. The filter remains largely unrecognized, and yet it is active to distort the events. Any comparison between them must drop incomparable features out of consideration, but this loss of information is multiplied when the number of comparisons is multiplied by relation to the filtering clock-system.

In addition, this piecemeal comparison means that the very nature of the events is distorted. In any relationship and encounter, e.g., a simple handshake, the parties experience one single event. But in timing that event, as by a clock, the comparison to that third event must be sequential; first one and then the other is compared. Instead of one event which is itself a relationship, there are two events originally unrelated and then related together only as afterthought and indirectly. While the encounter organizes its parties' activities as well as being organized by them, differently than each would alone, the clock makes the encounter only a sum of two separate and independently directed activities.

This makes clear that clock-time cannot handle events without distortion, since as will appear any action is relationship. A project of process can exist properly in time only in terms of reference to its own perfection and its own timeliness, i.e., a qualitative timing and not a quantitative; this "discerning the times" and "having good timing" has been the mark of wisdom, while watching a timepiece is scorned as "mere clock watching."

Another sense in which leisure-time is found antithetical to leisure-activity is that this reference to an unrelated and so irrelevant standard also inserts the suggestion of modern work right into the heart of leisure. This can be seen true even of human projects, which call for measurement in their own terms. It is even more true of natural processes, which are cyclical while clock time is linear. "Diurnal" time returns; and so it cannot be wasted now once and for all, nor can there be radical novelty which one can bend his efforts toward accumulating in the future. But clock-time never returns, and so can be used or wasted forever; every moment is radically new, and something new in the future may be planned. Because the future is a given and all activities go into perfecting it, arriving at its "virtue," natural time penetrates all activities and is all mixed up with them, so that no leisured domain separate from other domains is visible.

But clock-time both requires planning and the contriving of the future, and makes this possible by facilitating the coordination of human activities (of course, at the cost of their differences) on a large scale.[22] It is possible to distinguish sections of time, and in fact even to conceive of leisure-time or free-time, as well as raising the problem of how to "occupy" it, productively, so that it is not wasted, just as work-time or unfree time. While the clock begins its history as a toy, it makes modern work both possible for the first time, and then inescapably necessary.

While clock-time seems not to permit of leisure, process-time does not exclude it; and perhaps it can even penetrate and redeem clock-time. Still, neither of these is classical extra-temporality. The possibility for anything that fits the classical description of leisure depends upon the universe being as claimed and upon there being access by man to such activities and faculties as are claimed. Such objects and faculties are much in disrepute today. But even if one is a believer in a self-sufficient God who carries on as does Aristotle's, he may still have problems. God is not reached by man in the same way as God is reached by himself, but only haltingly and by steps; and, in fact, there is analogy to parts in God himself, viz., the persons of the trinity. So if leisure is to be given its same sense as distinct from leisure-time, some other way of discovering self-contained activities is necessary; of course, another alternative would be to find another meaning of leisure while still keeping that sense different from leisure-time.

Perhaps one way into this would be to investigate what is felt to be insufficient about leisure-time, but satisfied by leisure-activity. Leisure-time is harassed, because it continues the attitudes and goals of the non-leisure-time activities, chiefly of job, in terms of which it is defined.[23] To the tension is added either the enslavement to a prearranged life or the degrading stultification of being led to expect and so experience enjoyment while there is no objective correspondent to it. While the leisure-time activities may be enjoyed, they could contribute neither to human betterment nor to any recreative function, in critics' eyes.

Leisure-time is stressful not simply because competition is present, but because the competition regards the same objectives as does that foisted upon man by our post-industrial employment. The competition is for elusive goals which evaporate even when within the grasp, because the goals are not intended to satisfy the achievement but to keep the activity going. Satisfaction would terminate it, while dissatisfaction matched with common expectation of satisfaction keeps it going. Because leisure-time is governed in its existence by the work-time standing over against it, it has no autonomy and self-definition, but exists in the attitude of the anxious glance over the shoulder. Not only does it end when the work time must recommence, but the events which fill it up have no internal coherence to give rest in the interval, no occupation of the attention, only frenzied cramming to "waste not, want not," for "time is money"— a criterion whose origin is easy to find.

Whatever leisure-activity would be, then, it would have to be something other than what makes up these degeneracies. Because the inner coherence of the activities, there would be no reference to employment, its criteria nor its mode of competition. Instead it would offer confidence, absorption and integration. Not enslaved, it would be free.

Now in order to achieve such desiderata it may both be necessary to have either the object or the faculties of classical leisure-activity; and if we do not, then it is doubtful that the ancients did either. Instead they may have been performing activity much like ours in exercising leisure, although they experienced it as something else entirely. The exercise of leisure, as of most other things, need not command only one experience of leisure; to have leisure one need not know leisure. Whether these sorts of objects and activities are available to us will have to be decided by continuing to look at what we do in fact do, and at how we are able to think about this.

Clocking Sports Events

We shall look later at the bounding of sporting games by a starting and a finishing time. Here we shall direct attention to the impact of noting the passage of time within the sporting event. While a boxing match has its own time given beforehand, the effort is directed to packing accomplishment within these limits, and while the shooting or jumping contest may include a penalty or disqualification for too long a delay before starting, i.e., for passivity, the race has a much different time relationship. In such events there is no pre-assigned time for start or finish, and so no time-"outs" in the course of it can be granted, or even conceived. Instead, there is a constant stretch of time running from start to finish; the temporal boundaries or at least the final one are determined by the participants and their performances.

There is a serious technical problem of just whether a touch of a finger or even an electronic pulse over wires is fast enough to discriminate truthfully a hundredth of a second difference between contestants. Neglecting this the difference between clock-time and diurnal time, and their effects upon leisure and recreation, can be highlighted around this kind of sport. The race can be run with no clock, and of course was first done so; or it can be run with a clock, with far different consequences. The first differences appear when changing to a more common expression. The race is run "against" the clock, not with it; or the race is run against other runners, but it is equally correct to say "with" other runners. Each races with the other, one against one, and one against all; but in a clocked race all race against one, the clock, and only secondarily does each race the other runners. The fastest time wins in this race; the winner has the fastest time, in the first race. The one race is interpersonal, with the criteria being the other persons present; the other race is impersonal, such that the others' positions are only a sign of the clock-criterion, and are no more than the rabbit—a fake rabbit at that—out ahead of the greyhounds on the track. Perhaps more stimulus would come from posting the runners' times for each other, and keeping them from viewing each others' positions. Passing "like ships in the night" could be more effective than passing the other rowing shells in the daylight.

This changes the present event directly; there is an even greater effect from the change in historical time that this promotes. Under interpersonal time, each race is separate; under clocked time, all are continuous, since all performances can be compared, and the single race loses its confines, identity and importance. Under interpersonal time, the ideal lies in the persons concretely present, a concrete ideal; under clocked time the ideal lies in the nature of man not yet achieved or manifested, an abstract possibility. In the first case the ideal is higher or lower each time, and is always achieved; in the second the ideal is always higher, never lower, and is never achieved. In interpersonal time the external conditions are all important to changing the performance, for the racers perform all under the same conditions; in clocked time the real conditions are irrelevant, for only the clock time goes out and this is not indexed with some coefficient for weather, equipment, stimulants, amateurism, etc., whereby conditions are included within. Therefore on the clock these do not matter, the particular contest does not matter, and the other racers are not even necessary. The result is that performances are improved to an astounding degree from year to year under clock time.

This phenomenon of the changes in the quality of leisure-sport is just a matter of keeping records, and the same occurs in records of other sports. But because *altius* and *fortius* not to mention the number of goals or points can also be recorded by means other than inscription, they are more naturally amenable to it. It is *citius* which is utterly dependent on the machine for a record, and would vanish instantly otherwise. It is also for the reason that the race is most deeply affected by recording clock-times.

Species Time

In the same way as it seemed inappropriate to our study to engage upon comparisons between the species of humans and animals, so it is unnecessary to work with the manner in which not the time of the human individual begins but the time of the human species, i.e., to belabor evolution.[24] In principle it comes to the same thing as we have discussed regarding the individual, since we acknowledge no issue of appreciating a kind as different from individuals of that kind. Perhaps the sole reason for consideration is not to leave a distracting curiosity over the occurrence of the human remains at a certain point in a vast cosmic development, and not before.

For this is the sole argument for evolution of the human species, that the continuum of fossil remains contains nothing like human bones before a certain time, then approximatively and progressively similar bones, and finally remains of the very same sort. The argument is weak, because it appeals to an absence rather than to some presence; but under the most likely available hypotheses for explaining this fact, the argument seems sustainable. Note that all other arguments for evolution show only its possibility, not its occurrence, e.g., the continuity of human bodily structure and behavior with the bestial, the ability to produce new species artificially evolved from others, the devolution of certain other species.

Taking this to be a factual occurrence, we would have to know more accurately what the occurrence consists in before knowing even what might be seeking explanation about man in it. First of all, evolution is not progress, which goes on within species and consists in its individuals maximizing the realization of their specific potential; instead evolution goes on between species, and consists of a secured set of likenesses between individuals being modified in isolated individuals who then initiate a stabilization of them into a new species. The species does not evolve; the individuals do. Stable species precede, continue through and follow upon the individuals' modifications. The species from which the individual mutates may continue subsequently, if conditions are favorable; but the same is true for the survival of the mutant individual and the tenuous new species. Environment neither leads to nor guarantees the mutation; instead, it tolerates it, or does not, just as it may continue or not to tolerate the earlier species. That the individual mutation need be not in gross form (phenotype) but primarily in genetic structure (genotype) is of no particular importance; we know excruciatingly well today how minor are the events needed to affect genetic endowment.

So what is the question remaining and needing explanation? It seems to be whether there is truly a change of species from animal to man; and this it would be rash to examine before concentrating upon man, whereas it may seem idle afterwards. Nonetheless, we might well ask why this would be such a threat anyway. The threat (or promise) which elicits response is that, when specific similarities are added to specific continuity, the sense of human distinctness may disintegrate and the special care accorded humans may be no longer justified. But, first the sense of human distinctness is a given to be explained, not a hypothesis or an illusion to be explained away. Next, perhaps the special care should quite properly be extended, at least so as to leave behind carelessness and contempt for the animate universe. And, most basically, the metaphysical principle involved is misunderstood: *nemo dat quod non habet*, "no one gives what he lacks," does not mean that the earlier species must have in a realized and recognizable form all that the later one does, nor does it mean that even the unrealized and potential presence of a capacity is ready for immediate exercise. The correct meaning is that the causality of the earlier is needed for the later result; it is also almost always the case that more than that is needed. This addition may be a completely external input, or it may be the passage through many intermediate stages at each of which a possibility for the next arises which had not been present before. The primitive possibility for humankind cannot be leapfrogged over these mediating developments so as to be alleged as a real ability to act humanly present in the animal species as it is in the human.

The only other question might be why the mutation happened then and no other time into man; and to this the obvious answer is that there is no reason at all why it had to be so, and no indication that it was the sole time. Nothing stands in the way of there being polygenesis of humans which have either not been discovered deep down or which were not ripe to survive in the times or which produced only one sex, etc. As said at the start, it seems neither necessary nor profitable to dwell upon human time in this sense. For us to have a memory, as it were, of our non-human ancestors if there were any does nothing to add or detract from the continuity of existence in the individual human or in the human species, nor to reinforce yet further the sense of precariousness as humans that our daily life offers us quite well enough.

Survival Play and Evolution

Among higher animals appears a vigorous analogy to human play, whose repetition in humankind cannot be well distinguished at this point in our study.

The young animal confronts his fellow offspring almost immediately upon birth with tooth and nail. The teeth and nails are shielded, however not too much. The animals wrestle about and nip at one another and give chase; they turn belly up at the end of a skirmish. All of the attack and defense techniques of maturity are tried out here. The young animals' activity is incessant, and whatever one can say about the pleasure it brings it is certainly evident that it is exciting.

It is alleged that this activity is a practice for adulthood, that these attacks and defenses, thrusts and feints, will serve the serious purposes of maturity. In maturity these no longer young animals will be called upon to protect their young and themselves against dominant animals of their own species and marauders from other species. Their activity in youth, which resembles so much the rough and tumble play of human youth, is seen as a functional activity. While there is no attempt to claim that in the animal species there is some intent to perfect this activity to the end that they will be able to be dominant as mature, it is still alleged that this is what as a matter of fact it does; and since among the animals there is little more that can be ascribed than this by us, since we lack their own consciousness, then this is all that their childplay is. The impetus to extend this analysis to human childplay is almost irresistible; even if not taken as complete, it is taken as either basic to any other higher analysis, or as accompanying such, or as a stage which is no longer dominant in cultured play.[25]

What is overlooked in this swift transition to the human condition is that in fact this is not at all what is happening among the animals. The play is ostensibly in training against enemies. But animals within the species who are dominant are not fought with; they are submitted to. Among dangerous animals a pitched battle is extremely rare; very few of such species indulge in it—almost none of the great cats, canines and simians, some species of sea animals but only once a season and with only a very few participants, the great reptiles but again only outside the band and infrequently. Among the battles which do occur, fights to the death are almost unheard of. It is again tempting to project the intention of caring that the species survive; and, while it is unrealistic to see things that way since defeat means that one does not propagate that year, still what is true is that major injuries are few, although blindingly rapid and bloody self-destruction of these species was within their reach long before our own was within ours.

But fights are few, although threats and retreats are many. A clear loser, usually determined by no more than roaring and pawing, seems unable not to withdraw; a clear victor seems incapable of finishing off a contestant disabled, withdrawing or giving signs of submission to the more dominant. Even this occurs as infrequently as their mating, and as its accompaniment. Beyond this the only intraspecific attacks seem to be by a band upon a single member expelled; again, the battle does not occur but is only threatened. Aged animals are slain, but this is no battle and there is no resistance; it is very clinical, with no need for training in combat.

It appears, then, that the youthful play is no training for anything but the same sort of activity in maturity; nothing more serious than the same feints and thrusts, the same aggression and submission occurs. If anything, the childplay or pup-play could be called perhaps a preparation for the rituals of dominance and submission, for the proprieties involved in maintaining the order of the band, of keeping everyone in his place. But even this is not a practice of mature actions in youth; rather it is their exercise in fact during play. One or the other alternative seems to be demanding: either both childplay and mature confrontation are playful, and then the comparison to human childplay leads to vastly different results; or both are serious, and then the comparison to human childplay is manifestly empty.

The other possibility, of training for combat with other species, is more plausible since of course such combat even to the death occurs as the normal way of life for species whose food is each other. Again, however, some hesitations are in order. First, it is seldom the more healthy members of other species who are successfully attacked, and therefore seldom those which are approached at all; the usual approach is to an invalid or immature stray, whose slaughter is less an attack than a butchery. Secondly, the combat with other species is not something for which practice with their own kind could have prepared the animal, for the other species simply do not combat in the same way. Their organs of combat are not the same, their moves even with comparable organs are different, their vulnerable spots are peculiar to their own species. At best what mock combat in one's own species could have done is to tone muscle and to perfect movement. But to identify their play with this, the demand of the organism for exercise of its powers and development of the skills along lines of criteria involved in that very exercise, is another set of assertions entirely, not at all continuous with a comparison drawn within the range of combatively functional play.[26]

Energy

While body is the source of our singleness and individuality, and therefore our separation from one another, it is also the only available bond between us. Only over such a bridge can we contact each other. There is no content to our imagination of what bonding would be like without bodies. So being outside of one another makes us separate and single but also makes us available for joining each other. The image of the human species is of a planetary oneness: of the individual humans turned in upon one another in a bounded universe.

This is to say that the volume and depth which give us individuality are also the source of energy. The energy is that of relationship among the electrical charges in our mass. Individually the direction of our energy flow is outward, as bodies are drawn to the most weighty. The energy of our bodies takes place between bodies, an energy not just of attraction but of repulsion, such that everything stands in its place due to the tension balanced between attraction and repulsion. Though this is not peculiar to the human body, it offers some sobering anticipations of human peculiarity.

Entropy of our energy and disintegration of our body is simultaneous.[27] Once disintegration occurs there is no center, no pole of attraction for energy; and once energy is diminished there is no binding force to provide the tone needed for individuality. The winding down is continual but so is the replenishment; there is always something present to replenish it for me, although there is not an infinite energy reserve and even though it will be exhausted eventually. The replacement occurs by accretion and assimilation of new energy sources from outside, by outside pressure, as in the case of diamonds and coal, or by the input from another yet higher system taking over the lower, one of a different order. This would not alter bodiliness but supply it with energy resources from beyond it, once these were accommodated to its own form. Already within the basic form of bodily energy, of attraction or drawing power, we have a model for the most lofty form of energetic exercise, called exemplary causality.

Enjoying Sickness

A standing joke is that the only time one relaxes is when he is sick. It is no joke, not just because it is true but also because this is a point of importance in the notion of leisure. One cannot do anything productive; he is forced to contact his own self and its resources, or to be amused, i.e., distracted from himself. Does the fact that the inactivity of sickness is enforced make it incapable of having the features of leisure which would otherwise be open to inactivity? Perhaps better, are leisure and pleasure so closely connected that it would not be possible to have leisure in the discomfort or pain of sickness?

First of all, it is evident that along the spectrum of seriousness in illnesses, there are some which do no more than offer an excuse for withdrawing from activity; no one would hesitate at giving these a leisure dimension. If we take this as the starting point on a spectrum, then whatever this shares with more severe illnesses might be a basis for ascribing to the more severe the same if reduced leisure features. The dominant feature of the simple state seems to be that in it one is acutely aware of the problems being faced by those whose daily activities are continuing. Because of his proximity to those activities there is no jump to be made into being delighted at release from them. As one's condition worsens and his distance from ordinary activities widens, it will become increasingly difficult to get a sense of his condition as one of release from burdens. Yet one expects of the healthy man that he make just this projection which will allow him to enter into the experience of the sick man. He is doing wrong if he does not appreciate his condition as benefiting from the access to activities, by reason of being removed from debilitating illness.

There seems little reason why the same demand, in reverse, should not be made upon the sick man. Otherwise, he is ejected from humanity by being deprived of the sort of demands we make upon it. And, since we never really do think he should be so freed, when we have done so and he sinks morosely into his illness we are disturbed at him and feel guilty over it.

Negentropic Renewal: Forgiveness

Energy expenditure may seem like the gravest threat to activity but in fact it is the very condition for it. If the energy put into an activity remained unchanged and undiminished, then there would be no possibility for movement and change at all. On the model of the pebble thrown into the water, if the ripples kept rolling out indefinitely from this then there would be no going back, no escape from the activity performed. But in fact the activity dies out and diminishes; I no longer need fight everything which has ever been done nor push aside all of the energy which has been expended. It has returned to other forms and no longer stands as an obstacle to my own activity. While I might like the effects of my own activities to persist indefinitely, I would surely not wish this for others since it would inhibit my own.

The humanized form of this remission in energy is forgiveness.[28] Unlike nature, our memory makes it possible for actions once done to stand in our way without end; they are there and there is no way around them. Once again, however, the faculty that cripples us provides us the crutches, too: since our memory is not dependent on the remission of energy in nature, neither is it held down by the factual presence of the effects from actions. For the effects remain effects and not just facts only so long as we remember their sources in action. But we can forget; Nietzsche stresses this as the human activity which alone permits health, and saw the big problem in how to train us to remember.

We can forget, and we can forget upon will. This is forgiveness. The same lack of necessity which introduced the inhibiting action can dispose of it. Only this can clear the ground for a new start, for action free again from the weight of past action. Forgiving both ourselves and others, healing our memories permits the newness and freedom which makes up leisure. It goes one step beyond the *lex talionis*; for while "an eye for an eye" at least matched the punishment to the offence instead of it overflowing its bounds and continuing forever, forgiveness clears our environment even of the obstacle of punishment.

Recreation

If there is an expenditure of energy or matter which is needed for the continuance of something, then that energy or matter must be supplied from somewhere or the being ceases to continue. The model for this happening is that a hole is created, and unless that hole is filled in the being in which the hole is found cannot continue. The sequence looks as if one thing follows another; but of course that cannot be, for then the being would not survive past the end of its expenditure in order to be replenished. There is not an emptying out of one thing, followed by a supplying of more of the same thing. If there is to be replenishment, it must be simultaneous with the expenditure and of a different mode than it, so that it can be made at all, input while output is still going on.

If one looks upon stamina as a quality which can be emptied out in kind and then restored in kind, with as it were the bodily structure, the frame, supporting itself with creaks and threats of collapse until it is restored, then there is a wild metaphor indeed which has taken over the scene of recreation. Stamina, of course, is not a certain kind of thing but rather the condition of some thing; and so it can neither be lost nor restored in kind. Only what has been used can be restored. "Energy supply" has the same metaphorical structure. When we speak of restoring energy, we are in fact talking about putting ourselves back into a condition where we are capable of certain kinds of activity once more. How we restore the condition and what we restore it with depends in turn upon what kind of activity we are to restore ourselves for.

Recreation, then, will be differential, something different from the activities in which whatever kind of stamina we are speaking of is lost. In some cases it may be anything different, in others it may have to be a special kind of activity different in a special way from some other and debilitating kind of activity. Often activities which appear superficially different are the same in the relevant aspect and so they do not recreate. Whatever else is to be said about recreation, it is relative to the activity from which one is being recreated; leisure, which may be different from recreation, can instead at least as a possibility be seen as a certain kind of activity, from which as well as from anything else one may need to be recreated. If leisure is seen to be distinct from work (which we are not claiming but only raising as a commonly made relationship), then recreation will not be necessarily associated with a cessation of work; it may be a return to work. When however recreation is designed as a differentiation from work, obviously it would be a case of leisure, if we keep the work/leisure contrast going too.

Recreation is parasitic upon creation (and suggestive of creativity, to be treated later), both etymologically and for its meaning. Recreation is activity intended to create again the person the person once created. There are differences: one does not create himself, but does recreate himself; the person to be achieved by recreation will be different than the one achieved by creation, at least older; recreation intends to restore parts lacking, while creation provides the whole with no parts preceding it. Recreation is more akin to the notion of creation as a rearrangement, forming up or juggling with realities which pre-exist the act of creating, than it is to the notion of creation as the giving of existence to both parts and their whole after nothing at all preceded them. The first notion of creation is bound by its building blocks, the second is not, as recreation is a function of whatever absence or deficiency the preceding activity produced.

Recreation is not free in any ultimate sense; instead it is absolutely required for the continued existence of the being, if given the meaning it has been given above. While alternatives appear in how to effect the recreation, one among them must be chosen, and only at the cost of his life is one free not to chose among them.

If recreation can cope with our requirements globally, such that many different recreations often can remedy the same lack, or any single recreation may remedy a variety of deficiencies, then our energy expenditures are relatively undifferentiated, and so are their recreations. Both physicist and railroader may enjoy soccer during time off from their fatiguing activities; and either physicist or railroader may be refreshed as much by chess as by soccer. Of course, each of these may be false. If false, it is not because the recreative activity was unfit to recreate from a general type of activity, although we could not exclude that, but rather that the singular person who is physicist or railroader does not take to it. Or, even more correctly, he does not now care to recreate by it, though he often does do so. So, although the activity may expend energy in an undifferentiated manner, this will be determined one way or another by the present choice.

However even if no particular form of recreation is sought one may need only cease doing an activity in order not to "break" under it; he need not replace it with any specific form of recreative activity at all. Of course, truly ceasing it may involve replacing it so as not to continue in the same habit despite cessation, and involve replacing it in fact with a considerably different activity.

But quite clearly this often does not happen; one often recreates in a very similar activity; one often recreates with a similar intensity, weak or strong. So common is this that it is tempting to suggest that no one is lazy or industrious, but that one performs according to his differential energy level and can no more help his vigor than his lackadaisicalness. This is to say that "lazy" and "industrious" do not find their meanings in the context of the physical or mental vigor with which activity is performed, but only in the context of the moral or virtuous rightness of the activity selected to be performed, whether weakly or strongly.

If the recreative activity is frequently so similar to the recreated activity, is there in truth any need for recreation at all? Would one truly "break" if he continued? The answer seems to vary: laborers would, professionals would not. Or at least their interests manifest that they think they would.[29]

At the very least, recreating activity may sometimes be a necessity only for the humane living of vision expanded beyond the recreated activity, and perhaps not for the continued healthy living of human bodies and minds. If we accept for now this minimalist position, which may still be going too far, it means that recreation is less a matter of physical necessity than of cultural perfection, and that the content of recreation is to be designed accordingly.

Having discussed recreation-from certain activities as a feature of recreation, we must inquire whether recreation-for other activities is equally essential. Is recreation not simply pushed from behind but also pulled from ahead? The most frequent suggestion is that recreation is for the job, for restoring one to the condition where he can return to the job and again perform it effectively. Recreation may indeed contribute to this, and it may be designed and permitted solely insofar as it heads toward that goal. But there seems to be no necessity that recreation which is from work must also be for work, except in the case of the cyclical activities which we shall see. There may as well be activities for which work unfits us and recreation fits us, which are neither. Such activities could readily be seen not to be work, but they could be distinct from recreation only if they did not restore from work, and we have seen that not all activities do so for any given individual. That is to say, work and recreation are not categories exhaustive of the range of human activity, even if we admit them as categories contrary to each other. By suggesting that recreation need not be for work, we may expand the possibilities for human activity, certainly the possibilities for its qualitative variety.

· 3 ·

OUR ANIMATE BODY

The distance is short from gravity to life. Instead of being moved and moving others by all that we bodily are, but despite ourselves, now we move ourselves and others by part of what we are, by organs. The result is that there is something about ourselves which can stand outside of the activity and give a whiff of freedom and transcendence. Instead of being joined to the world by losing our identity in it as sheer bodiliness would, or by being juxtaposed with other items among its furniture, we now make it part of us rather than being just a part of it.

The sort of activities performed are ones which are tightly integrated into our living existence. The only source out of which they are done is so that they can continue to be done. The activities are ends in themselves, and are identified with what it means to live at all. "For the living, to live is to exist": there is not something yet further which is being accomplished when, for example, we eat than that we now may continue to eat and to live.

Our living surface is overgrown with skin, and our depth is a group of further organs. As living we are made up of organs or parts functional and "responsible" for continued life in some way; of course, what is continued is those same organs as functioning. Our surface and depth now are to be seen as permitting digestion to take place and movements to be made. The shape or form which was looked at for its own meaning as a structure of spatiality now is seen to consist of protection for soft organs; this is the first entry of protection, for the covering and appearance of our surface did not have to be read in this way. This is not so sturdy a protection, to be sure, but it suffices for normal life circumstances. More accurately, normal life circumstances are to be defined as what do not threaten beyond the protections, threaten either with attack, inaction or stress. The normality is our normality, not that judged upon some other criterion. The areas of vulnerability—head, chest, abdomen, groin—locate the centers of our life interest.

The material which makes up the living man is not just located there but lives there; bone is not just matter but living matter. Nothing that makes up my living body is not living; anything that is not living does not make up part of me, although it may accompany me more or less constantly. Still, these are portable environments which it may be difficult to distinguish from the living body, organic flora and fauna which though living and making it possible for me to continue living do not live my life but their own.

Our lived activity is a rhythmical one, that is, it comes and goes rather than being a constant insistence. Better, the constancy with which it operates is two-phased: a beating heart, circulating blood, periodical ovaries, inspiring and expiring lungs, a hungering and satiated stomach. While each of these organs could as well have the citing of its activity identified as that of the whole, e.g., I hunger and not just my stomach, and I beat my blood around rather than my heart doing it, it is nonetheless clearer when put in organic terms. Again, my skin continually absorbs energy; but it does not do it as a capacitator up to a brink limit and constantly, for besides the expenditure in activity it is also just true that the sun is not always up. Non-human nature matches my bodily rhythms. Once again it appears that I am a being of repetitions and whose only constancy is to be doing it over again after stopping. What the meaning of this is escapes me, but it is surely important that it is not otherwise when the whole alternative is completely excluded. Might it be that I would not notice constancy, as I do not notice the constancy of other features like the nervous systems? These cyclical activities need to be noticed, so as to be cared for. As with phenomena of non-living nature, one phase induces the next instead of simply following it; unlike nature, our input is demanded at one or both phases.

These organs are produced by myself as part of the exercise of them. They are not pre-given their exercise, arriving full-blown from elsewhere, but are functioning as soon as they are appearing; and since that functioning is our living, ourselves, we cannot say but that we produce them ourselves. As noted earlier, no one is formed before all the others; they advance together, and no one is formed apart from the simultaneous formation of the others. The consequence is that neither could they be operationally separated.

Since unified exercise is their reality, not each organ for itself separately but for the whole, i.e., itself indirectly, then their failure can be called anything that stands in the way of this; we call this sickness, illness or disease. It is necessary that sickness be possible in order for the functioning to be possible; for the functioning is done in terms of a criterion to be met, even though that criterion is indirectly nothing but its own existence. And wherever criteria are being met, failure to meet them is a built-in alternative resultant.

Organically we do something to our environment because we cannot continue unless we do so. What we do to it is to make it part of ourselves and then release it. We are distant from our environment and not immediately satisfied by being within it; we can be in our environment as what we are, namely living humans, only at the price of doing something to this environment.[30]

Food

The activity of bodily organs for their own sake is most commonplace in nutrition. In feeding I change reality other than myself into myself. The chemicals and atoms which make up food are altered, sometimes only in appearance and sometimes in their chemical or atomic identity, into my own chemicals and atoms, and their transformable energy. Changing them into me has no other role than to permit the continuance of the very same process and thereby preserve the organs of nutrition; that has been dwelt upon earlier. To say that I am what I eat is not as accurate as to say that what I eat is what I am, i.e., becomes what I am.

This is what, in fact, constitutes the very notion of food. What makes the world food for me is that I change it into me. What is not food is excreted, because it has not become me, along with what has ceased to be me. My bodily reality is just what it is, living; and nothing that does not belong persists in its company. Food, then, is only what becomes part of me; properly speaking, not everything that enters the mouth and digestive tract is food. Prior to consumption the world has the possibility of becoming me; but it only becomes food as it does become me, in the process of its assimilation and destruction. The status of food, then, is a precarious one: only what is well along the way to not being itself any longer has become food.

The object of consumption is to make the consumable disappear; if it persists, the consumption and nutrition is unsuccessful. The character of food, then, is not in anything that is, as it were, to be framed and preserved. The best of food is what disappears the best, on condition that the disappearance is meeting the needs of the organs.

Not everything can be changed into me, which is a puzzling fact. Am I more alien to part of the world than to other parts? Am I less akin to some reality, since I cannot make it part of me? Surely the range of food is limited by my ability to disintegrate and assimilate it, as an absolute limit, and by what meets my organic needs, as a relative limit. Even more relative a limit are the habitual modes of consumption I engage in, such that some things are not acceptable; but this dimension is outside our scope for now. Perhaps the response should be that the world is no more alien to me in one part than another, but that it is accessible not all in the same way. In particular, objects which will themselves persist and endure if not consumed seem the least fitted for food but the best fitted for other relationships with me.

Whatever else is to be said about food, we eat because if we do not we die, and this is in turn because the organic life is the activity of carrying on just such activities as eating, repeating them endlessly. That is what life is. It is not simply that we are not fueled for other things, as though fueling was something to be gotten over and done with so we could go on to other things. Rather, death is the cessation of these activities precisely because we have ceased to perform them; for the activities, present in cyclical repetition, are the life.

Excretion

Besides food in the normal sense, our nutrition is also carried on with world-products assimilated in other ways: radiant energy exposure, inhalation of oxygen, etc. But it is improper not to continue the examination of nutrition, of whatever sort, by noting that for it to be repetitive we must provide room for the new activity, by excretion. Besides bowel and bladder movement, exhalation of air and perspiration are also excretions, as are the growing of hair and fingernails and several other processes to be mentioned shortly. The activity of using up food cannot be complete without disposing of it; we are not solely involved in making the world part of us, for then our individual limitations would be burst. In order to remain one reality in the world, we must again pass the world on through us. The picture changes, then, from a world at our service to a world flowing through us, made into us temporarily, and disposed of in turn so that we can become something yet further.

The poisonous and hence repulsive character of excretion to us is a result of its fertility: non-food for us, excretion is food for other living beings. The same is true in reverse: plants' oxygen output of the daytime is essential to our life. Our excretion generates multiple organisms which simply do not fit, however, into the limited and defined system we are; they do not fit among our flora and fauna, though they fit quite well with others.

We must use great effort in some phases of our organic activity, effort fueled by that very same activity, however. Mostly our effort feels expended upon one part: excretion, exhalation; in fact, exhalation is considerably more demanding, as the inhalation after death suggests. Excretion seems also the more demanding, but this is likely a cultural habit of control which cannot easily be dispensed with, just as the tensions from expectations surrounding birth.

Sleep can be looked at in the same light, as a form of excretion, since it stands in structurally the same relationship with wakefulness. Regarding sleep, the question which may have suggested itself about feeding becomes more pronounced: why bother sleeping? In turn, why both excreting? If one were to consume just the right proportion of food, to just balance the net bodily needs as they arose, would he not be able to forego excreting? The answer is, of course, that among the bodily needs is the requirement to be rid of portions of the world which have formed our organs and by so doing to be able to replace them.

By the same token, sleep might appear as the condition which should be able to be remedied by wakeful replacement of energy. If it is just a matter of diminished energy, then I should be able simply to eat more or better, or otherwise to supply my energy needs, and thus refurbished to keep right on going without the need for a complete stop. One thinks of yogis, whose sleep patterns are hardly normal but who are entranced for years and even undergo burial, or remain sleepless through impossibly long periods of time under certain conditions. Actually this is a very helpful comparison in making the point, for the states in which a yogi can undertake such activity approach sleep so closely as to be indistinguishable, even from death.

But there seems to be more than just input and output to the organism; it is not just an emptying and refilling process. Instead, the exercise itself of organs tires them out, in a way which is not simply equivalent to the diminishment of their energy supply. The state of the organs begins to render them unfit for continued exercise, e.g., by contraction of the routes of oxygen supply in the blood. Again, the cycling is more important than what ostensible function, otherwise manageable, the cyclic process fulfils. The impossibility of getting our bodily activity completely under the control of independent purposes seems important to our way of life.

Likewise the process of reproduction and generation is not just for the sake of relieving tensions nor just for the sake of offspring, but for both, and for both in the sense of bodily life. Firstly, the importance of excretion is shown by the excretion of our very life, in menstruation and seminal emission. Our eggs and sperm are our greatest fertility, but they are being cast off as unused potentialities, irrespective of the pleasure which sexuality and all other natural processes brings, done in fact in some cases with severe pain. The wastage seems horrifying, but it is the repetition and renewal which is more important to the organism. There are no persisting bodily tissues to be framed for keeping, but only such as whose sole activity is to change, for the sake purely of that changing activity itself.

The fact that I am generated in a genetic fashion emphasizes this. Every cell is a repetition of the single flesh, the single genetic endowment, formed of the parents' dual endowment; every cell of the body contains the same structure found in the generative tissues, sperm and egg. Each cell is formed of a replication of RNA upon DNA, and is so formed and formed again with each bodily renewal, continually. The repetitive character of bodily activity goes this far down, as well as in the more grossly observable forms.

The second point of view on the reason for reproduction falls within the same camp. Just as the fluid transfers occur independently of the pleasures of sex, so does generation by sexual intercourse occur independently of any intent upon procreation. The repetition which goes on in procreation is a more broadly based one; for what is being effected, quite apart from what is being sought, is a repetition on the level of species rather than on the individual level. Renewal of the species is necessary as individuals who bear life depart. Species is, in fact, able to be described as the continuation of life, among mutually fertilizable individuals; it is this before it is a separable kind, a generalisable essence, although this follows immediately from the fact that the essence of the living is their life. To put more bluntly this need to continue life through procreation, we reproduce because we die; to exclude the intentional element, reproductive encounter functions to offset death, whatever else it does. I may be born in complete unconsciousness, in an act concerned not at all with me; in fact, it is unlikely one's parents would succeed in reproducing him otherwise. I may be born with a complete profligacy of reproductivity, as from the millions of sperm one alone fertilizes the egg. But through all this it is human life continuing itself, with no outside intentional help required. As Aristotle put it unimprovably, we try to keep our life going in the only way we can: by repetition, of ourselves in nutrition and by replacement in reproduction.

Birth itself is indeed labor, as the contractions beforehand stretch the tissues to enlarge the exit. But the intensity of this event takes over and seems to make of it a single distinctive occurrence. In fact a little reflection would bring back that this is part of a cycle which was equally intense at its commencement; although public documents ask only for date of birth, not date of conception, the birthday is only the end of a repetitive cycle. (Somewhat scurrilously, the male has been defined as what comes out of woman and spends the rest of his life trying to get back in.) This cycle, as others studied, is associated with pleasure in natural cyclical performance; only the imposition of cultural expectations or the inadequacy of physique, which can either be trained away or remedied, stand in the way of this.[31]

Pleasure and Pain/Displeasure

The performance of these cyclical self-maintaining activities are associated with some recognition of their accomplishment or failure, and these recognitions are known as pleasure and pain. Their structure is such that achieving any part of the repetition will bring pleasure, and being apart from any part of the cycle will be accompanied by pain. These two states are the presence or absence of our body to itself and to its continuance. Apart from maladies wherein the bodily conditions are not accompanied by the appropriate pleasure or pain, these states are not so much signaled by pleasure and pain as they are united and identified with them. This identity of our bodily states with our pleasure and pain will be continued in discussion of feeling. However, here it is worth noting just what is identified with what. To have to make this identification we are presumed normally to think or imagine that we are not so identified, and indeed in pathological conditions we are not. But this points up less the absence of identity with body than the fact that there is distance between the object of thinking or imagining and our pathology, on the one hand, and the bodily states and the pleasure and pain on the other. We are as identified with the former as with the latter, but differently. It is surely conceivable, then, that bodily states of necessity could have been gifted with no such concomitant as pleasure and pain; but it is not so, and for us as we are it could not be so. Our existence is cyclical and bodily, i.e., it lies across time and space; and this distance which we are incorporating is the very distance which pleasure and pain represent, or better which they are. The presence and distance are not dimensions of ourselves vis-à-vis something other than ourselves, but a presence to and distance from what is ourselves, a presence and distance which are our existence.

If pleasure and pain stand on opposite sides of the wheel in this way, it means that the pleasure is never occurrent without the pain; for any position is both an accomplishment of some point and an absence from some other. However, the phasal activity of organs being not instantaneous but time-consuming, if not time-measuring, they can persist in a condition before moving over into the opposite condition. More accurately, there are three conditions: the pleasure that is arrival, the homeostasis that is persistence in the state that the body is in, and the pain that is the absence of satisfaction for the next requisite position. Pleasure considered as the absence of pain can be either the burst into success or the gray endurance in temporary balance. In the first case it is dependent upon preceding pain which is now escaped, in the second it is not a recognized condition at all but is rather a "condition" in a different sense—a prerequisite for forgetting momentarily about bodily needs and for doing something else. In neither case is pleasure the enduring experience it is idealized to be, but is either not enduring or is not an experience but a condition. As a result it cannot be sought directly, but only the events expected to relieve pain can be sought, with only an indirect hope of pleasure. Although the bi-phasal structure is true also of pain, it is in our discourse non-symmetrical to pleasure, for only the distressed absence rather than the homeostasis is felt opposite to pleasure; of course, it is equally sensible to consider the homeostasis, then, as pain.

Labor[32]

These animate activities contribute directly to life and to their own maintenance. The time in which they must be done is a cyclical time, for they must ever be redone. There is no final termination; in this sense they are futile even when successful, just as the "old army game" of busying servicemen by digging holes and then filling them back in. Futile though they be, they cannot be foregone or life will cease; they are necessary, and our prime model for necessity. We say "as necessary as breathing," rather than "as necessary as the laws of nature." Yet the latter expression would convey the same meaning, since it is just this feature which makes breathing "natural," which makes it an activity inseparable from our "nature," and which makes up "nature" (from *nasci*, Latin for "to be born," as in Greek from *physis*, for "growth").

Our lifestyles are oppressive and futile because of our life activities, whether or not we feel them to be so; they are a burden, even the rest they include. For this reason they are activities which ought not to induce pride, but only relief and gratitude for their continuance. Even the infant is proud not of eating, etc., but of eating in accord with our adult rituals, which lead us to superimpose our approval on the mere facts of eating. We do not show off these activities, i.e., we do not show them in public. On the contrary, we keep them carefully private, and redeem their shamefulness—their futility and oppression—only by the rituals already mentioned, of which more later. In addition, because these life activities are "wrapped up" in the depth of our volume, they cannot be shown anyway, with again a reservation for the showing of the hidden depth, as hidden, by surface. For both reasons, our life activities are not only oppressive and futile but also private. The attempt to show them freely intrudes upon the privacy of the person who is exposed, as well as the persons to whom he is exposed, shaming both.

It is no accident that one phase of the natural activity of reproduction is known as labor. For the word itself can be used with no other meaning than the life activities' characteristics we just discussed. Used as a verb, the word of course signifies an activity; but used as a noun it continues to signify an activity, i.e., there is nothing the activity ends in, for it must be redone. Even the term "laboring class" is used to refer to persons so employed, in non-salaried but wage earning positions, in repetitive activities or activities tied to satisfying physical needs. The activity is "laborious," which term is in turn applied to similar experiences found in activities other than labor. For there possibly are activities other than these animate ones; in fact, their characteristics fairly demand that there be. Nonetheless, these persist. If there were nothing else, or if they lay unredeemed by other activities, human life would be one of labor. Any respite from labor would be part of its cycle, part of labor; any sense of leisure would have to fit under the limits of recreation, and both under labor.

It is not inconceivable for this to happen. All that would be needed would be to assume the moral ideal of life as the highest good, and continuing organic activity, i.e., pleasure, as full happiness. It is a posture not just of "better Red than dead," but better anything than dead; it is the deification of the labor movement as the sole criterion of human truth and virtue. The appeal of these views suggests how prominent is the ideal of labor and how inconceivable not labor but leisure may be.

Consumption

Consuming of goods and services is such a dominant part of our activity that our society calls itself the consumer society. It is one in which all realities are presented as objects for consumption, objects whose sole existence is to be used up and destroyed (fungibles). Besides this they have no other role remaining; to the extent they would force themselves upon us, they are ignored or if possible processed out. Clothing is to be worn out so new can be bought, and so is made to that end, of paper; cars are to be exchanged as used up, once the ashtrays are full, and are planned accordingly for obsolescence; works of art are marketed and stored, like so many grain futures, and the art world responds with works which propel themselves into degeneracy; buildings are intended to be ready for tearing down in a brief history so as not to encumber the ground for new needs, and the quality of construction needs no comment. The brilliant recovery of the most bombed-out countries of the Second World War, Germany and Japan, proved the truth of this expectation.

Consumption is modeled upon consumption of food, it is probably not necessary to note; there is no reality to food but its destruction in a particular way. In eating there is no intrinsic termination of the process but only adjournments until it recommences; the same is true of consumption in the wider sense, but it is also engineered so that there is no extrinsic termination either. That is, the process has any bounds from without taken off of it, in particular the determinations that would come from pleasure. The aim of consumer society is to provide pleasure only in order to keep consumption going; and consequently if it is possible to keep the pleasure confined to the very act of consuming rather than attached to the character of the objects consumed, this will further the aim. One way of achieving this is to advertise a sufficiently broad range of products and varieties so that the selection among them is made to take up all the time that would be spent on consumption, and thus the selection becomes self-satisfying even without the use. The pleasures that are advertised lie in the anticipation and in the moment of terminating these anticipations, rather than in the actual process of engaging in what is anticipated. Of course, this can be done only if irresistible needs have been satisfied, and only non-essential needs are involved. Thus the article is over with when acquired; its value on any market is halved or lessened even further.

However, as has been pointed out,[33] the needs that might otherwise not have arisen have been roused by advertising and, although one may not perceive that this is why the consumer stays dissatisfied, he is not satisfied in these needs by his mere following of an advertisement. The consumer's tolerances are continually led toward expanded limits. For there is no end, and consuming cannot terminate anything, any need. Although it is activity performed on the model of natural necessity, as consumption in eating, it brings a natural process beyond its natural parameters, using the natural in a way that goes beyond its nature. To the extent leisure and recreation are looked at as being the consumption of goods and services, leisure then bears the features of necessity, and is indistinguishable from any of the poles it is usually set over against by reason of their necessity.

Luxury

The experiencing of luxury is taken to task as being not only a scandal to others too needy to experience it, but also a degeneracy of the one experiencing it. Taking the cue from this mode of presenting the question, we will consider not whether luxury is an affront to others, but only its impact upon the one who lives luxury.[34]

There is first the distinction to be made between luxurious events and objects, and the luxurious life in its integrity. It may well be impossible for there to be any such reality as the latter, but we shall take it at first as an hypothesis. The luxurious life would likely be one nearly all the occurrences in which were describable as luxurious ones. Both have been attacked, but it should be sufficient simply to consider the luxurious events if the life is only an accumulation of these same.

The luxurious event can be either an unnecessary event or else a necessary event which occurs in a special manner, a manner different and beyond what simply supplies the necessity. Each event is a flourish or an excess, or what is added to each is such; this is one way to present it, and another is to say that the luxurious but necessary event is one in which attention is paid not just to getting the need satisfied but more to the perfecting of the particular activity which satisfied it. This duality of patterning to luxury shows not only its many dimensions but rather its incoherence, since the rococo and baroque flourishes on luxury of the first type stand in blatant contradiction and affront to the simplicity, quality and craftsmanship of the second. Schools of aesthetics and classes of society have polarized around these alternatives. Either of them is difficult to obtain in our culture, although for reasons discussed under fashion the rococo is less unavailable than the quality. Both have been criticized as luxury, although the former more than the latter.

Luxurious but necessary events of the qualitative sort are an attempt to perform the execution of the object in such a way that all of the demands for it are met. This is somewhat deceptive, for once the object is available for use and can be so used, is there any sense in saying that its demands have not been met? It cannot simply mean that it is made to be longer lasting, for this is not always an advantage to the object's own demands. It cannot mean that the materials used in it are of a superior quality, having dismissed "enduring" as the meaning of this; for the only meaning that could have is that the materials are more striking or expensive, but this would be one of the ways in which the object would become one of rococo luxury, from which we are trying here to draw a distinction. Even the touching fact that more care has been lavished upon it is not the determining factor, for unless this can be related to something of use, it remains the baroquely labor intensive, as a form of showing off, which we shall return to.

The demands and details cared for, then, can only act as distinctive of luxury when they contribute to the use. But since the use is to a large extent determined socially, including economically, the consumer society's insistence upon the rapid degeneration of objects would make the luxurious object conforming to this demand of use precisely the opposite of the image held of luxury. Nothing is opposed to quality more frequently than consumerism and a conspicuous consumption for its own sake.

If we do not, then, want to surrender the meaning in our references to luxury of this type, simply because of not meeting success in this track, we would have to go back a step to the exercise of craftsmanship. An object produced in this way is made without necessity; there is no need for it to be so made. The details and flawlessness of the masterpiece are ends in themselves. There is no reason for them but that they make a world in which care is exercised, in which tasks are taken seriously and therefore the commitment of persons is forthcoming. Their commitment means their whole self is inserted and turned to the execution through both the exhilaration in the project as well as disgust and cynicism at it: because of not taking oneself seriously through the immediacy of shifts in temper and enjoyment, one can take the object seriously. This is gratuitous; one would do it even without reward, in fact often at the price of reward, or else would be miserable doing otherwise until he could cast the object produced into some new light, some new context of meaning.

Although this is not done for the sake of show, it is eminently able to be shown and public, at least to one who is initiated into the craft; he can point out the stitched seam, the dovetailed joint, the smoky taste. The same is true of the less respectable form of luxurious necessary event, that which is embellished and flourished. To the necessary is added something which in some way points it up, if only by downplaying it; embellishments sometimes have the purpose of drawing attention off the object and onto an accompaniment for it, something silly even, whence the object of concern is put into perspective and its eminent sobriety is made mock of. The embellishments are the fool who must always puncture the pride of the king and is immune to do so only because of his office of fool, since dignity is a necessary attribute of a king because his rule must have the respect and honor of everyone excepting someone removed into a never-never world, however cagily.

The addenda and flourishes may make a commentary upon the reality of the object, providing the context in which to view it, or the likely consequences of it or the origins of it. While these are no more necessary to it than the crafts-manship, their addition causes no more degeneracy than does the crafting.

This brings us back to the unnecessary event as the model for luxury. This has already been cared for in the preceding: the unnecessary may contribute value by its very gratuitousness. Consequently, the inner degeneracy of luxu-rious events is not founded. The same can, in turn, be said for the life of lux-ury, since it adds no new principles.

To go any further requires turning outward toward the external determinants of luxurious events and life, for these may flaw what carries no internally neces-sary flaws. If necessities for some are deprived by the acquisition of non-neces-sities or luxuries by others, then there is a causal relationship wherein some unnecessarily cause deprivation to others. The lack of concern for the others might appear to be a definitional feature of this relationship, and this in turn is an ignorance of the realities of human personhood, to be seen. If on the other hand the concern for causing others harm is not something called for, then it is open to reevaluation.

The ways into this are that: it is not harm; it is not impermissible harm; it is not irremediable harm. To keep one from something other than necessity is no damage to his necessities; and to think that by depriving one of non-necessities one is depriving him of necessities does not follow. One may well have none of the non-necessary fulfillments of necessities that the luxurious life contains; but there are ample movements beyond necessity, even in the non-necessary play sur-rounding the absence of non-necessities. Next, there may be no reason why one should not harm others; if he is engaged in performing his own activities, the unin-tended side-effects of those activities are sometimes permissible, up to a point deter-mined by shifting social conscience. It is not a necessary conclusion that social conscience is developing as well as shifting. Social conscience is approximately uni-form in all social members, and is not at all the same as their individual con-sciences. Rather than the following of social conscience being an excuse from one's individual standards, it may well heighten them; even if it is lower than one's own, it may well place a practical limit upon what one's own can achieve in action.

Finally, if the activities which cause the deprivation are not a necessary cause of them, then the abstention is an act of gratuity; it may be noble, and in some circumstances and for particular purposes indispensable (e.g., if living and work-ing among those deprived), but it is not called for. Other causes not related to the luxurious cause may be determining the very same result; these would con-tinue unabated upon ceasing the luxury. In fact, if ceasing the activity would not be able to remedy the alleged result of it, the allegation of causality is suspect.

In summary, then, luxury is not degenerate for any reasons internal to it; it may be degenerate by reason of its external setting, but this is not an unavoidable relationship. This conclusion applies both to the luxury as one form of leisure, and also to the exercise of any leisure activity. A still internalized work ethic considers leisure as a degenerate luxury;[35] and classical doctrine considers leisure also as a luxury, but admirable by that very fact.

Drug Consumption

Substances which modify physical form or performance and mental or emotional experience when consumed, we call drugs. Small quantities produce major changes in the balances of chemicals upon which performance and experience depend. A continuing question has to do with the propriety of such consumption for the sake of altering experience or of improving performance; the question is highly relevant to leisure forms, because this experiencing is done for its own sake, usually, as a self-contained activity and because the performances altered are frequently those of competitive sports.

The issue centers around the question of whether it is proper to permit alterations which arise in ways other than the agent's habituation of his faculties by practice of exercises, even when the habit may produce the very same shift in balances that the drug does. This is the sole remaining question because there seems no way of continuing to consider the use of a drug which results in a deprivation of the faculties it is meant to enhance, or which cripples other faculties. We are, then, talking of the "soft drugs" and hormones.

They seem just like food, since drugs are consumed for the same bodily result, achieved only more quickly. But this quantitative difference may manifest a difference in quality, insofar as the food contributes to the organism indiscriminately and only indirectly to the specialized organs of the experiences and performances in question. As a result, the greater length of time needed to come into effect is, with food, tied up with the need to practice the organism in its newly recovered energies. Thus, the shorter period is indicative of a different mode of operation of the substances. They cannot be looked upon in the same light as food.

Their leisured use may be compared perhaps to the use of the use of the same or similar drugs for medical use. The intention there is again to alter experience (alleviate pain, generate labile states in mentally ill persons) or improve performance (in physiotherapy). The immediate response from this would be that these are necessary uses, intended to alter deficient conditions back to normality.

However, this does not in itself touch the issue: alteration is the point, not alteration from what to what. Also, the levels of consciousness and performance reached in drug-induced conditions might well be the normality proper to human being which he would not glimpse otherwise. Something the same might be said, in reverse, also about normal athletic engagements: many of the bodily situations any athlete puts himself into threaten as much injury to his health as the amphetamines or steroids of drug-taking athletes.

Playing with one' s mind or body needs to have the same conditions upon it as would play of any type. Among these was the note that play is not directed toward the accomplishment of some purpose external to play. The drug play, however, is undertaken precisely in order to bring about a specified mental condition or a specified physical accomplishment. The consumption is a means to an end, which stand apart from each other; and, on the other hand, the ends reached are taken not for themselves but as something to be consumed—the participants are experience-junkies and jump-junkies much more relevantly than they are drug-junkies. However these promotions of activity rate on general moral grounds, as forms of play or leisure they rate not at all.

Fashion and Uniform

Presenting of surfaces is the home of fashion, high or low. "Superficiality" is its name; it is a science of appearances. If that were not enough to condemn this "phenomenology," its service to consumerist vacuity completes it, along with its fostering of corporate dominance by renewing inventory for a never-satiable market.

While none of these is false, the importance of surfaces to our animate lives gives pause. We have to do something with them; will that be always the same uniformity, or always fashionably different? Fashion's supposed unimportance as a freedom of expression is belied by the enthusiasm with which the citizens of newly liberated societies embrace it, no less exciting than a newly freed press. Off with the uniforms, on with the fashionable!

Fashion is being looked at here insofar as it is a continual alteration in the manner of dressing or furnishing, even though the activity remains the same. The continual shift requires that one must change the manner of dressing and furnishing if he is to be up-to-date. Being up-to-date means that one is coinciding with the now accepted canons or examples of what is the way people carry on such activities at the present time. The activities can be carried out in a way which will meet the needs regardless of the fashion, but this way will be viewed by observers without admiration and pleasure; no respect will be given to it and the out-of-date person will be viewed as in some way strange and not fitting easily into the milieu. Over and above this, it may be no longer possible to service out-of-date furnishing and dress, nor to keep up its condition if it is designed to perish as rapidly as its fashionability fades.

Fashion is of value because the variety it offers exercises more of human potentialities and develops more of the possibilities open for structuring our human world. It would be improper to praise the perceptual value of its variety at any single time, however, for the variety is only a sequential and not simultaneous value; at any one time, persons are reinforced in all behaving the same way. Yet even this temporal variety is worthwhile, since boredom sets in with any fashion and the dressing and furnishing ceases to give pleasure, becoming only surroundings. However, the expectation of boredom as a positive experience rather than merely as the objective condition of life is not to be taken for granted; one would not feel boredom except for the expectation of change, and one would not expect change except for the acceptability and even the very concept of fashion.

Of course, fashion enforces the uniform of the moment, by requiring that each adopt it, or be shunned for skipping it. Even those who cannot afford it are forced to buy into it. Because its essence is visibility, it cannot be ignored. The imposition which fashion wreaks falls upon those who can barely afford to attain clothing and furnishings, and who are penalized by its becoming outmoded, since they cannot replace it. In this respect, fashion becomes not only the prerogative of the well-to-do, but also becomes an instrument for economic oppression, and in our frame of reference a loss of leisure, since it requires that work continually be redone both in order to make the new goods and services and also to afford them. In effect, the less well-to-do person is expropriated: his property becomes a loan from society, ever to be paid for anew if he wishes to keep it, as he must. To this extent, work must be the overriding concern and leisure is impeded, despite the fact that fashion and conformity to it is itself a leisure activity.

It is not wrong to enjoy fashion. At least, one can be respectful of others' wishing to play at it, be humble at one's own, and exercise imagination to lead and change the fashion cheaply rather than to follow it. At best, one must resist fashion's extension to areas of life where more than pure appearance reigns, as in doctrinal and moral fashion. But here, too, due to the ever responsive call between our surfaces and our depths, we cannot expect to expunge it. Nor can we expect that all the facets of reality will be caught in any single moment of approval.

Profligacy and Waste

Our Western cultural world is consumed with the problems of disposing of its waste. Where the problems of nutrition are not paramount, the problems of waste products' disposal takes over. Whether this is an embarrassment in itself, or only in the comparative light of those who have nothing to consume much less to waste, depends on how natural the process of waste is.

The issue might be reformulated as a problem of profligacy. Is there any inhumanity in making use, particularly a consuming use, of the reality we find, throwing ourselves into it with no thought, for the economics of profit and loss, preservation and future necessities? If there were, it would seem to make anything approximating leisure a moral scandal. For within the confines of the game or the sport or the play, only the demands of the game come into effect; whether there are sufficient materials for this leisure purpose is the sole concern; whether these draw from other worthy calls upon their use, whether they are consumed with the more effective destruction, are matters which enter not at all into the leisure. If they did so, the rules of the game would be distorted by external matters foreign to the purposes at hand and probably ruining them. The path of non-human nature seems to be followed in the millions of sperms produced unnecessarily to die without ever fertilizing, the millions of ants destroyed in their sheer profligacy of building a bridge across a river or constructing a portable chambers for their queen.

The economics of leisure are an economics of giving, not of saving.[36] Everything put at the disposal of the leisure is expended, with no thought of preserving it nor any thought of capitalizing upon it, boosting one's possessions or supply of energy and goods, as perhaps one might for recreation. It is unquestionable that if this were not able to be done, leisure would be impossible.

Any restrictions, then, must arise externally. If there is a limit to what is consumed in the game, the limit can only arise from what was put at the disposal of the game in advance. There are factors outside the leisure which govern this disposal. Only the pre-game decisions may be faulted, not the game's expenditures. And if there is a limited amount of materials or energy available, this must come from limitations outside the leisure.

While this makes leisure seem impossible, since there are always limiting factors severely controlling the allotments, the contrary choice might equally well seem available. For no matter how tiny the allotment given to leisure, once made it allows total freedom in its expenditure. That is to say, necessity itself may enforce the need for leisure or playing, games or recreation, as a way of coping with that necessity. But once allotted, the necessity is excluded and, within, all is as if the world were unlimited in resources and the economic decisions were not grueling.

Release

The expression of excretion as "easing oneself" is packed with meaning. For it takes clear notice of the fact that there is pleasure and a particular kind of pleasure in this activity; and that therefore it stands in the same structural situation as recreation and possibly leisure. In activity, release is as important as continence, control-over-control as control. Granted, this is an activity on the same level as nutrition and reproduction: an activity tied to necessity, something therefore of which we are not proud as of our peculiar human freedom, something which we either keep private or share only with those we trust, and even then surrounded with ritual. But despite this there is pleasure in the release. The point being emphasized here is that it is a release: one lets himself be controlled in movement by something other than his own doing and making, his body takes over and he is moved by what escapes his conscious control.

This is the sort of dimension which is essential to leisure and to play, that one be released and given over to what encompasses him. Again, the training toward privacy in excretion is an important dimension of leisure, since one will not give himself up but to those he trusts. When we look for reasons why leisure may be difficult to attain, we will want to look among other things to whatever reasons one may have for not trusting himself over to the context of leisure.

Breathing

Breathing is not one of the activities we ordinarily are aware of, at least until it is even the slightest bit threatened, by cough, smog, disease, or mechanical obstacle. Then it emerges into the forefront of attention. It is possible to keep it there and use breathing as a model for leisure and recreation, at least as a trial model. The relevance becomes clear when we consider the status it is given in Hindu thought. Breathing is Purusha, the penetration of Atman by Brahman, the world whole; Atman in turn is but the local habitation and name for the world whole. The *pranayamas* or breathing exercises of yoga are the concrete attempt to realize this penetration of the individual by existence. In Western thought, as well, the Latin *spiritus* is paralleled in the Greek *pneuma* and the Hebrew *ruah* as the principle of life while also having the meaning of breath. If the view of the world whole is important to philosophy and to the worldviews of leisure and recreation, as we have discussed above, then the model of world-liness in our breath must also be important.

Becoming conscious of and attentive to breath is an experience which closes one up into himself and acts as a centralizing point for consciousness. He becomes aware of the passage through him of the environment, of the fluidity of the environment into him even if not of him into the environment.

Waste Decor

The activities which we perform at leisure may thoroughly reinterpret the way we see our being. Take, for example, our waste products. Most of us would think it abhorrent to keep such around us, to hang onto them and to play with them. Our toddlers are spanked and trained away from this abomination. But consider that in fact we as adults do perform such activities, and in fact wallow in them. For our hair and the nails upon which we expend such care are waste products. They are not living, injurable nor sensitive. They are the castoff of our metabolism, as significant of its state as are our stools. Yet they are more closely attached, the body pushing them out only a little at a time. Yet when we paint our nails and manicure with great pleasure, and when we coif ourselves, what we are doing is in fact to decorate our waste products and to make them decorate us. Waste is cultivated and beautiful. It appears, then, that the only "natural" thing about our disposal of waste is that we dislike it when it is too repugnant to our senses; the fact of it being a waste product is rather unimportant. Our uses of hair and nails would suggest that leisure can well be spent in the treatment and recovery of waste, rather than simply in its creation and disposal.

Movement

If the ability to be moved is a necessary feature of spatiality, the ability to move oneself is a necessary feature of animateness. The organic activities just studied all imply that there is movement, for there is an absence which has to be achieved at every point, the absence of the remaining points on the wheel of repetition. One can move parts of himself and thereby move the whole, it seems from a partial viewpoint; but the direction is toward moving the whole, for the activity of movement is in relationship to the whole.[37] At this point we need consider the movement of body only as a repositioning, for without introducing cognition it is not possible to speak further on movement as being toward something.

The positioning of limbs in space is the same as the positioning of the whole in space, for doing one effects the other. Movement does not occur by one part pushing another part, for one part may well move and not bring about the subsequent desired movement, while on the other hand movement occurs in which the awareness of the parts is missing. In fact, in the latter case, such awareness is unavailable in most movements since the number of physiologists is small, although larger than the number of physiologists who must think of their parts before moving their bodies. In addition, in most circumstances the awareness of the parts impedes movement rather than effecting it; not only is activity crippled by focusing upon the pleasure as a goal, it is also impeded by breaking apart the movement. The point is not that this should have to be the only way of moving, upon the hypothesis; surely there is room under it for habitual ability. The point is rather that if part moves part, this aware way of performing the movement should be open, as well as the forgetful mode; but this does not seem to be the case. Thus the comparison of the moving body's muscles and tendons to a rig of pulleys and ropes is out of the question, for our bodiliness is not just more complex but more integrated.

The exercise of any movement is one alternative out of a variety of possibilities, gradually giving a set of contractions and releases precision from other ones. If any muscle has only two states, it does have various degrees between the two states; and complexifying it yet further the variety of muscles each with these degrees interacting expands enormously the range of possibilities to be selected from.

The occurrence of movement by means of muscular contraction and release is taken for granted as a fact; but given the other features of human bodiliness there seems a necessity inherent in that fact. For something to move through space, something else must move out of the way, not only beyond the organism but also among its parts. That is, movement must occur into "empty" space, space emptied in that very occurrence; and so organs must flex, stretch, bend, fold, expand and move out of the way.

While no part may be said to accomplish the movement, it is possible that the failure of a part may impede the movement. Included among these separate movements are those of the vital systems, heart and lungs and brain, blood and chemical and hormonal. While these do not effect movement, they are what move and so must be reckoned with; while limiting what we can do, they expedite the very possibility for us being able to do anything of the sort. Since the vital systems' organs are not self-sufficient, in the sense that they need to be determined out of their indeterminacy of operation, out of the variety of possible modes of operation or non-operation open to them, the range of possible movements is expanded by the performance of movements beyond the customary range. Thereby, alternative means of effecting the same movement are developed and the failure of any single part will not have the impeding effects it would have if it were the only means of operation available.

Interoception

The determination of the position of our body in space, i.e., in the space of relationship to itself, is not something which must be accomplished by faculties other than the very movement. While the nutritive and reproductive activities are integrated with pleasure and pain experiences (although we have seen the limits upon calling the former "experiences"), the movements of body are integrated with experiences of location. This is called interoception. It is perhaps best shown in the observation that, in order to find out where parts of our body are, it is unnecessary to exercise any sensory capacity to discover it; we need not be spectators of where our kneecap is located by looking at it or by touching it with our hand or with some other distant bodily organ. Its location is given relationship to me at all times, even when relationships with surroundings is unable to be determined. Bodily movement is integrated with the existence, and the existence I am is not foreign to it; I do not have to approach it as I would an object distinct from me.

The fact that I can be mistaken about both pleasure-pain and interoception does not go to prove that these recognitions are faculties separate from the objects they dwell upon. The inappropriate feeling of hunger is either something learned, in which case it can be unlearned, or else is a pathological condition. The inability to locate myself in respect of myself is either a pathological condition or the location within unfamiliar media, as when twisting in the air during a dive or when rolling over in the water: I may not know whether I am oriented up or down, and one or another of my limbs may escape control and act eccentrically. However, when the recognitions are not succeeding, neither is the activity; they do not part from each other here. In cases where learning a response to a medium is involved, the cognition returns as soon as does the activity to its proper function; and in the pathological condition neither one is effected. There is no room for error, here in a cognitive sense; activity matches the sense of activity. There is function or non-function, not malfunction. Nor is there an object mis-known in reality and an object known separate from it and replacing it.

Aerobics

The exercise of bodily organs is fixed upon nothing more than that very exercise, in accord with the needs of our whole organism. But this exercise does not only now bring into movement the organs, but by their movement ensures future movement. Such is the mode of exercise known as aerobics, which uses this fact to establish new tracks for the vital system's operation so that, should any of the channels become inoperative, alternatives would be available to set free the operation and not have it dependent upon a single means.

Imitation and Creativity

In the light of the importance that repetition plays in leisure, it should not be thought that imitative movement is either uncreative or improper. In every imitation there is something irrefutably new, which appears in its novelty however slavish the imitator even intends to be. This is due to the fact that the movements imitated are not imitations of themselves, whereas his imitation is an imitation of that original. This makes of the imitation something other than the original. It is not possible to expunge creativity and innovation from human activity. We often insist strongly that creativity is essential to human activity; but this could not be true unless we were unable to get rid of it.[38]

Equipment

I face out upon the world in my movements not immediately but mediated through objects of my own making, in some sense mediated through myself without this reducing back to sheer immediacy. The instruments with which I contact the world make the world's availability to me the result of my own doing. I not only enter into a given dimension once I have made myself an instrument for doing so; instead I bring that dimension to be in making the instrument for it, and then explore with it a territory which I have myself created.

The mediation which sports equipment places between and binding me and the world is also a bond to others. By reason of the equipment they can enter into the same universe defined by that equipment, since as fellow humans they can share the purposes which designed the equipment. Equipment, then, always carries with it the reference to purposes which can be commonly shared and not purely private; they contain implicit references to fellowmen. The team is called l'équipe, the equipment consisting of the other persons whom all equipment refers to. In this inclusive sense, equipment has been made the very criterion for distinguishing sport and non-sport.[39]

Catch

Throwing a ball back and forth does not seem to contain immense riches of leisure illustration, but its very simplicity shows some things that more complicated forms obscure. There is an objective of keeping the ball going, but it is not of overriding importance since there is little failure felt by the throwers if one drops it. There is competition, and the throws tend to become more fancy; but primarily there is cooperation since both are more interested in keeping the ball going than in making the other drop it. If there is competition, it is with oneself, not to let down the other one, rather than with the other, not to let him do better than myself. The repetitiveness is essential; nothing is done but to move the ball back and forth. As a result although there is no internal definition of the time spent in the activity such that the activity itself wants ending or cannot continue past a certain point, e.g., someone winning, there still is no external definition either, such as that the participants continue until they have to stop or until they are told to stop. Instead, they start and stop throwing according to their own desires; when it is no longer rewarding, they cease. The activity itself is rewarding; the exercise of a human potentiality, it is preferable to there being no exercise at all of it. The throwers are delighted to have enough basic skill that a power does not go to waste, even though they have no particular interest in perfecting that activity. Although the activity can be done out of training for some sport in which throwing is a means, not an end, the participation of people who have no interest nor involvement in going on into the sport shows that this means-end relationship is something added on and not basic to the activity, as does also the throwing by experts when the sort of throwing they are doing is not capable of perfecting or sustaining the achievement of their throwing skills.

Skill

Exercise can be pushed by practice into perfection. The limits upon the exercise are overcome, and satisfaction follows. But the satisfaction and the skilled activity are different now from the simple exercise. How to start the activity, stop it, and continue during it are no longer determined by continued enjoyment but by advance of skill far past the point of enjoyment. This is almost the definition of skill, in fact. This experience is not displeasure, for it is no longer being done relatively to pleasure. Rather there is no monitoring of the feelings about the activity, only of the activity taken objectively; and any feelings permitted are relative to the quality of performance.

Two alternative positions are open regarding the perfection of movement in sport.[40] In the first perspective, in sports young men try and older men share the pursuit of excellence. Both seek the excellence of human existence, in a certain order of movements and circumstances, what man can be and do. What he seeks is an excellence greater than that attained up to this time, by himself, and by anyone else. This is an action carried out in a focus upon the present moment, the now, as emphasized by the fact that athletes often have little or no future to ripen into. He does not count on actually reaching man's outer limits; for if performances seem to have reached a plateau, then the sportsman modifies the circumstances and goes further, by improving fitness, dedication, environment or equipment. By devotion to this pursuit, the sportsman shares perfection in a limited and distinct way: because he holds himself off from other activities in order to devote himself to sporting perfection, he becomes aware that his being is as contingent and temporary as all others. This is the contemplative turn which finds the whole of existence in individual existence, and by totalizing contingency becomes freed from it. He *has* being, and *is* not being.

On the other hand, pursuing the perfection of activity which one knows to be beyond him and not in his grasp, which is not a real ideal for him, is to live falsely; and this is always the case when one tries to live up to an athletic goal, i.e., a record, whether already achieved or not, for the completeness of one's existence will always elude him. It is to substitute an essence for one's own existence, to try and become something one is not, to grow out of self instead of being a growing self, to go through steps of development rather than to live in stages of development. Instead of mimicking another's perfection, the act is to be "perfect," i.e., present and altogether with existence, where the circumstances of the act comprise a whole together with the movement, forming the nature of that act, rather than being extras superadded to the precision movements. The perfection is personified, rather than the person seeking another perfection. While the unity of being altogether is more tightly integrated at higher skill levels, this is a perfection of the self and not of the sport. While the greater self-perfection is not possible without the higher skills, these latter do not guarantee the former. Instead of pursuing the perfection of the activity and making the activity only instrumental to the perfection, the perfecting of his activity is sought as the person's own becoming real.

Perhaps the intermediate position is that the perfection we pursue beyond our present selves is ourselves but is not present. Just as one is contingent by only *having* his present existence instead of *being* it, i.e., he can die, he was born, and he is spread out over time rather than an all-at-once event, so also his perfection, i.e., future existence, of movement in sport is something he has but is not identified with. It is a matter of degree, of greater or lesser distance from ourselves, of having an existence distinct from what we are in both circumstances.[41]

Dilettantism

In dilettantism the feelings about the very performance of the activity are monitored; these feelings, or some social conditions external to and competing with the activity, govern its starting and stopping, and the initiative with which it is pursued. The adjectives with which dilettantism is derogated include "birdlike" and "inconstant," "childish" and "inattentive," and especially "not serious." The objectionable feature in this surely cannot come from doing the activity at all; the activity may be quite worthy or permissible, and its mere exercise without perfecting it may well bring pleasure. The only objection would seem to be that each activity carries an implicit norm of perfection within it: the definition of the activity is given in terms of the successful and perfectly skilled activity, not its fumbling beginnings; and so the dilettante appears to be violating the nature of the activity, striving to be no better or else not making improvement all important, as the condition for continuing with it. Simply to exercise without practice toward skill violates the norm implicit in activity, wronging it as much as a carpenter is pained to see a chisel being used to open a can of sardines.

This persuasive observation, which is relevant to everyone since everyone is better than someone else in something, needs to be made more pointed. And the point is that one should not do this activity unless he is giving it and its perfection priority of importance over everything else. The upshot would be that everyone would do one thing, and God help him if he chooses wrongly something in which he has no grace. All one's other possibilities must be lived vicariously through that one activity or at most a very few activities. This is true; but part of making an activity primary is that perfecting it requires periodic if short-term departure from it, for recall or maturation or to allow it to set. While other activities will be analogized to the primary one—everything is somehow like wine to the wine taster—the primacy demands secondariness. So it is disgraceful to be a dilettante—about everything; but being a dilettante about some things is essential to one's not being a dilettante about everything.

The two alternatives have formed social models for the most influential philosophers.[42] The alternative that "something worth doing is worth doing well" is the driving presupposition of Plato's *Republic*, wherein guardians, soldiers and laborers are freed from engaging in each other's activity, indeed where such meddling is the most socially disruptive sin. Once this basic option has been taken, it is a matter of indifference what the particular functions may be that the fathers of the republic distinguish.

On the other hand, More's *Utopia* and Marx's classless society of "communism" do the working out of the commonplace that "anything worth doing is worth doing badly" (Chesterton). From the narrow toil of a unidimensional occupation, the citizen is freed into the breadth of human activities and fulfillments. While this is not a major objection to More's feudal corporative society, it seems to pose problems in Marx's society of industrial workers; for the technology which is the key to being freed from function is dependent upon high skill and expertise, i.e., upon narrow specialization in function.

Growth

Movement is not just the movement of organs in their bodily space at intermittent times; movement is also and primarily growth. Not just local and manifest, growth is movement vital and imperceptible. I do not grow quickly, but slowly. The slowness of movement here implies that it is not to be over and done with, as each specialized bodily movement of the limbs and organs is; rather this is a condition which takes as long as I am long, as enduring as I am, and so no faster or slower than the life which I lead. It is a mode of existence; it is the lived existence, not a limited event within that existence.

Growth occurs for all parts at once, not some now and later others. Some organs and parts mature in advance of others, while those others continue abated and later hurtle forward in the vanguard of growth. For example, fetal and post-fetal head growth is enormous, with body and trunk growth catching up later, while genital and sexual growth only bumps along until of a sudden it bursts forth as the eminent focus of life temporarily. But despite these different rates of growth, all are present and active simultaneously, only in differing degrees.

The movement of growth goes on within the limits of the species, of the entire sort of existence which is living in its own unified way. It occurs within specific dimensions, such that the human world is a world some five to seven feet above the surface of the earth. It occurs in a specific form and shape, given by genetic repetition, which defines human capacities. It is not just particular human relationships which is thus designed, e.g., two arms instead of four, and so many millions of brain cells rather than so many other millions; rather it is the wholeness of all the parts within the whole which are designed.

What this means in practice is that abnormalities which do not fit this wholeness are abnormal precisely because of that fact. One is less humanly whole on account of them. But it also means that their reintegration back into the whole, when the person is made whole again, is the re-achievement of full humanity. The capability of this reintegration, which is not equivalent to cure, is what guarantees the humanity in abeyance. Human reproduction, as we have seen, is the activity of the whole bodily person in the repetitive patterns which constitute himself; and so it is not the case that there is any possibility of producing anything other than man in reproduction. Men make men, not muskrats; no matter how far from the appearance of man the reproduction may be, or how early and distant from completion, it is a reproduction of man and not of something else.

Growth is a movement of one being which remains the same through complete alteration of all tissue and form. It may be tempting to try and assert that, although all the human material changes, the form of man remains the same; but form which is taken in the sense of shape and even of pattern or outline itself changes. Only if the form it taken as nothing different than the growth movement which is going on, not with anything that remains behind it, still and unchanging, can the pattern of man be said to remain the same throughout all his change. It is not a case of trying to find something stable and identical alongside the movement of growth, since this is never the same; rather it is a situation in which we have to take the growth movement itself as the identity of the being, for this is the only referent we have for the term "identical." We take the meaning from the being, rather than imposing it upon him from elsewhere.

Although it is true to say that the growing being is one by aim, it is perhaps more within the reach of imagination to speak of it as one by termination. The fact of growing up to a point and then further growing while at this point constitutes the terminus of growth, and is a unification for the process. Bodily maturation is acquisition of better movement, greater bulk, more sensitive and resistant tissue and bone. The direction is shown by the fact that all children want to grow up, that no adult wants to be younger or older, and that while most elderly envy youth they do not want to relive any other youth than what they did, which brought them where they are and so lets them look back upon it. All this, of course, is on condition of healthy and happy life at each position, and is rent askew by abnormal conditions at any stage. In summary, the termination of all life is adulthood, and life does not descend again from that. To raise the question whether life is made absurd by the fact that adulthood ends in dying is premature now and will have to wait for the end of this study.

Reaching and passing time in adulthood is not a matter of an accumulation of events. The lines do not match neatly if we were to wish to see life and growth as an up and down again. For example, nutrition and excretion persist throughout life, without becoming better, although they usually become worse in advanced years. Reproduction is a way of growing beyond myself; and so if death were the nearing of my end, the reproduction should occur in the proximity to death. But instead reproduction usually occurs in the strongest and least threatened part of adulthood, or even before that. So growth is not an accumulation which I bring with me into later life, for as a vital process growth too demands an excretion of what had been and no longer is part of me. Rather, adulthood is a continuing mode of having experiences, of facing upon the world. Towards this terminus, whether it be called a completion or a continuance or a perfection, body grows itself and its growth is nothing but itself, what it is.

To take these notions of growth and to put them into a systematic form applicable to other realities, is to produce a developmental model. The dynamics of the model are not accretion nor addition, but unfolding; something is present but is neither patent nor potent, and becomes gradually more pronounced. There is a commencement and a terminus, and there are stages or levels. The levels are conceived of as the unchanged presence through a period of time of the same function or degree of function. While other factors in its milieu change around this level, the function is not required to change noticeably. During this period at a level, the conditions of life which were precariously reached and in danger of being lost are secured by being made the sole mode of functioning. This continues until that mode of functioning is no longer adequate to the further demands for growth; and then the level is abandoned.

This model of growth is graduated, i.e., consists of stages or levels; but the growth does not consist in a leap from level to level. Rather the bodily growth is a continuing event, identical with the body, which manifests a major change periodically, and a foundering in between. The structure of stages implies some order among them, but the order is not necessarily hierarchical, with a higher value set upon some than upon others. Each is a meeting of demands rising to the fore at that stage; the functions are all present at every stage, and are refocused at each. Only those demands arise at any stage which are able to arise; there are none left unmet, for no others arise. Those demands which arise can be handled; others cannot, but they do not arise, at least for this given existing human.

There is not, then, a hierarchy of perfection, stage to stage, but an ordering to different dimensions of existence.

Irritability

The moving body's self-movement, local and developmental, needs not to be undertaken so as to effect anything, but may arise only to relieve something. These movements are not moved by the motives of the whole organism. The motives of reflex responses are constant conditions for exercise, not distinctive events which set into motion the living body by pushing or pulling it.

What the movement responds to may lie outside our living body. Yet while different from the mover, the motive may be indistinguishable from it, such that the movement is as if to itself, as if some part of itself was needing attention. The response is not a seeking response, but is one concerned to restore homeostasis.[43] It is not sensation; there is no knowledge, no distancing. All there is, is immediate adaptation of self-contained bodily conditions to various alterations in the immediate environment it provides for itself.

PART II
HUMAN MENTALITY

· 4 ·

SENSATION: FUNDAMENTAL
FEATURES

It was difficult not simply to take for granted the life features we have been considering, because they dwell so close to us, as the very activities which we are. Even more difficult, perhaps, is it to concentrate in turn upon the condition of our being which made the bodily activity available to us by permitting some distance from it, which bodily activity does not do. This is what is meant by mentality, in all its dimensions; and it is nothing but this which must also become our access to itself as well. This is what constitutes the difficulty now: not any longer having something about ourselves which resisted being separated from us, as too identified with us; but now having something about ourselves which is already at a distance, and has to be brought close to become accessible.

One could have performed all the bodily activities spoken of in a state of senselessness about environment; all were internal, or at least appear to ourselves experiencing them as internal, self-contained. Body is not inert and senseless of itself, but there is no distance which it can take up from itself, because it has none from its environment. Not being concerned with environment, it is not involved in distinguishing itself from environment, either. With mentality, however, we meet our processes and transactions which are not just self-maintaining, but are relative to others—active upon them, and submissive before their reality. That these are "not just self-maintaining" does not mean, of course, that they are not self-maintaining. They are; however, the "self" they maintain is not vegetative functions alone, but their own distinctive mode of living sensorially.

Mentality is multi-faceted depending upon how that distance is achieved. Gradually the mechanism of distance making for closeness of myself to the object makes it clear that oneself, too, becomes clear only distant from and over against the other from whom I become distinct. Ultimately, the human being in his mentality by becoming all things does not lose self-identity but sees that: what is all things cannot be any of those he knows.

The features which characterize mentality have to be given in a set of metaphors: transparency or reflectivity, possession of a substitute or of media without identity of their own. To penetrate these and, more difficult, to understand them aright we must move step by step. This joining with reality, however, wrought by human mentality has no other dimension but itself, namely, mentality is one of our means for living real, for existing. Although it is an effective means of living, since it is a most adjustable way of being, it is not necessary to consider its accomplishments, in order to study our mental activity. Even if we were able to accomplish all our needs and purposes without mentality, we would still value it in its uselessness.

Feeling

Feeling seems like the basic sort of mentality, the feeling of the general bodily state and its condition. This is generalized as a state, in the sense that it can be described independently of any objects known. It is an object-related condition, insofar as it is feeling about objects; so it is not self-contained. But the object appears in it only as a referent of the feeling, whereas the feeling is my own. As a result, we can recognize ourselves to be responsible for feelings, even though their source is external to us. For example, when feeling hurt I do not feel the hurtful object in my hurt; at most I feel hurt from or by the hurtful object, which itself I do not feel. And often not even this much is present. This is a report on the condition of the body, not insofar as itself hale and hearty, but of its condition precisely insofar as I am, by reference to an object, distant enough to relate back to it.

Feeling is part of the makeup of man, and it identifies who he is perhaps more indisputably than other claims about himself. When one announces that he feels hurt, sad, ecstatic, no one is in a position to criticize the propriety of his claim nor to say that he is incorrect in it. There is no difference between claiming that I am sad and that I feel sad, nor between either claim and the present feeling.

Nonetheless, unlike pain and pleasure claims, these may be wrong, as well as being inappropriate: one may have misidentified his feelings, or have been feeling a condition entirely different. Still, this correction can only be suggested to the subject of feeling; his own claims have always to be the final court, because no one else can feel for him since the feeling does not identify an object available to others.

While this is eminently my own, this is not to say that no one else has better evidence for my feelings than I do. On the contrary, only others have evidence for my feelings, while I have no evidence of them at all as a means of knowing them, since I have (and need) no "means" at all for knowing them. It is not an access that I have and others don't, for it is not an "access" at all.

Sensoriness

Sensation is my power to be in relation to the features of material existence, and this in contact with that existence. For the essential character of material existence is to be a bearer of such qualities and to exercise them, just as my sensory existence has its essence in exercising sensory activity.

In sensing, however, I do not have a bare contact with such qualities; only in abnormal and negative circumstances do I discover such contact, and then more as a deficiency than as a normality. Normally in the operation of sensation I encounter the qualitatively modified object, not the qualities; this shall be called perception.

In attempting even to imagine the event of pure sensory contact, for example, color, the color would seem to have to fill the whole environment, so that nothing within the environment could be discriminated; if I cannot distinguish the source of the color, this is because it must be manifested as equally present throughout the visual field, omnipresent. If I am able to distinguish the object so met from myself, this is only because I find it unusual; the usual is overlooked as part of my substance, for my substance has its objectless status. The same happens with external continua, such as the objectless sensation: it gets ignored, gets assimilated to what is discriminated. Only the unusual could appear in this way; as I can distinguish unusual inner noise or smell, so also I can ascribe some unusual things to the external.

If I experience pure sensoriness, the input is global, a surrounding milieu, pervasive upon all my discriminations. In this situation I can eventually separate off the input from the environment; for example, I can approach the environment and find the input no stronger there, as in a game of "hot and cold" search for the source. I can do this even without experiencing the sensation as an output from the source. I locate the environment by discovering its extension—by echo, by touch, by seeing texture—and this extension identifies the environment off. It is the boundary of my space, and from the boundary as a medium I am receiving the sensation. Thus sensoriness even when perhaps not liable to being objectified as the sensing-of some object, can be identified as the sensing-in some environment. In that environment I may be unable to differentiate body noise and environmental noise; but there are available tests for doing so, if I am in a position to make them. The tests are tied up in the nature of what is being tested and what is performing the test; total distrust of senses is impossible, even when the tests cannot be made.

In recapitulation, the fact that sensoriness has degrees of input seems an essential feature for performing certain discriminations. Discriminating an object at all need not be a discrimination between the presence or absence of its sensoriness, but equally well it can be located as now more, now less influential. Instead of the brown-patch-here-now to the left of a red-patch-there-then, I find a pattern, almost a quilt, whether the pattern is a symphony or a cacaphony. By advancing or retreating, the source of the parts of the pattern may be discriminated. So the experiment of what pure sensoriness would be like shows that, even granting the hypothesis and what it would have to be like, it is still possible to locate the object and break the purity of sensoriness.

As a result, sensoriness is not a substratum of knowing, but instead is made sense of by other ways of knowing, instead of giving them their sense. Because there is no claim-like experience which occurs in sensation, on the few occasions we encounter it pure, there is no possibility of error in it. We sense the relationship with an object, but that object is not identified in sensoriness.

Sense Organs

Sense gives possession of objects in a way beyond the spatiality of body. Instead of simply enclosing the objects of experience, and even assimilating them, what sense and mentality generally do is to model itself upon them.[44] This is possible because, as we shall see further on, the structure on which both are built it taken from the same set of possibilities. In this representation, something stands for something else in the absence of the second.[45] What is held onto is the exercise of an organ, held not for itself but for something else, that upon which the organ was active and vice-versa.

Sense is a power, not another organ; it is a power of men, and not of an organ. Still, usually the sensory power is not exercisable without the organ commonly identified with it; but all that this means is that whatever parts of the body are required for the exercise of the power make up the organ. So in some cases the sense organ may well be the entire neural mechanism. On the other hand, it means that at some more inchoate point in sensation, a substitution among organs could be made and the sensory operation continue.

The sense organ is required as a medium, for in sensation we are distant from the object and can relate to it only through something. This is a minimum meaning of "medium," and for some senses a special and separate medium is required as well. The reason is that sense is a power, and is known only from being exercised, although not equivalent to the exercise. As a power, sense does not come into play until activated; and for it to be activated it must be placed in contact. Contact can only occur through a medium suitable for being affected in the manner relevant to the sensing in question.

The organ serves as a medium for sensing in the same way that the tool serves as a medium for moving. The tool extends the moving part beyond the range of movement it would have had by itself, and the sense organ extends the living being's relationship to the world beyond the relationship it could have had through vital operations' movements by themselves. Sense surpasses movement, which the tool only extends; but the tools of bodily movement cannot help but bring along the senses' bodily organs, and thereby extend the senses as well.

The action of a medium or means, both the tool as a medium and the sense organs, is to retain as little identity of its own as possible, so that its alterations will alter the sense object as little as can be. For the character of the medium determines how closely it can give access to the sensed object without running up against the fact that it exists as itself first and only secondarily that other. This is achieved in tools by them being as unusable for anything else as possible, by being so specialized that their existence is inconceivable apart from the purpose for which they were designed, and unrecognizable without knowing that purpose.[46]

On the contrary, this is achieved in sensory organs by their being as unspecialized as possible, so able to become the other that it does not even exist actively as an organ seeking sensibles until it is brought into activity by the movement of a sensory object. The only limitation here is that one sensory access is not another, even if perhaps all together exhaust the character of material objects.

But whatever be the medium, tool or organ, there is some limitation which it places on the accuracy of sense, by its own features. The natural tendency is to berate this feature of the medium and to supersede it by intellection. Yet it is this very feature, again, which makes sensory life possible at all; for sensing is extension of life, and requires more distance, non-identity of senser and sensed, than do vital operations. Without the distance, no sense; and without the medium, either no distance or no bridging of it. In metaphor for this, Kant recognized that the light dove flies higher and higher to reduce wind resistance, but finally falls from no air support; and Wittgenstein imagined the walker improving speed on less bumpy surfaces until he strode on ice, and then has to regain solid ground to move at all. The medium, then, must set limits upon what message can be delivered, and the same goes for the organs' tools. But neither would the sensory messages be meaningful without this limitation.

The relationship between tools and organs as media is incomparably well analogized by Aristotle: as the hand is the tool of tools, so sense is the "form" of sensible things; and so also, he adds relevantly to our coming discussion of intelligence, is mind the "form of forms" (*De anima* III, 8, 432 a1–3). Hand with the potent results of its opposability is able to use everything which has already extended the hand's own abilities; its non-specificity makes it surpass its own tools continually. Sense is the gathering place for its objects, because its organs are in an indeterminate condition and can be determined to either of the opposite qualities which make up its objects (424a 3–7); again, it lacks specificity, and so can be almost infinitely specified. The only limitation is the specialization of a sense to each object; but mind does for the variety of senses what the senses have done for the sensible objects, due to being set not for a particular quality but for all being, and thus having no identity of its own at all.

Sense Objects

The only limitation upon sensory power is that it is divided, in that it is not a unique power of sensing material reality but a variety of faculties each of which is competent for relating us to a single dimension of material reality, called the object of that sense. We need not presume that they exhaust the qualities of material reality, and nor that a "sixth" sense is needed or therefore possible. At least, if such is needed, it is more difficult to conceive of a sensory dimension we have not experienced than for a blind person to conceive of vision, some of whose effects he can experience in other ways. There is little help in those claims made for a "sixth" sense which only affirm a more effective means of attaining already given sensory objects or even concepts.

The fact that our sensory powers are distinct one from another enforces our bodiliness, as another dimension of our spread-out existence both in time and space. But it is the unity which is realized out of a variety of sensory capacities that redeems our wholeness. Touch seems to be a model sense in this respect, as studied by Aristotle in *De anima*. For on the one side he finds touch to be more related to the object's radical materiality of having part outside of part (435a20), as well as by having no other medium than its own organ; and on the other side he considers that this very feature is what makes touch most fitted for analysis and discrimination, passing our part over each part of the object under study, a feature which is the very reason for our being called intelligent (421a15–25).

This wholeness will appear again as we study each sensory capacity in turn. We shall not look closely at either taste or smell, despite the depth of memory which smell induces and the basis which taste lays for a criteriology in aesthetics; for it is difficult to gain insight into them, and also these senses are more integrally associated with other senses than are those to be studied, so that they may well be exhausted in studying the others. Regarding hearing, sight and touch, and their organs and the physics of their medium we shall touch briefly;[47] then we shall concentrate more upon the spatio-temporal character of the object yielded up by their exercise, and the causality of the object upon them; in each case we shall conclude by anticipating the relation of their objects to imagination, the conceptual possibilities each offers, and the social environment each suggests. While many of the features of hearing and touch coincide, we shall look at touch last, and discover there some of the healing of our wholeness which Aristotle anticipated.[48]

Hearing

The organ of hearing is the entire aural mechanism associated with our ears. The most striking feature of the ear is that we have no "earlid" as we have an eyelid; there is no device we have developed for stopping the input to our sensory organ of hearing.

The medium of hearing is sound waves of large amplitude in the vibrating material, usually air. Because of their size, it is difficult for sound to travel long distances without distortion; in addition the speed with which sound travels is relatively slow and can cause as much disturbance to the material through which the waves travel as does the material to them. For both reasons, the distance over which we can hear is cut down. The audial object is a momentary event, a point-experience. The contents pass away as soon as they are heard, and are replaced with other contents. Its duration is the duration of the act of hearing; nothing of the object transcends the sensory event, nothing beyond the event lies within the event. While hearing can be given a reference point, an object apart from the hearer, and while it does have the intentional structure (a hearing-of-something), this is a consequence of memory. Thus memory can be seen not just as an event subsequent to hearing but as constitutive of that sensory act. The object of the act does not represent something other than the experience, and even when reconstituted by memory it never makes another object fully present as a whole. It refers only to its own order and internal interconnection. There is no spatial character given by hearing, but only the character of time; it is a presentation of "sequence by sequence" (Jonas).

With no reference to wholly present objects beyond, the hearer has the impression of "looking" in upon the object; its vanishing point is off in its own distance, and the sensing person appears as the source and forum of the sensible features. The objects include all possible moments of their activity when they are given, for nothing more is given of them than the full activity of hearing which exhausts itself in being carried out, to be replaced by another. Each object creates each its own area, and different audial objects do not exist in a single slice of time containing all of them. Their location is autonomous, bounded and patterned into an unconnected and sequential mosaic. The hearer is immersed at the centre of an audial field which surrounds us without any bounds, extending both indefinitely far away since there is no limit encountered to the field, and also deeply into the hearer himself.

The variety of objects heard are indistinguishable one from another, when heard at the same time, unless they are qualitatively distinguished in their sound. Each with its own area does not "keep its own place" in continuity with others, but imposes and intrudes itself upon other sources, as well as upon the hearer. They are close enough to us that each sound blocks the other, so we cannot hear each separately, or often at all. The strongest sound seizes the attention, whether or not it is the most important or the most meaningful. The sounds impose themselves upon the hearer and upon other sound objects, and thus act as an environment which remains unrecognized. The hearer may not be absent from the whole field of hearing but only from one or another part of it. We may gain a sound experience at all by becoming somewhat more distant from the sound source, since we cannot hear it at all if we are overly close; but distance gives us no better point from which to experience the sound altogether. There is no increase in the unity and setting of the sound to make up for the loss in detail which distance brings with it. In addition, when set at a distance from the sound source the hearer is given no details of the intervening space; only the sound has character, and the space of distance has none. It is as though the distance were silent, non-existent for hearing.

All that the hearer can do with sound, in hearing it, is to respond to the activity of the sounding object. We can only keep ourselves at readiness for the event, for it is not the permanent activity of the sounding object to emit sound; this occurs only occasionally. We cannot wander over the hearing-event and examine it bit by bit, with the remainder of it still kept available to us. Since we cannot anticipate sound experiences, we must always be at the ready to catch them, so no "earlids"; we are approached by them as interested parties, not as their contemplators. We are dependent upon the sound, for everything is done by the sound and nothing by the hearer. This is also true in reverse: when I make a sound, or speak, there is no assurance that I will be sounded back to or spoken to.

If memory is essential to constitute the sound experience, imagination is essential to complete the experience and fill in all that is other than the point instant of the hearing experience and sound event. Constructs of sound may be freely composed in imagination; but they have no cognitive value, for they offer no reference to the world of things. While no sound imagination is impossible to realize, there is no guarantee that it is realized because the sound events are all separate and do not necessitate one another.

Such an experience is related to a specific set of conceptual tools.[49] Philosophically the notions of becoming and change are made available by hearing; heard existences are events. They acquaint us only with temporality, moving presences. In addition, they suggest infinity, but with the peculiar twist of a successive infinity changing with us, identifying with us in all our changes: a process, infinity by pervasive immanence. The operational correlative of this is that "making" is the activity that beings carry out; they are act, and their being is totally efficient. The social model for sound experience consists of a small number of persons accomplishing the predominant portion of the results in society, for they are the creative ones.

Personal existence as delivered by a hearing-event is a participation and an involvement deeply into others' lives. The experience is impossible without it pushing other prior ones off, and thereby "trespassing" upon others. Persons live in a corporate existence, a mass, with individuals profoundly involved in one another. In this framework the discovery of a private identity is a terrifying experience. The person is embodied vaguely at the location of his body, but is diffuse around it, absorbing us in his sounds; but this is no less embodiment than other alternatives.[50]

Sight

The visual organ does have the capacity for interruption, by closing of eyelids, contrary to hearing organs. Visual media are electromagnetic waves, very small and very fast, which disturb and are disturbed by material media only slightly, but which allow much greater distance and minute precision.

Although vision gives only one side of an object at a time, that side is present in its entirety all at once. All the seen parts are integrated and related one to another, without a subsequent act being required to experience the next part. The present is the object's presence, not that of the seeing-event. "Now" is a dimension which endures, a lasting of the same, a continuing identity. Returning to it only makes articulate what is already present. No memory is required to have all parts together at once. These parts are continuous one with another, and the order is one which they dictate. The parts already lie given outside of other parts, and spatiality is given as their co-presence. This is a simultaneity (of object) through simultaneity (of the visual experience).

Because of the order the parts impose, the looker has the impression of looking out upon the object; we the lookers form the vanishing point behind which we do not see nor even suspect, and the objects appear as the sources of light. The persistence of their enduring present suggests future possibilities of movement, so that their whole existence is not tied up in what is in this present, but has direction into the remainder of their duration. Sight shows a uniform space and time into which objects are fitted. Everything is connected by being juxtaposed, and nothing is out of perspective; perhaps better, being "out of perspective" is itself a position connected to parts in proper perspective. The looker stands outside of this visual space, at its terminus rather than its point of origin. Our visual field is limited to what lies in front of us, not behind; it is limited outward in that we recognize its bounds and the possibility of something beyond them, and inward in that it does not penetrate us but stops at the eye, itself unseen. We drop out of sight, and are not explored. Vision remains at the surface of both ourselves and others.

The objects seen stand beside one another, and retain each its own identity even if there is no qualitative difference between them which we can see. Each has its own place and keeps to it; none intrudes upon the other. They are sufficiently distant that they do not block one another. The looker is not seized by

the most forceful input, but can locate whichever is most meaningful or important. This distance permits the viewer to terminate the visual field entirely; not
only are we absent from it, but it can also be absent from us. But the distance
also permits the intensification of the sight-experience: not only may we withdraw from the object so as to experience it at all by sight, rather than touching it; but that withdrawal has compensations for the loss of detail it involves.
For distancing from the object gives, first, greater distinctness to the detail since
each object has its proper viewing distance; and, then, it puts the object into
its accurate proportions, allowing it to be seen more "comprehensively." This
tactile metaphor means that, by motion, the object can become more continuous with other objects. In addition, the intervening distance between viewer
and object has a character of its own, present within the attention which is paid
to the object; it is out of focus, but nonetheless present before or behind or
beside the object as an alternative focus which we can take. This is a really present possibility, not one which only becomes real when we relinquish the first
visual experience and take up another upon the new object.

The viewer not only is able to do something with the object, but must do so;
it is impossible for us to remain passive before it. Because the field contains multiple possible focuses simultaneously, choice is required in selecting a focus. This is
not imposed upon us by the object, which remains at sufficient distance that it does
not invade our body's space. It belongs to the object to reflect light, so it is not
affected by my seeing it; and I can choose or not to see it, so we are not affected
by its merely being present. Because the object remains self-contained, so can the
viewer; the object can appear without engaging our intercourse with it. The
time-margin between seeing and acting upon the object gives room for adaptive behavior, and is a foreknowledge that allows a contemplative attitude to
be assumed, one which does not have its truth or falsity consequentially
responded to before the object is reconsidered. It is no more necessary that the
object act upon us than that we act upon it.

Since the object of seeing is delivered whole, memory need not constitute
it but only retain it, and imagination need not fill it in but only vary it. Although
this variation can be performed freely, it does not lose its reference to reality;
rather it reveals properties as possibilities which may be realized or not, but which
on the other hand may be found to be impossible. The objects are limitations
upon each others' possibilities, because they are all given together.

The conceptual correlatives of this faculty parallel the features of its objects'
duration and relative permanence: being, changeless essence and form; and at
the outer limit of these, eternity now becomes conceivable as the never-moving

present of a being. The coordinate kind of infinity here glimpsed is that of an existence stretching beyond us without end, a simultaneous infinity which is transcendent to the sensory events of our lives. Operationally, this suggests that
"matching" is the prime mental function: fitting the self-contained objects all
together in a logic of interconnection. The normal curve of distribution becomes
the model mental function, such that where there is an accumulation of objects
they should be matched by an accumulation of their consequences.

Because all the details of the object are present in the visual experience,
the viewer needs become less involved in laboring at continually representing
them. As visual persons we become less involved and participant in each others' lives, because vision involves us less in others' things and persons; these
remain visual objects at a distance. It is a public in which persons live, as separate individuals each with our own point of view. To discover herein that we
are or must become involved with any other is to experience a loss of personal
selfhood, an alienation from ourselves into those others. As ourselves, we are
embodied at the boundaries of our skin with great exactitude, such that neither
can we go out nor can others come in.[51]

Touch

The organ of touch extends throughout the whole body, not just in its complex
processing but even in its end organs. But, while many parts of the body surface are more sensitive to all objects of touch (pain, temperature, pressure), the
hand is preeminently the organ of touch, for reasons to be seen. Tactile media
are no different from tactile organs, i.e., there is no distance between the tactile object and organ. The input by the tactile object is massive, however slight;
for not only is there disturbance of the touched, but the sensing is made up of such
disturbance.

As hearing, touch delivers only one portion of an object at a time; its primary objects are time-entities, just as sounds. However, the toucher by moving
brings together an object with some co-present spatiality. In fact, were it not for
touch the spatiality and co-presence of vision would fold back into the viewer;
for the spatiality which vision delivers is immanent to the viewer, the extension
of our visual field and not of the viewed objects, which remain at a distance.
Nonetheless the toucher never so fills up the object's space as to supply all areas
at once. What is rendered is a simultaneity by sequence.

There is no vanishing point in touch, for there is no distance to vanish into
during the experience. Movement is not only a future possibility, but takes place

within the present held open as a dimension with connected parts, part of which the movement is involved in connecting. There is no field of touch-experience, only the independent extension of the touched body. Other objects, i.e., the remainder of the body touched, are present but not presented; they are involved as boundaries and the support of the touched surface, and always available to be brought forth from within the touch experience, but they do not announce themselves an anything other than a relationship with the touched object. They are not even marginally present, as in vision; their possibility of becoming content is abstract, for they are not already the content. Any future whole that touch delivers must add something new, not already given; but, unlike hearing, it is added to what continues to be present as another part of the whole.

Throughout the foregoing few paragraphs on touch, it would have been possible to replace the words "toucher" and "touched," the two poles of the experience, by one another. Touch does not leave the person uninvolved, as does vision; touch is the actual intercourse between them. But neither does touch consist in single causality exerted upon the person by the object, as does hearing; instead, the subject and object are always doing something to each other, changing each other's situation. The toucher is always touched, whereas the speaker may not always be spoken to nor the viewer always viewed. The toucher is involved both beyond himself into the other, and within himself by being touched back: the blind man feels with and at the end of his stick, as does any tool-user; the touch of the physician upon our skin feels our inner organs, and the safecracker's upon the dial feels the inside tumblers. One is never free of this contact; it cannot be ceased.

But this inescapable touching into depth remains under the control of the toucher; we feel-for the object touched, as we touch it. The touch-event is not involved with distinguishing among objects so much as it is involved in distinguishing object and subject. Our own reality is disclosed in resisting the object, beyond our absorption into sound; and the object's own reality is disclosed in resisting us, beyond the abstractness of vision. This can be magnified until no doubts remain of our reality, ours and the object's. One is never sure of vision; that is why it makes possible contemplative activity, not already swept into self-interest with hearing. The reality of both are confirmed by the test of effort against resistance; any quality encountered in touch is inseparable from the experience of force.

The memory and imagination active on the basis of touch do the jobs of both audial and visual imagination: we retain what was touched, not as constitutive of the act but both to fill in what has been touched and to vary the possibilities of what may yet be touched; we develop those possibilities only on the basis of the experiences, and tested against them.

Conceptually, touch yields us reality we know, rather than either the becoming or the being which we do not know apart from reality. It relates us to events neither as purely active creation from nothing, nor as totally foreign data into which we have no input, but as results (effects, consequences) of our putting designs into movement upon a reciprocating and resisting material. This is the experience of causality: one activity between one set of the touching and the touched, another activity between another set of the touching and the touched, and the two activities connected only because one activity relates to the other (as its cause or model or goal or possibility, etc.), but not because any of the elements are themselves connected one to another. Neither audial conjecture nor visual logic, this mental activity is called "analogizing" or metaphor: not just the three-place metaphor of sensation, in which the activity of the organ is held by the subject for the object, it is the four-place metaphor known as analogy of proper proportionality, which constitutes the character of intellectual activity—artistic, scientific or metaphysical.

Finally, a social emphasis upon sense of touch will urge that society toward community. Object and subject are not uninvolved and separate, not involved only the first in the second, but involved mutually, each one in each other. This changes each, and does not force either, for the resistance may be higher than the effort. Each confirms the other by involvement, rather than absorbing him or ignoring him. This mutuality is known also by the term "intimacy," hardly a surprising term in the context of touch.

Attention

To watch or to watch- (listen-, feel-, sniff-) for something is not the same as to see it. While both are an exercise of the faculty of vision, or another sense, they have different standings. Watching or looking is carried on in two different ways, in the absence of the object and in its presence. I may watch for or look for an object, and either not see it or get to see it: I may or may not catch sight of it. This beginning of seeing, which itself continues without internal demand for cessation, is an impermanent and momentarily distinct event. The seeing which I do after catching sight is not, however, the same as the continued exercise of looking or watching in the second sense, also a continuing state. I continue looking and, only if I do so, do I see; if I look away I pass through the endpoint of seeing and lose sight, I no longer see. The looking is an accompaniment of the seeing, one which can be dissociated from it when the looking is unsuccessful. The looking is a brooding presence over the seeing, a *doppelganger* which is the direction of the whole being toward the object and the seeing of it, which anticipates this happening and so conditions it with past experience, common categories and personal purposes regarding the object. Occasionally, the sight may be caught though no looking is going on; in fact, this is indispensable, for no one would "look to see" unless he knew what to look for, i.e., unless he had seen already. But the sight will continue only with the coming into play of the looking.

It is curious that "look" and "watching" have a present continuous but no present simple form, whereas "see" has a present simple but no present continuous, while both have a past continuous and a past simple form. I am looking or watching, but I do not say "I look" or "I watch"; and I see, but I do not say "I am seeing." ("I am seeing him tomorrow" is really a different action.) Once into the past the distinction between them makes no difference. But in the present this lexical peculiarity highlights the structure of seeing above noted: looking and seeing continue; but looking does not just happen, while seeing does. Looking is something I initiate, whereas seeing is something that comes upon me, although as the one seeing I perform the activity. The distinctiveness of attention requires the complementary features of sensation.

Taste and Preference

Taste is not an exercise of one sensory organ only, but is also its redemption, by growing a normative judgment on top of it. Taste in wines or soups introduces a human element into a beastly consumption. Taste is not mere preference, but is learned, with discomfort, attention and effort. It is learned so as to enhance enjoyment, but in fact the enjoyment overall is lessened because fewer products of the kind remain satisfactory any longer. The growth in taste is also a social dimension, since it makes possible a discourse about the accuracy of judgments, their justifiability in the face of criteria, where prior to the acquisition of taste the only communication regarding the objects could be grunts of approval or disapproval.

Taste is the tuning of other appetites and appreciations in turn. Taste in books or art, in political parties or companions, relates to objects now already articulated. Here taste seems to run in the opposite direction: not to further articulate, but to provide a reliable response such that it need not be fully articulated and rationalized, before it can be trusted.[52]

Study as Tactility

Study in our sophisticated educational system means an activity performed by the scholar or pupil, in making discoveries or in learning by rote. In a less categorized intellectual world, one more leisurely, the term instead refers to the whole range of activities in which one pays attention, broods or meditates, from "brown study" to studying a proposition. If we refer this sense back, in turn, to the intellectual milieu, we get the following.

Study is an activity in which tactility is the best model for intellectual activity. In study one does to the object of study what the lover does to his mistress, running his fingers lovingly and searchingly though her hair, over her lips and eyelids, throughout her body, exploring by touch all her reality. One does not feel able to rest in a quick glance; in order to remain with the reality of the beloved, the lover must slow down his exploration and use a sensory medium which does not reside in an all-at-once explosive contact. By using the medium which places part in touch with part he modulates and prolongs the discoveries for both himself and his mistress. Otherwise, it would be all over and done with as soon as they began.

Intellectual study and brooding is of such sort, too. The object is seen at a glance; but either it is too complicated to be adequately taken up in one glance, or else it is so enticing that one cannot bear to depart from it and so must find a means for staying with it. Either way, particularly in the latter, one is in no hurry to have this done; instead of measuring his activity up against some external criterion of how late it is getting, he will continue and would continue for an indefinitely long period if he were allowed. There is nothing more needed to justify the activity to him than the doing of it, and only when he has traveled the whole many times does it cease to be rewarding to him, for now—and even then not because the object is exhausted but because his own intake is exhausted. But he will come back later and complete the activity, by doing the very same thing. He will make the leisure for it, as it makes possible leisure for him.

Tactile Intimacy

The surface is something which makes possible the sense of touch. The act of touching in turn makes possible the human surface. It is difficult for one to discover to himself the reality of his body, the ins and outs of it. When he touches it himself, he is feeling himself touching as well as feeling himself touched; the activity is one of preening, enclosing oneself more fully within by closing down the surface, finding where it ends from within. The toucher and the touched are the same and there is no outside contact; there is no confirmation of one's self.

When my skin in touched by another, this ceases to be the case. I am located in terms of some outside, something which I do not initiate and do not monitor but something which comes from beyond me. Not only is it an indiscriminate touch and an indiscriminate beyond, but a human touch. Knowing me as I would have known myself is another; but instead of knowing me in the very same framework as I would have already known myself, I am known as new territory for the other. I am to be explored, and by being opened up for the other I am made aware that I am not all patent but have depths to reveal through my appearance. Stroking me confirms this, calms it back down into an openness which can be left vulnerable since it is being cared for precisely in its vulnerability.

The different ways of touching (with what, upon what, with what movement), its occasions (with whom, in what contexts, how long and how frequently) and its effects (organic health, emotional balance, personal stability, social intensity) are still not amply documented.[53] The net result is that there are distinctive patterns of cause and effect, all referring back to the great importance of tactile intimacy for human well-being. As well as the near-magical potency of touching, the reverse is true as well: touching is not a piece of data-gathering immune from the human interpretation of what it is. The lover's touch is sexual and pleasing only under conditions of an erotic nature, i.e., whatever conditions make the touch able to be a sexual stimulus. The handshake today is a statement of closeness, whereas in its origins it is a statement of the distance between parties. A pat will not always satisfactorily replace a stroke. The tactile experience, that is to say, is a meaningful one because it is a human one, i.e., it is not a basic building-block separable and more elemental than the whole human experience. Touching shows how integrated is the human person.

The recreative effects and the leisurely setting for touching that gives pleasure must be generated from this consideration. It is insufficient to promote the activity itself; all that can be done is to provide a context and atmosphere conducive to its occurrence. Otherwise, whatever physical contact occurs is not a carrier of the meaning promoted. By the same token, however, it is not impossible for a comprehension of the meaning of the experience to induce a person to engage in the experience, since they are bound up in the same context. Often enough, the meaning thus acquired is inadequate and stilted; but imitation of what one wants to become does eventually induce the personhood corresponding to the behavior, since again in the other direction they are not separable features of the person.

Connoisseurism

The connoisseur is one who knows, who is in the know, about something sen-
sually perceptible. He is one whose delight in the experience is used as a measure
and criterion for any practical judgments about the quality of the objects, such
as pricing and labeling; it is upon his decision that prizes are awarded for superior quality. His activity is one which is done for the sheer pleasure of experience,
not for the satisfactions of completing a sensorily felt need by filling it up. Instead
the whole concept of what a sensory need is undergoes change: from the image
of a hole which needs filling in any way and at any cost, it becomes a string
which needs plucking as well as possible.[54] Getting the best tone from it is more
important than the intensity or prolongation of the plucking; better not to
pluck at all than poorly. The exercise of the sensory appetite continues to be
its own reward, but for different reasons and in different ways. Sensoriness itself
undergoes transformation, being taken out of the order of a means serving the
end of survival by signaling dangers to it, and being made an end in itself with
no need to justify it on other grounds.[55]

Because of the intense dwelling in the object of experience required to gain
the insight into its qualities, it is necessary to spend considerable time in the
acquisition of the skill; either one is practicing it, or else is designing his life
so as to make most acute his time of practice. In order to do this, some other
dimensions of knowledge and activity must be neglected; as any other habit,
sensory habit requires a long time for its development. But no more than in
other cases does this imply a narrowness of worldview. The world seen from the
wine cup need be no more narrow than the world seen from the bench or the
commune. In either case all features of the world are being approached, but
they are seen in the minute area of concentration rather than in their singular reality, separately contacted. The metaphor for every existence is one or
another feature of the known object; that the comparisons may be distant is
only a credit to the insight given by this peculiar perspective. "To see the universe in a grain of sand" was the height of mysticism for Blake, the "inscape"
of the poet Hopkins.

People-Watching

Strolling through a park or down a busy street, or even watching just one single person, is an activity we can carry on almost without end. We find each
other interesting, not just with the analytical eye of the behavioral scientist nor

with the collecting study of a novelist, but in a more simple way. We can and do watch the trees, too, and there is something in common with the present activity though we cannot usually keep it up quite so long. Nor is it the very same as watching the girls, although this is probably involved in simply people-watching; no one really believed a friend who told us that watching a pretty girl was like watching a beautiful tree. It is; but . . . something isn't quite right in the comparison.[56]

What people do interests us, but so does what they don't do. Just as enjoyable a time can be spent watching a person alone reading a book as in watching teenaged girls in animated conversation. Nothing very gripping goes on with the reader; but, although our attention is kept better by the animated group, we return for just as long a watch to the reader.

Sartre speaks of the stare, the *regarde*, which reduces its object to a thing, non-human and with no further potentialities to change from what he has entombed it to be. This seems like the very contrary of what is happening here. In order to have this effect upon someone, I must approach him with animosity or at least the studied indifference arising out of my cynical or disillusioned conviction that there is nothing of worth about him; this follows, for Sartre, from our mutually threatening way of being. It is something which is done, rather than something which just happens; and so it is more a species of activity we are concerned with than with a deadened statue.

The interest which people-watching holds over tree-watching seems to consist in the fact that we can enter into the people watched. The trees or the butterflies or the earthmover which we watch either with contentment or excitement are related in the same way, insofar as we can enter into the movements and feel our muscles rise and contract and expand as our bodies act out their movements as if they were our own. But we find nothing beyond this with them: their grace and power. With other persons, however, we find that there is meaning even in what we cannot understand. There is trust by their willingness to be exposed to us; we are joining in their activity less than we do in the caterpillar's, simply because we have more sense of its profundity, however banal, and the depths of possibility in which it is enwrapped. I am much less aware of my own being, particularly my body, in watching a group or a person than I am in watching a tree wave.

I do not find my muscles rising of themselves to join or imitate the movements, because the movements of persons are so involved in the meaning the consequent response required that my movements would have to be those of response rather than of imitation.

The others feel this, too, that this is the way it should be. Catching me observing them, they feel uncomfortable and angle away or even give an unpleasant expression; their other response is to offer a smile or a nod to their observer, who can then return it. Both responses, however, manifest the same thing, that also the people observed feel that we have been having input to them in observing them. Either they resent the input because one does not trust strangers who are watching us, or they are complimented by it and acknowledge it by bringing me into action, even at a distance, even without making their acknowledgment an invitation to take a more active part; perhaps the possible misunderstanding of their positive response is what makes the negative more commonplace, unfortunately. But whichever it is, they acknowledge that I cannot keep out of them in observing them, that I specify some of their possibilities by doing so, for good or ill. They affirm in action that there is no way I can withdraw from joining them, and that therefore I should not pretend to do so by innocent observation. Either I acknowledge my responsibility, or I must get out of them.

Voyeurism

The discomfort which people we are observing experience is intensified into a different dimension when we are observing them in a context which makes it unmistakable that we are not going to reciprocate their activity but merely take up some other stance. Perhaps the best model of this activity would be perusing a girlie magazine. The editors, photographers and models intend it to be uninvolving of any but a narrow spectrum of human interest: taking on the picture as a stimulus for erotic desire. There is no question that so abstracting is a difficult skill. It answers to my own interest in having erotic interest aroused. To do so I need only just so much of a story on the subject as will more easily permit my imagination to fill in details at the very start of my interest in the subject. The tool can be used to stimulate an eroticism that is to be directed toward a partner with whom one's relationship is personal. Once initiated, the thrust of erotic interest even in a present partner takes over; and the subject becomes a nameless, faceless component of a global erotic universe with its own developments separated from any outside influence. In personal eroticism this is returned eventually to personal contact, and becomes an effective phase of it, whereas in the voyeurism of the girlie magazine no such return is usually undertaken.

Voyeurism is most properly used of a present meeting in which one person is treated as the subject in the magazine: the magazine is an instance, true enough, but since the subject engages willingly in the knowledge of a market of people such as the buyer, there is a two-sided relationship, if a stifled one. When the voyeur is involved in a flesh and blood meeting, the relationship is one-sided; or else, if both engage, then it is two one-sided relationships. The subject and consumer both restrict their input to the narrow range above mentioned. Usually of course the relationship is simple, one-sided and one-directional. The voyeur takes satisfaction from the use of a single sensory channel or at most only a few. He is content with the stimulation, without the satisfaction of engaging in the perception and then action with all of his sensory capabilities. Of course, one danger is that he will be sufficiently stimulated to go on and do so; but we will discount this not unlikely turn from our discussion.

What is happening is that the voyeur is not engaging in the interaction which his insight demands. He is dwelling in a limited dimension of even his sensoriness, not to speak even of his personhood. Such abstraction is normal and necessary, but normal to and necessary for a broader contact than he gives. Because he is unable to join in upon wider contact with the person viewed, he is not permitted the input which would have formed a part of that contact. His narrowness is both the cause of his exclusion and, if he persists, the consequence of it. He can be shut out and he is, due to his behavior and thus as a source of his behavior.

The general social climate which results from voyeurism is one in which, at best, people acknowledge each other's right not to be stared at but respond by then ignoring each other as fully as possible, averting their eyes from staring at each other. The situation is not the necessary sole alternative to voyeurism. Not staring is not equivalent to the action of ignoring; one will not stare, and not notice, if he is engaged in some other activity, even the activity of watching people if not his own concerns. Watching others with interest in their fullness and concern for their well-being is itself not well-received, since the recipient doubts its authenticity in a voyeurist climate; and therewith it can be terminated. But the silent cry for contact from those who walk the concrete and ride the bus can be given the offer of an answer; it may sometimes even be accepted.[57]

Spectating

Watching a sport or a spectacle of any sort may at first sight seem to be degenerate or at least imperfect in the same way as is voyeurism. Some have stressed this feature in the effort to disclaim spectating and encourage participation. However the comparison may bear up in the long run, in the particular dimension of voyeurism we have stressed there is no relevant shared feature. The spectating of sport or drama is not kept apart from the full person of the participants; rather the whole sportsman or actor is read out from and through his activity. He is not denaturing himself by amputation, and neither is the spectator doing that to himself or to the active party.[58]

With this out of the way, the study of spectating seems to be free for examination in an unprejudiced manner, despite the bad press it receives. The first approach has to be to ask whether the spectator is to have his activity considered on the same principles as the participant's activity or whether it is, instead, a distinctive activity not at all to be seen in terms of the participant. We have already partly decided this issue by considering above the propriety of the spectator's activity in terms of how the participant is offering himself for view.

On one view, if the activity is a game then the spectating is a game; if the activity is a play, then the spectating is a play. The spectating would have no identity as an activity but for that which filled it up as its object. Spectating is what is seen, not the seeing; the seeing adds nothing to the existence of what is seen, and therefore cannot demand any principles of its own other than those of the seen. On this hypothesis there is nothing more to be said; all we need do is to turn to the sections on the respective kinds of objects.

If, however, seeing is itself an activity which does not just reproduce but adds to the activity which forms its object, then it requires separate discussion. Seeing will be a peculiar activity, and differing objects will accord better or worse with its peculiarities.[59] Knowing does not just reproduce its object. However close the knowing is to the object it adds something which did not belong to the object previously, namely, that now it is known. The relationship does not change the object since it was already knowable; but in the knowing some categories independent of the activity and deriving from a wider interpretative context are imposed upon it. If the activity is one in which the participants know they are being observed, the spectating will enter into their activity and alter its features in addition to adding an external relation to the knower; this will occur quite apart from whether or not the participant and spectator are using the same shared set of categories for defining what kind of activity it is that is being performed at all.

The spectator is active in defining the pursuit he sees. He becomes enthusiastic or depressed over the outcome and all the events leading up to it. His involvement is structured by the same rules that the players are following. He may or may not identify with one of the players or teams. He will make appraisals of the players' skill during the course of the event. He is cut off from happenings beyond the game or play or performance, and is "wrapped up" in it, i.e., he is contained within it and also comforted by that containment.

None of this is different from what the player himself is doing. But in addition the player is bringing about the events which the audience and himself are treating this way. He is doing them, and the audience is having the events done for them. The "for" here is further down the line of agency than the actions of a servant are. The servant performs actions which his employer would otherwise perform himself or else for lack of opportunity omit. He is acting vicariously; by doing what he does for the employer, he does it "for the sake of" the employer and also "in the place of" the employer. Although both of these are true of the spectacle, there are differences of degree. The spectator sees himself vicariously acting in the person of the participant, but the participant does not see himself performing the activities in place of the spectator; he is performing them in his own right. And the spectator is served, he gets something, something is in some sense done for the sake of him; but it is not the player who does the activity for the sake of the spectator. The player does the activity for his own reasons, and the spectator happens to be served by it.

This needs to be modified somewhat. While the play and the game are worthwhile to the participants themselves, the play probably would not be undertaken without some audience of spectators; almost certainly the performance of other types of spectacles would not be. But the game would be undertaken simply on its own worth, even without the spectator. While both this particular game and this particular playing might occur only because of the spectators who expected and responded to the event, for which they financed it, still the genus of game might have occurred anyway, even if without the present trappings, while the play-type hardly would have. To generalize this, we could say that some spectacles are essentially shown while others are accidentally shown; some must be shown, and thus seen, in order to exist while others may exist even without being shown and therefore seen by spectators.

If in the play the spectator is not only possible but necessary, then the activity of spectating is as justified as the form of activity itself is. Simultaneously the nature of proper spectating in the play or performance is given, namely, that the spectating cannot be looked upon as something the spectator stands outside of, which goes on independently of him, for it is not. His role is constitutive of part of the activity. He cannot look upon it as something which he can spectate as outside of him, to which he may remain indifferent, taking it or leaving it; his presence places inescapably a responsibility upon him, a responsibility to penetrate the meaning by close attention to what is done, and to make his critique enter into the substance of the performance. While the spectator is a vicarious participant here, the activity is not being done as a service to him; his

indispensability makes him an activist, not a consumer. He does not stand outside the activity as one to whom it is offered and who can refuse it, or who can
take it and gobble it up and come back for seconds. The mode of consumption is
not fitted to play and performance, since the object is an end in itself even though
partly constituted by the reception of the spectator.

On the other hand, the role of the spectator in the game is determined by
his externality to it. He is an agent only insofar as he by analogy identifies with
the game's players. They do what they do regardless of what he does. Although
this is far different from the performance, wherein the existence of the performance may not exist without the spectator although the mode of what exists
goes on regardless of how he takes it, still the game is not far different from many
other human activities in this respect. Many acknowledge others but go their
own way anyhow, leaving the onlooker only as much relevance as he himself
can draw for himself from the others' activities.

His vicariousness is something added to the game, not required by it. Only
his possibility for doing the same is represented in it, and this allows him to know
the activity even when not performing it. If he can perform it himself, why does
he not do so? Besides the fact that conditioning and skill may be lacking to him
right now, he is able to exercise his emotions without the distraction of having
to act on them; and also by having one or a few persons acting vicariously not
for himself alone but for perhaps millions electronically, there is a greater bond
formed and unity established representatively. This is a satisfaction in itself. But
it must then be evaluated on how coordinated with human perfection is the
type of unity generated and the type of emotive specialization permitted by the
vicarious performance.

For every one of the outcomes which the few bring about, the many have
no choice but to be flung helplessly whichever way the game's results go. So the
unity is a helpless one. The emotions, too, are ones appropriate to the helpless:
hope, dread, relief, complaining, offense. In some games the activity is such that
even less advantageous passions fly, those appropriately ascribed to the helplessness of a slave class which has at its mercy a victim who must bear all the ills
done them and who therefore can be allowed no quarter; he must be dismem-
bered, since everyone wants "a piece of the action."

To judge whether this unity and passion is worthy, we could consider the
necessity and the function of them. They exercise one of the conditions in life
of men, a condition which men must acknowledge at times not to lie about their
life in their depths. The acknowledgment cannot be made in the midst of the
pressing conditions themselves, for there one is fighting for his life with no

chance for this acknowledgment. So the acknowledgment must come in inappropriate circumstances, ones where the necessity is man-made and not inescapable; over this men must grieve that it is not otherwise. The danger is that they deceive themselves into the thought that here too the necessity is real. Added to this is the danger that in the game the culprits enforcing their passions are identifiable, actors and directors, players and officials. While this is indeed better training than the faceless "they" at fault, it still does not go the entire distance of locating responsibility back with the spectator himself, either here or in the man-made circumstances of necessity which this models. The balance of these gains and costs will determine the propriety of spectating in any particular event.

Touring

Sightseeing and touring, taking trips and vacations in new places, have multiplied as leisure activities, and need to be considered.[60] One may go sightseeing just because others have said that this or that object or place is worth seeing. To take this at face value, it means that there are some exercises of the senses that are worthy of cultivation for themselves apart from any end to be achieved. Although it may contribute to world understanding or culture, it is too far a stretch of imagination to think that this is the end to be served by touring.

The objects that are worth seeing for their own sake are seldom things with which we are familiar, more of the same. Almost always they are things unfamiliar and unusual, surprising to us. When we see them we are supposed to be overwhelmed by them, reduced to speechlessness. Not everything that is novel will do this to us, only those things which break our expectations or supersede our dimensional framework, expected or not. Only the latter will make our tripping worthwhile if we have been anticipating the trip and its components eagerly, studying up on them and visualizing them.

A further dimension of touring is to be integrated into a different milieu and to learn from it, to have the boundaries of our experience expanded. With expansion comes the possibility for greater enjoyment because of greater receptivity, as well of course as of greater pain. The boundaries are not expanded by nationals grouping in a national hotel abroad, nor young tourists grouping in hostels for young tourists. Only an integration of somewhat more than a brief stay on the way to somewhere else will work to make this expansion; few achieve it.

Yet most enjoy their tours and trips. What brings that undeniable enjoyment? The very sense of throwing themselves open, as they see it, whether or not in the eyes of someone with greater perspective they really are doing so, is rewarding. Since, however, the myopia may be merely reinforced by remaining in it while thinking to have lived beyond it, it is a dangerous exercise which needs to be the result of a preliminary openness, rather than the blind charging into unknown areas as though they were simply more of the same thing. The touring of those who are installed in a foreign country and in a very foreign culture is notorious for its affront to those of the host culture, affronts which usually arise from invidious comparisons drawn between it and the mother culture. The reverse side of the attack, scarcely more approvable to thinking members of the host culture, is the predisposition of those for whom any foreign culture must be better than their mother culture. Apparently the only acceptable attitude is to recognize cultures as different ways of meeting some human potentialities better or worse, and of highlighting some to the downplay of others: the concentration of a given culture necessarily has to be at the expense of neglected possibilities. This allows both accurate comparisons to be drawn as well as respect to be given. The mode for exercising this in turn would have to be a non-judgmental one, insofar as the insights and perfections of a host culture are nearly the last thing to strike an outsider, just prior to the point at which he enters into the host culture fully and then by taking on its perspective loses the outsider's perspective and his sharp ability to compare.

One notable dimension of this is the contact with famous or historical objects in the host culture. One may know what to look for in this respect and have fully studied it; pleasure is found in contacting it at last. The pleasure seems to arise from having made real what was only a belief and testimony up until this point. Now the belief need no longer be held, for here it is in the flesh, or brick. It points up the setting of human life in the concreteness of body, such that beliefs can be held only as surrogates and not as adequate. The monument, museum or edifice brings dimensionality to our beliefs. It lets us put in a context containing ourselves the models we have developed. In the object are contained not simply the appearances but also the history of its construction and use: into its frame or handle or walls can be located the imbecility and nobility, the celebrations and the screams which have rippled out to resound through history as the origins of our own world.

· 5 ·

SENSATION: COMPLEMENTARY FEATURES

Perception

Sensation as so far described is an abstraction, or else the accompaniment of highly peculiar circumstances, even erroneous ones. As always, there is no reason for thinking that the primitiveness of the circumstance is any guarantee of the fundamental character of the event; it is always more likely that what is most fundamental is the normal, ordinary occurrence or exercise, not that which is analyzed out or which is peculiarly arrived at. The opposite point of view would have to be based upon the presumption that if one component of an exercise can be isolated, then that component even in the complex occurrence must exist isolated and have effects as an isolated and central feature; but this we have discussed in the introduction is a false perspective, ignoring the reality which the existing whole takes over its possibly separable parts, and even more over its merely distinguishable parts.

The normal sensory event is one played out in richer perceptual fullness. Seeing is our example of external sensation in grasping the relationship between sensation, perception and imagination. We can take the phrase "seeing" and develop variations upon it somewhat better than we can do with other sensory inputs, not because seeing is the more primitive sensory condition but because for us in our cultural setting vision is more characteristic of our perceptual and imaginative conditions. When we think of mirages and hallucinations, we usually think of visual ones; when we think of art, we usually think of painting; when we think of science, we see the light more often than we get the feel or get the point.

I can see, simply. I say that I see, simply, almost no other time than when I am affirming that I understand, that I get the point. There is an object all ready for me, and my only task is to get that object into focus. I am already active before I accomplish this. I am to some extent working toward the formation of the object, but this is just a matter of getting to what is there awaiting me, perhaps formed by another person who is suggesting that I look. The activity of seeing simply follows upon the activity of looking, perhaps without seeing. The activity of looking is an exercise of sensory capacity, because I am not doing nothing—I wouldn't see if I didn't look—and because the result will be a sensory result, not the result of some other faculty. Even where seeing is of the intellectual sort, the only meaning that this can have is from its likeness in structure to the sensory exercise.

Beyond this simple exercise is our relationship to seeing-qualities: I see red. Not even, I see the red patch, but I just see red. There seems no visual way I could move from this to seeing the red vehicle racing around the turn in front of mine. What would seem to be needed is some means of combining the visual, audial, tactile inputs into that car I see, so that I can move from seeing red to seeing something, that car. Some additional ability would seem to be necessary, not tied into any one sensory channel, to allow the coordination with alternative tracks. If, however, my fundamental operation is seeing the car, then instead the only reason for distinguishing the simple senses is to explain how I can happen not to perform in my full, usual manner. Only from the point of view of my full perceptual panoply does the inadequacy of simple sensation appear, because only thence does simple sensation appear at all.

One of the ways we can get to glimpse the reality of components in perception is by taking the example of miscues. Picture the football player of a defensive squad who is listening to the offensive quarterback's count for the snap. On a very simple level, if he has seen the ball snapped on the previous several downs, he will perceive the fourth count on this play as the signal for movement; it is no longer a sheer sensory input with solely as much information as it carries with itself, wherever and whenever it occurs. Imagine him, say following the count; is it only on the fourth that he will budge to follow the ball, because fourth has become a signal for movement? Of course not; instead, it is only in the specific environment of field position, count sequence and his task that the audial input of the quarterback brings the lineman across on the fourth count, rather than on the second or sixth. If the second or sixth count, however, is the signal for the snap, then the lineman is either late for the play or else is offside if he looks for the fourth count.

The facts of this simple perceptual situation are used by both contestants. The quarterback will vary his count so that the lineman will be slow or will give him a penalty, while the lineman anticipates that the quarterback will do this and so he restrains his response to the cue accordingly. He may try to pick up less manifest and so less controllable cues, such as the way the quarterback intones the sequence, with a hesitation on the count just prior to the snap; the quarterback, of course, may monitor his own tone so as to make this covert cue more controlled and thus yet another means for miscuing the lineman. Finally, the lineman may try to make his response depend solely upon non-auditory cues, such as the movement of the snap; he may screen out his concentration upon the audible cue so as not to be misled at all by it, instead gearing his energy for response to the event itself of the snap. He may, that is, now separate out a visual and tactile component to replace the audial one of the count which he had previously separated out. Alas, this abstraction, too, can be deceived by the quarterback's intentional miscuing; however, the quarterback's work upon the lineman can be matched by the lineman' s upon the quarterback, in terms of the defensive shifts upon a plan derived from the offensive quarterback's own actions, thus disorienting his control both of his offense and of the miscuing practiced upon the defense. Each side is seeking an initiative whence to wreak havoc upon the other's perception. The jockeying back and forth of the two lines is, from this point of view, an exercise in the rapid passage back and forth from completed perception to fundamental sensation, and from being cued to giving miscues to monitoring one's received miscues by taking the initiative of misleading the other.

If the quarterback were required by the game's rules to hike on the fourth count, then this would no longer be a perceptible feature open to being sepa-rated off. It would then be equivalent to the fact that the quarterback begins the play from the line of scrimmage, not from two yards on the defensive side of the line. No one notices the fact that he does this; it is hardly even notice-able in the game, to anyone but those interested in describing his sensation.

Similarly, the cues given by the prompter to the actors on stage are simple in comparison: the stage actor can hear and the TV actor can read his lines when he forgets. There is no attempt to mislead, at least within the proprieties of the activity. But compare this to the cues given by one actor to another. Not only is this not a repetition of the very line to be said, but it may in fact be varied in tone and speed and position considerably from performance to performance, all with the intent of eliciting the maximum impact from one's own lines and his respondent's. Such may, in fact, be misleading were an actor to be bound to a mere senseless delivery of his cues. If, however, the cues are meaningful not mechanically—that the occurrence of one precedes the occurrence of the other, separate parts with no internal connection—but they instead are points in a whole which, each of them, determine the meaning of what went before and in turn define the possible meanings which may follow during the remainder of the play, then such variation does not function as a miscue but rather as the only way a cue in a play at least could be delivered. Instead of them being purposeful attempts to mislead by one who is trying to control the other, both are the discovery, opening up and exploration of ranges of meaning which may disorient the other but which depend upon his response either to open it further or to branch off into an unperceived channel by his response.

Memory

Memory adds to an experience the dimension of the past; it is an absent object which I am knowing. My knowing of it is present; the knowing is occurring now. Error in this activity arises when one knows the absent object to be as present as his knowing of it is. In memory I recognize an occurrence as having occurred previously; I do not confuse it with one happening now, I do not make the same responses to it as I would to an event now occurring. My feelings do not go out to it in the same way, and my actions do not try to come to grips with it in the same way. There is no less contact with reality; but the reality is not present, only my knowledge of it is present. There is no error in contacting in the present an event not present; what I contact is as much a part of reality as something now present in perception. It is just that it is not before me, it has come and gone before what I am now doing. What I am now doing could not be done while the remembered event continues on, for then I could only perceive it.

Even in perception there is memory operating. It makes no difference that the present object I perceive has appeared a moment ago, while those I say I remember appeared an hour, day, week or years ago. Still I must relate my momentary perception to the object's appearing a moment ago; it does not now strike me as just coming into view, it strikes me as having been there in my knowing and now I am continuing to know it. There is a difference in stages of sensory knowing: the appearance is not the persistence nor the ending. What these depend upon is the behavior of the object known sensorially; it will be "comin' round," there it is, it's passing by, it's just about ready to go around the bend, there it goes, goodbye.

Now when I know it, there is not the freshness that its rising before me had, as distinct from its turning to me of ever new sides and aspects. I connect back the event now occurring with that aspect of the same event which preceded. There is a breaking point at the start, when my experience which continued before the rise of this object is now specified by this object. In a sense there is no break in my experience; I perceive now this new object only because of the context which preceded it in my perception. This background renders the new one now possible. But in an even stronger sense, there is no perceptual experience but insofar as it is specified by objects; there is nothing flowing like an electric current from the perceiver which is shunted onto only now this, now that circuit. This analogy is impossible, for the circuit does not flow until completed by the interjection of some specific resistor, which then in turn determines the current, weak or strong, bearable or causing a blowout. Even more true is it of perception that it does not flow continuously, only specified by each passing object; it does not flow at all, and does not commence at all but in terms of some object. The fact that there is seldom lacking an object, and that each perceived object is, indeed, only perceptible in terms of background, makes it appear that there are no real entries nor exits. At the same time, there is a real continuity of perception of my one object studied, despite the various hues it turns to me, for I am persisting in awaiting it to turn itself so to me.

The continuity of perceiving any object requires, then, the continuance of sides already past of the very same object. Since the object is not now freshly appearing, it was perceived a moment before; but that moment has passed. This passed moment is not immediately preserved as past; instead, it is preserved as the more expansive present of the object, although perhaps not of the perceiving. The object is present throughout the perception and the act of perceiving is also; but the perception moves in a way that the object does not, for while the object remains what it is as it turns, the perception is defined anew by what is perceived in passing over the turning object.

To perceive, in summary, I must remember what I perceived; memory is not always a separate exercise, but is an aspect of our perceptual exercise. When I do remember separately, however, that something is past, rather than just continuing to operate on that fact incorporated into my activity, I do not fail to note any of the features it had when occurring; in fact, I may even note some which I did not recognize when it occurred. This shows that the pastness of the object is not a new feature added nor an old feature subtracted from it, but is simply the reality the event has; it is past. No sum of features can give it its pastness, anymore than some extra feature gives perception its presentness.

How, then, do I distinguish the event as past in memory from the event now present in perception? I can confuse them, and misjudge which is which. Perhaps this confusion will give some glimmer of what would happen were I to judge them aright.

As we stand before this neutralized past, distant or proximate, it becomes an object of contemplation for us. This stance has several postures it can assume. In psychology, these are called recall, recollection and recognition, as varieties of remembering; sometimes remembering is identified with one variety, the second. Re-collecting is bringing back the scattered pieces of an event into the whole; we have a set of glimpses of what happened, and then as we dwell upon them they begin to take shape, with some gaps that we suddenly fill in, some which remain persistently unfilled. As we put the pieces together, we re-member it. On the other hand, the whole event may sometimes be educed by the mere delivery of a key word or occurrence; the key names the event and calls it before us in its own person, re-calls it. Finally, we may have no keys at all to the past occurrence but may only be able to be certain of our presence to it at some earlier time, should the event be presented to us in image or in detailed description. We can only re-cognize it; although we have not yet broached intellectual cognition, it is all we can do to say that we have been before it. These varieties of memory surely are different ways of living our time. They bear little relation to how important a past event is now; for one may desperately want some recall and have no more than the barest recognition when it is shown him. The past has here taken on an importance for the present which it never had in its own occurrence. Although a recalled event may have been striking in its features, it may nonetheless have been highly unimportant then. The difference seems to lie in what we do to the event between then and now, how we endow it with meaning which we only now glimpse. Memory goes beyond perception here.

Collecting as Hobby: "Pastimes are past times"

Collecting appears to be an activity closely connected with memory, because it keeps objects from the past. Looking at the faculty and the activity side by side may reveal more about memory and also give some guidelines to the performance of collecting aright, not as "The Collector."

Collecting can focus upon any object, from the traditional stamps and coins to pancakes and tin cans. In the objects collected we have items whose meaningfulness, if their meaning is their useful function, is ended; one does not collect legal tender, although he may save it, something illustrative in its own right as the accumulation of trust. But the coins collected cannot be passed and used at face value; even though their value is greater than their face value, they cannot be passed at all, even at only that value. Their life as instruments has expired; they do nothing.

There is here evident the observation long since made by McLuhan, that something is not noticed until it is no longer living a functional life; when it is useful, it is simply used as part of the transaction, not noticed. When it becomes dead enough to have its boundaries set with stability, then it is fit for framing, it is seen in a rear view mirror

If this is the case, what is there that is attractive about the objects collected? Infrequently is there sheer beauty of design; perhaps of Tiffany lamps and the works of the masters, but not of old coins. Surely it is not the unwillingness to let something be destroyed, for collectors are not usually avid conservationists or environmentalists; frequently we would sacrifice the preservation of the present to preserve the past objects. Nor is it important to the collector that each of the relevant remaining objects be maintained; it is usually sufficient that only one enter his collection, and any further exemplars may be kept only for bargaining with fellow collectors who have none of these but who have others he lacks.

So it appears that the collector keeps his objects in order to have one of each kind, that is, to have that kind. It is of no value to him to have many of a kind; the collector of Heinz soup cans is thought insane, but not the collector of labeled cans of the widest possible variety. It is the kind which is worth remembering to him. What he ends up with is not just the memory but the very object remembered. He does not have to rethink the object; he has it before him. He does not need many objects for him to be able to do this, but one will suffice. The past is made into a present for him.

Perhaps he finds that the past, at least, is able to be controlled. Neither the myriad individual coins in circulation nor their sparse variety is interesting to him. What attracts is the large variety of past kinds and yet their impossibility of expanding further. Past types are limited, they do not threaten to run away with a life of their own. It is usually essential for the collector to have the collection ordered, and this order is able to be exhibited, at least to himself; he is proud to exhibit his pages, cases or shelves, all in order, but is continually suspicious that all these outsiders lack the appreciation he himself has of them. The exhibition is for his own sake, or even more likely for the sake of the objects, which as kinds are interrelated.

So, although stamp and coin collectors tend to sell their occupation on the grounds that it teaches one history and abets intercultural and international understanding, which it does, this is simply the external side of the activity, just as anyone makes a case for his activity on the grounds of what he feels the outsiders hold dear since they cannot grasp what he holds dear.

The collection is the past made present, the past in its nonfunctional meaning. The meaning is its place within a system of types, types not important because of their representation of human imaginative possibilities—for one can collect wood samples of various types, as well—but because of their permitting the coherence of a closed set.

The collection is not, then, like the nest of a bird, which is the remnant of the past, something to which the bird returns year after year. The bird builds anew on top of the old; he is not unaware that the old nest is not the new layer, although it is the nest, the place he returns to. It is not that the bird does not know while the man does know that the past is no longer present; neither responds to the past as though it were present, even though what is present contains and refers to past events. Each so responds that what is before him is not something utterly new; nor does either of them so respond that what is present is disinteresting because old, functionally of no more use. To the extent that each so responds that the object has a place within present life, they both are remembering.

Collecting and memory have some features of common root, then. Neither is an indiscriminate assembly of atomic individuals, which speak nothing but their individuality. The individuals in a collection are there only because their present meaning derives from the way in which they are past, viz., as samples of types mutually exhaustive. The past recalled in memory is meaningful and functional in the present because the present must displace it, thereby giving the present both support and possibility. Memory begins organized, and bears no strict correlation to the intensity or then-present importance of events when we encounter them.

What collecting does is to put one's stamp on time. If there is no attention paid to the notes, events and items which mark the passage of time, then our sequence begins to look like just one thing after another. We are spread out, only; we are not unified at all. We are reduced to the barest features of our bodiliness, that of having to live by displacing a prior condition. However, once we begin to pay attention to the items which surround us, we see the continuity which unifies our existence. There are events which are not simply over and done with, but which instead form part of the present whole which we are. They persist not as threats, not challenges, but as facts which we can acknowledge with more equanimity than we can do regarding upcoming and current situations.

For example, should I collect stamps from the end of the First World War, I do not perceive that here is a period which my family has lived through, and which has been punctuated with events memorialized in an institution which continues and changes throughout and in function of those events. My past is not lost but is solidified forever.

Perhaps the perversion of the collector's memory is nostalgia. It is one thing to ensure the past will not fail to take root; it is another to whine for it at the price of the present. The past suffers a sea change by being transported into a comparison to the present. Being subjected to the necessarily pressing concerns of the present, the past events take on a flavor of content and peace which they had none of in their own time, subjected to the pressures of their own dying present. Only because it is past can we look upon what we remember with equanimity; were it to be represented, it would tug with the same pain at our yawning into the future that our real present does today.

Imagination

The situation is much the same in regard to imagination as to memory. What each adds over simple sensation is something that ordinarily forms the context for our sensory activity; in any imaginative exercise what we encounter is the aspect of possibility, while what we come up against in memory exercise is the aspect of temporality and necessity. Not only is what I perceive sensorially a combination of inputs which from an artificial point of view look independent, but I also know things sensorially as coming at the point of time subsequent to prior occurrences and prior to subsequent ones. I also know my relationships in terms of the possibility for them being there or not, for them occurring or not occurring, for my production of them or my refraining from so doing. Because the event is set temporally, it contains the possibility for it not being, since once it wasn't. And the temporality which makes up what we call our memory is estimated by, even if not consisting in, the passage of time, the occurrence of change, the appearance and disappearance of various possible events. We do perceive not on the basis of determination and necessity, but rather in the context of possibility and openness. Just as the combining of sensory inputs into the one perception is a basic activity, so also the operation of memory and imagination are present in every perceptual act, and only become separate and independent operations by way of exception and on peculiar occasions. One of our chief enjoyments, however, lies in so separating them that they can be taken separately; thus we simplify and appreciate their wonder by detaching them from the everyday habitual or even functional usage we make of ourselves in normal perception.

The remarkable capacity of imagination is a problem. In every major philosophy this exercise stands at a critical point. It is eminently sensory, for it is, as any artist would urge, exquisitely concerned with the individual; and, on the other hand, as any scientist would affirm, unboundedly directed toward the universal. Urged by some to be purely sensory and by others to be the essence of intelligence, imagination also mediates out of cognitive powers and knowing faculties into the active alteration of existence independent of the knower. It is a considerable stretch of the faculty that it can also be claimed as being either a correspondence to what is or a coherence with what is already known.

The initial encounter with imagination seems to occur as Aristotle suggests: with perceptual exercise we sometimes doubt the deliverance, and ask whether it merely appears; with imagination we have no such doubt, for the objects presented are presented precisely as appearing. Perhaps it is this overlap which is the strongest suggestion that imagination is a knowing power instead of an effective one. If sensing was, e.g., a seeing or a seeing-red, and perception was a seeing-of-the-red-car, imagination is a seeing-the-car-as-red or a seeing-the-red-as-car.

Imagination first appears to be a human exercise carried out while sitting back, freed from all commitment, and making gray study. However if imagination is looked at in terms of its object, the possibility for an individual to exist, then it can be seen to be inseparable from any straightforward perceptual exercise. If perception requires that we set the object into the context of its present surroundings of other backgrounds and differentiated alternative sensory forms, and also as we have just seen that the object must be set against the past out of which it appears in memory, so also perception requires that any perceived object be one among a variety of alternatives which could equally well fit the remembered past and the surrounding present. There is as much a definition of object in terms of its alternatives as there is in terms of its horizon.

Imagination is a crux in other ways as well. There is first the distinction between reproductive imagination and creative imagination, which gains the feeling not of a distinction of exercises of the same faculty, but rather of a complete opposition in kind between the rote learner and the romantic artist. In addition, but in many ways the solution to the problems of the former crux, is the difficulty to define just what is the object of imaginative exercise.

Starting from the Parmenidean presumption that non-being is not a possible object of knowledge, we can take it that imagination has an object which is real. More basically, we can take it that imagination has an object, being an act of knowing. But this makes the point vague; for if the object of imagination is nothing but itself, then it is not meaning the same thing to say that it has an object; and then it is improper to call it an act of knowledge.

By working out the notion of an image as the object of imagination, it is possible both to validate the knowledge character of imagination and to reconcile the two views of imagination, as reproductive and as creative. Until this point it has been possible to skirt a controversy deep in philosophical history, the issue of sense data, since it was only improperly placed heretofore; but with the study of the image this is no longer possible.

The issue of sense data is the following. If the object of any human knowing faculty is merely a modification of that person, and if other knowing faculties depend thereupon, then all we ever know are our own modifications, ourselves, never any world apart from us; however much that object may seem to stand apart from us, or even resist us, that resistance also is a modification of ourselves. The issue has been avoided, properly, up until now because both sensation and perception and memory were taken as concerned with concrete existence and demanded no object other than the distinct object known; no product appeared in the knower from his operation, except the fact that he knows.

With imagination, however, the problem is that there is admitted: from the start that perhaps there is no such a thing past, present or future which the person is knowing by imagination. Surely one can and does approach his imaginative activity with no expectation of finding the corresponding object in perceptual experience. Of course, most frequently the image is stated in a form like this: "If he were here, he would. . . ." That is, we have seen him in like circumstances, and while not simply remembering them now, as past we are banking on them for what is now seen. Somewhat more distant and using the same phrasing is the case wherein we judge from past circumstances that he would so act now, even though as far as we have seen he has never encountered just this situation. Again, more closely to a real object, we simply imagine him now: "I'm thinking of him," and I see him, perhaps just as he is, but certainly with no intention of projecting his existence beyond its proper standing, in fact quite the opposite, except that his presence is included in the image but not in the existence. Finally, and much less frequently, we are asked to put ourselves or someone else in a spot we or they have never been in, or are required to develop a sensory appreciation of an object or situation given us only in description.

Progressively, through these cases, does it become clear that there is no question of finding any existing individual with the requisite characteristics, except our imagining selves. That is, there now must be something of ourselves which we know in imagination, an image.

How can we describe this image? The usual method is to call it a picture, and then proceed to describe what a picture is and then what one of this sort is. There are some problems with this procedure right at the start; for we do sense a picture, but we do not sense nor perceive an image. We imagine it. It would not do to resolve the peculiarity of the image by assimilating it to self-perception; the very reason for introducing image was that the circumstance is a non-perceptual one. We have already seen what it would be like to perceive ourselves, our bodily selves.

In addition, none of the features of the perception apply to image. In perception we see one side or otherwise sense one dimension of the object, and then move stepwise to bring to awareness the features implicit in that side, or rather we then find out which to select from the possible range of features implicit in the initial contact. The table is rectangular, flat and elevated, so it demands a support; is it on legs, a stand, or hung from the ceiling? But an image does not permit of this sort of research. The image is presented all at once, and nothing is implicit; what would be implicit in a perceptual experience, is impenetrable in an image, for we cannot discover, only add on. On the other hand, what we can do with an image but not with a perception is to carry on research of another sort; we can, as said, add on features at will. We can try out a variety of possible components, plugging them in and pulling them out if they do not work. Whether they work is dependent upon whether the image will bear the weight of them, or whether upon other grounds than just their presence to the image they are withdrawn.

The image appears absolutely, without the possibility of further knowledge-acts supplying something it lacks. Perception is always lacking yet further perspectives to its entirety to complete it. While perception never anticipates further content, imagination always does and its entirety is simultaneous with its imagining. "One sees a specific face vaguely, but one imagines a vague face."[61] This all-at-once delivery is what gives the imagined object its absolute certainty, and also makes imagination fantastic: we are fascinated because we are stuck on the image, and cannot bring ourselves to anticipate anything more, only to vary what was already presented.

Over and above this, the image bears the features only of auditory perception, not visual, even when the image concerns an object designed to be known visually. Imagination can approach any sensory mode. but only imaginatively. The spatiality of visual perception places the object within the confined area in front of the perceiver; we cannot see what is behind us, unlike auditory perception's placing of objects all around the hearer. But it is possible to imagine visually objects in any position, even behind us and inside us; imagination exceeds its perceptual base.[62]

As yet a further distinction, Aristotle made a distinction between knowing which requires its object to be present, and knowing which does not but has its own form as object. The first is always true, but the latter often not if aimed at an object to which it does not correspond. The first only "seems" to be true when it is confused, whereas the latter "seems" to be as it is no matter how clear the knowing is.[63]

The ability to construct imagination to direction is a limited capacity. Not only is there an inability to supersede the limitations of sensory logic, such as imagining two colors in the same surface in the same way; there are also limits which are more simply factual and which can be extended somewhat with training and practice, viz., the common limitation in the imagining of discrete quantity. Most persons have no difficulty with three items, no hope of three thousand, some possibility of thirty and a strong confidence that five would not be beyond the scope of practice.

These features separate the image from the perceivable picture. However, the image bears in common with the picture the fact that the same perceived object can be perceived now as this, now as that. The suggestion is made that this implies a disintegration of perception into imagination; the more correct solution might be that perception is made possible in an expanded and alternative manner by reason of an imaginative projection. That is, in the famous duck-rabbit, the figure is seen as duck, or the duck is seen; for the figure to be seen as rabbit, or for the rabbit to be seen, what is required is that the rabbit-schema[64] be superimposed wherein the figure can be perceived as rabbit. It is not an exercise of imagination displacing perception, for the object is present and the image is a vehicle to widen the perception to include a like object, not its replacement. Alternatively, the duck-rabbit may be said itself to shift; the only obstacle to this would be that this would require the very same and unchanging reality to be two things at once. But this does not happen; it is two things consecutively, and the agency for altering it is the perception. Now the only obstacle would be the claim that here perception cannot have the same agency as, say, a pencil in altering the picture; but this is true only of the design, not of the picture. The two are not the same, as shown by the fact that one can see a design and not see there any picture.

Image, then, does not have the same features as does picture. Instead of providing a specified object for perceptual knowledge, its character is in accord with the way of operation; the image-object is a possible object, not a general possibility for some kind of existence but the specific possibility of this particular existence. It is not perceptual, and it is not something done to perceptual experience, even though the possible characteristics are ones that could be verified also of some perceivable object or event. The perceivable object as well as the remembered object have a straightforward indicative modality of being there, albeit perhaps as past; the imaginative object, on the other hand, has a subjunctive modality, as something that might be but which has never been, so that not only does imagination add futurity to sensory exercise but also makes the futurity conditional, and so equally applicable to present and past, too.

Imagination does not negative perceptual experience, or do anything else to it. Although this is a popular position after Sartre, in fact after Kant and Hume, this is not the way imagination operates. Our imaginative activity is not negativing but varying. The special feature of imagination is that we can plug in and pull out components, depending as they do or do not work. As a result, it is not true to say that imagination is foreign to truth and falsity; when the composition works, it is a real possibility, and when it does not, then it is a false possibility, an unreal one. The correction, of course, is done by the very same varying activity, not by some other judging capacity; image is both the provision of the object and the check upon it. The check comes in the very activity of trying to put it together.

This is the position imagination holds between sensation and intellection in human mentality. On the one side we provide schemata of possibilities making perception possible and providing it a context, just as does memory with a temporal context, and just as we as perceivers give sensations the only reality they have as knowledge.

On the other side our images set the scene wherein the classical questions about intellection arise, whether our knowing is best viewed as a nominalist, idealist or pragmatist activity, whether our ideas correspond to words or things or actions. The operation of imagination suggests all three: our first test is an attempt to fill in the blanks of what we start by merely naming as an essence; we then try possibilities into what have the feel of prearranged slots and evaluate them according to what in retrospect has the feel of prearranged possibilities quite apart from the given individual; but while carrying out the exploration, the immediate criterion is whether they work, whether we can continue to imagine the individual once the prospective characteristics are plugged in.

This description also appears to satisfy both the side of reproductive imagination and that of creative imagination. The former involves rote learning and bringing experiences back, but without any temporal setting, not as past. It is carried out with experimental suggestion and then retraction or confirmation of the suggestion. The creative act is notoriously, on its side, a beast of brazen confidence alternated with withering doubt. Images for either activity supply no more than possibilities, possibilities for the past in the one case and possibilities for the future in the other. The intents of producing or of reproducing do not arise from imagination but are directives injected into the exercise, whereby we bring ourselves to exercise imagination upon this rather than upon that. Both are quite commonplace, though some persons have specialized in the exercise of the one rather than the other.

Imagination, then, allows us to widen yet further the space opened up in perception for varying our existence beyond the confines of biological activity, however much life activity already frees us from inanimateness. As in the case of everything about our bodily and now mental existence, our movement is one simultaneously of opening and of control, of self-control. Not that the control is exercised according to any criterion but ourselves. Rather, we step further out of immersion in activity and encounter more distance between the activity and ourselves, while we simultaneously can now more fully claim to appropriate the activity. So, too, the rules by which we control the activity become more and more objectified, more and more stabilized independently of our choosing. The rules are both less preformed and more stringent; they do not exist prior to our forming them, but once we begin their formation, as we must, then their demands are all the more pressing, although we still retain the option of closing them off from ourselves. Imagination is not an exception to human activity, but one further movement in a thrust to our being which is beginning to disentangle itself from the distinctions and detail.

Artistic Creativity (as causality)

The imaginative object was said to be conditional; and what it is conditioned upon is activity. The object needs to be caused in order for it properly to exist. Here more than in other products it has been suggested that there can be free causality of novel objects; this constitutes artistic creativity. Creativity will be considered under a limited scope, here; the problem-solving which is a large part of its activity is excluded for now. What is to be studied here is the notion of causality involved in artistic creativity, i.e., in what sense creation is causality, how much and how it can cause effects.[65]

Some limitations upon execution and conception appear immediately. The artist is limited by his materials; he makes not (the materials of) the materials he works upon, but only what is made from them, and not everything can be done with every material and tool. The artist is limited by his society, i.e., the point at which he stands in tradition; some conceptions are not available to him because their underpinnings have not been laid. Even within the rearrangements of materials and the conceptual limitations available, making is not fully free in the remaining area, the giving of new form to the materials; the combination must as well be something possible and recognizable. The possible forms to be given the material are not only dependent on the possibilities of each individual material but upon the combined materials as well. Their form in combination, while not dependent on each alone, is dependent upon them all even though they may have never been an "all" before, i.e., never had their possibilities together as anything other than an abstract and absent possibility.

With all these strictures, where is the creative causality of the artist to be found? The artist works with those possibilities which have not been actualized before. This is not to say that novelty alone constitutes artistic creativity. Skill of execution is necessary. But on the one hand a low level of skill may make possible many artworks, and on the other a deceptively simple work which seems to demand only a low level of skill may require exceptional selectivity and long experience for it to be designed. So novelty is important; excellence of execution alone may realize borderline work, but while admirable it is not intensely creative.

Novelty and skill are insufficient for creativity, however, for many pieces executed with these qualities are unworthy to be called highly creative To finish the definition, the possibilities must not only have been unexercised previously, for many are overlooked purposely as not worth exercising; they are bypassed because the difficulties or novelties they would incorporate have been solved in principle already. What adds final value to artwork is that fact that the very social conditioning which acted as a stricture is also the boost to something new.

What is worthwhile doing is whatever has not yet been managed but almost has, whatever the thrust of artifact-making has been towards. The pool of possibilities is not given for unlimited access at any single moment; but what is available is both restricted by and made available by what has already been accomplished. Perhaps the thrust has been towards not just the continuance but the negating of what preceded, particularly after a period of consolidation during which the problems and suggestions attending a technique or a novelty have been fully worked out; nonetheless, the negation is as much a function of the preceding as the continuance.

The artist's creativity, then, consists in his expansion of what exists in a manner that the present has made possible and only slightly incomprehensible, i.e., recognizable as meaningful with an uncomprehended meaning. His creativity is continuous with his society, its cutting edge also cutting back into it. His novelties arise less from clarified conceptions than from the suggestions of material which in constant association with him refuses to yield more than it has, but suggests more.

Mathematical Creativity

Unlike artistic creativity, it is not one's first reflex to look upon mathematics as a leisure activity; but the flood of mathematical games and puzzles on the one hand, and the early history of mathematics among the leisure classes of the Fertile Crescent on the other hand, should give us second thoughts.[66]

Some ground for those second thoughts are given by Thomas Aquinas' analysis of the various sciences.[67] Aquinas sets off practical sciences which depend upon alteration of the real individual's existence, from theoretical sciences which ignore increasing degrees of the individual's limitedness and so do not act upon it. The latter include natural, mathematical and philosophical studies. While the first and third are uncertain but can be learned by oneself, mathematics can only be learned from another person and is the most certain kind of knowledge. The reason for these surprising features of mathematics is that, while it requires the individual mathematical object's bodiliness for the object to be realized and to exist, it can be known apart from the individual's bodiliness. In this it differs from natural science on one side and metaphysics on the other; in both of these the way in which the object is known is the very same way in which that object exists. In mathematics there is a distinction made between the mode of being and the mode of knowing; this is easily appreciable in an age when macro-astronomy and micro-biology both predict the discovery of entities corresponding to calculations long before the discoveries occur. The reason for this, as again we see more clearly today, is that the entities and rules of mathematics are freely posited ones, checked only against criteria of the same standing. It is easy to see why one could not discover such rules himself, but only receive them from whoever constructed them; of course, however, here each could construct his own. Both the most excessive sociability and the most excessive alienation in knowing are possible here.

What mathematics is concerned with is the structure of reality, not its fillers. The structure is the constitutive rules internal to what knowable objects are. Aquinas calls this their "quantitative matter," i.e., the subjection of the individual to always having some structure able to be set out in a definition.

Mathematics so understood is the work of imagination. It is the furthest our intellect can penetrate in the present life (VI, 3, resp.). The only movement beyond imagination is metaphysical judgment of separation, saying that things not the same are not the same, but not saying what they are. But this is an act which is real only in the moment of its exercise, a climax to the analysis which precedes it, ready to begin again for ever-new reality. This latter is the proper business of thinking, "mathematics"; and this is the business of imagination, of working out images. Freed from the conceptual strictures of science into its own self-creation, imagination as a higher faculty creates what are play environments in their satisfaction and game environments in their freedom. And this is man's highest present intellectual operation.

Meditation and Contemplation

The Hellenic tradition in philosophy sees leisure as inseparably tied to contemplation, and intensifying the leisure the closer that any activity approaches to contemplation. But far from this being the retreat from daily reality which is usually thought of the Hellenes, contemplation was the hard work of theorizing about the most eternal and pervasive things. The stillness came from the objects, not from the still all-too-human activities.

Meditation and contemplation today continue to bear this objective delineation, as sources of refreshment by withdrawal. Two modes are characteristic, the focus upon nothing and the focus upon something. These fall out as Eastern and Western modes and, within Western religious traditions, as Benedictine meditation and as Jesuit or Franciscan modes, respectively, to oversimplify of course. That is to say, while the rich diversity of Eastern practices is known in the West mostly through Zen Buddhism's focus on the sole reality of emptiness, the Western practice has often been focused upon images in order to plumb and assimilate to their resources.

Common to any, however, is focus, the limiting of recognition to a range of attention less than the boundless and changing multiplicity of daily experience. Any of the disciplines called yogas or taos take this focus. Whether it be the visual or tactile focus on a mandela in or out of body, or the auditory focus on a mantra of one's own or exogenous, the melting of boundaries and identities into wholeness is the objective and outcome. The experience of totalness is then easily rethought into religious terms, but that need not be its only interpretation; religion may not even be thought compatible with the experience, as some religions insist, as do the pragmatisms and systems theories which applaud this result.

This experience is the recreative dimension of meditation, whether or not heightened by religious intimacy. The contact with the singleness of eternity is what makes this recreation into leisure, for Hellene or for contemporary.

What repetition of the focal object does is to make available by repetition a constancy unavailable to us by endurance. None of our objects remain unchanged. So as the wild cat constantly moving only its eyes over its prey, in order to remain still but keep the prey in sight, we too achieve the eternity which is foreign to our worldliness. A vacation from our experience, this recreation can mislead us that the world too is like this.

· 6 ·

INTELLECTION

As a result of giving more scope to sensation, the need to pick out perceptual activity became more questionable. The same thing happened to imagination when perception was allowed more variability. So now the same is true of the relation between imagination and intellection: what need is there to speak further, when we seem to have supplied all that is needed for full human mental activity? The pattern thus far, however, has been that what was at first glance primary and fundamental, and which in some other life forms may so be, is for us on closer scrutiny not even meaningful until it is seen as a partial activity abstracted from our real and concretely exercised whole of activity. We may now approach intellection with at least the possibility that this is so.

For take the main examples of what pass for intellectual activity: sciences, arts, professions. What about them lies undescribed once we have described imagination as above? What else remains beyond the formation of hypotheses and spinning out theorems therein contained, beyond the construction of models and the continually readjusted monitoring of their realization, beyond the projection of the future and commitment to the client within it?

We might again attempt an answer in terms of error. What becomes more and more clear at higher degrees of knowing, and what probably in fact should serve as a criterion for their degrees, is the increasing ability to be wrong. Corresponding to it is an increased ability to be right, to know truth or know truly. There is no way in which we can be in error acting sensorially, those few times we seem to be, although it is the event of error which lights up the reality of sensorial acts. There is little possibility for perceptual error; remaining within its scope, we do of necessity recognize some object with the features we perceive, although simple insufficiency of perceptual investigation may leave this partial perception inadequate, and false when pursued as adequate. But there, as with memory and imagination, the correction arises from the same facultative operation wherein it was induced. The very conditions which induced error are those which can and alone can rectify it. We check what appears with what else appears, in alternative sensorial channels; we check what seems past with what else seems past; we check what we imagine against what we can imagine. Herein, however, there is no room for the more profound errors which we make. There is no possibility for their frontal failure to match what is, nor for the extravagant introjections of what is not. To allow for our constant experience of such error, we must open up negations in mental reaches beyond those of imagination.

The features of any form of mentality which fills the bill will be determined by the aspects of the need to which it is to be an answer. What is lacking thus far is some means of throwing our support behind the fact not just that something appears, but that something is. There is no way that what appears can not appear, nor is there any way that what is can not be while it is; but the opening for the error we are convicted of lies in the possibility that what appears can not be. The human operation we pursue, then, is one concerned with the claim that what appears, exists—not just that the appearance exists but that what that appearance manifests exists.

Perhaps not very noticeably we are primarily concerned with our ability to make a claim at all, since the claim of existence is not just the situation claimed but is the action of claiming. What is required to launch the claim is that we are set outside of what we are concerned with; here the import of the progressive distancing from the knowledge-object becomes clear. We must be distant from what we claim not in space or time, that is unimportant, but distant by our lack of identification with it: we are not it. We are all the more capable of finding that the object is not a modification of ourselves, even though all the more something for which we are responsible, again in line with developments thus far.

The requisite distancing is in continuity with the description of imagination. The only way to be in position to make claims regarding existence is somehow to stand beyond it; and the only taker for this condition, is to have it described as standing in possibility. But now the possibility with which one is concerned is not the possibility of this or that individual, its singular albeit internal consistency. Now it is of question whether there can be the species of individuals and of their qualities, whether in turn there can be individuals at all, and what else there may be, and at last what their existence might be, whether the same or different from these individuals and types. Such questions are clearly philosophical ones rather than being the issues taken on by the sciences, the arts and the professions, which supplied our preliminary examples of possible intellectual questions. But then from the start we have suggested that philosophical questions did in fact underpin more common intellectual activities, in the same way as, for example, imagination underpinned perception, and as we shall see judgments underpin conceptualization.

Returning to the point of contact with imagination, we recognize the need for a faculty which permits of the error we experience. Once given a satisfactory representative, we can proceed to fill in the features which it must have in order to be able to do this. Intellectual operation consists in working variations upon the possibilities of existence. The process is usually looked upon as having dimensions known as conceptualization, judgment and reasoning, with the formation of concepts being the most fundamental. The suggestion could be made, however, that the operation is single and unified, and that these component operations are moments distinguished reflectively, i. e., after the fact from the totality.

Ideation

Conceptualization is taken to be the formation of ideas or concepts by means of which we know reality. The threat of the image is intensified here, and more frequently succumbed to: that the concept would be taken as that which we know rather than that by means of which we know. The issue might be resolved if we could have the experience of a concept or idea, and examine it for just this character. But under either hypothesis there is no such access to the concept; either it is only a vehicle with nothing of its own to be approached, or it is all that we know and then we would not be able to know it in some other way than the way in which it lets us know.

The only sort of circumstance in which we come even close to a direct grasp of the idea is in the condition of doubt or uncertainty. When we hold up uncertainly the issues that this either is an X or is not an X, we seem to be presenting purely the idea of Xity. In fact, of course, what we are working with is the inchoate judgment, formed in structure but not yet executed; the idea is only given access within that structure.

Again, we seem to be standing still before one of our ideas when we name, or when we provide a definition. Our naming, however, is exercised upon an individual, not upon an idea; we name the individual and attend to his features, and at best can be said to be using an idea rather than knowing one. And when we attempt a definition of some kind or class, we have until the definition is complete no idea but only a set of elements for one.

It might be suggested that this is missing the point, that the elements of ideas are themselves ideas; and if ideas are objects rather than means then this surely would be so. But to avoid missing the point and have to ask, "Then what is the characteristic of the ideas at all, whether component or compound?," we are embarrassed back by our failure to experience any ideas into a reference toward what we do when we name: ideas must be what we name.

The difficulty here is that there is no agreement about what it is that we do when we name. The most telling arguments for the characteristics of ideas thus reached are those of Plato: when we name and claim we are not speaking of the characteristics of any particular individual but rather of a characteristic which could equally well be shared by many, which is stable through all their multiplicity and change, of which each partakes to attain the reality it has. Thus, ideas may persist beyond the individual and exist purely; however, even if Plato should be right, this does not meet the issue, for the question is what our ideation consists in and not where its objects are. This solution merely makes singular objects the means for knowing ideas rather than making ideas the means for knowing the singular objects.

Aristotle, followed by Aquinas, looked to the ways of reaching idea, which in general come down to leaving out of consideration the various particularizing factors of the individual: especially its numerical singularity, and in other ways its perceivable qualities and its mathematical configuration, i.e., its placement within a set of heuristic hypotheses. One is taken thus to have attained what Plato characterized; this may very well be what happens. But this explanation leaves out the reasons for turning attention in this direction, and what such attention is. It seems that this attention approximates the commonplace attention, where we are interested in one individual and not in another. But that sort of attention cannot be a means of explaining ideas, for in ideation it is the capacity to cease attending to individuality that is up for explanation.[68]

Whatever it is, the result is commonly agreed to be a movement beyond the individual, or rather an interest in it always through non-individual factors, and perhaps only because of such factors. We are brought full circle back to asking why we would not be satisfied with sheer individuality, or better what is available other than it. And the answer that comes back is: nothing. What is must exist as *an* existence; and while this escapes the confines of individuality, it places confines no less stringent upon what is possible as existing. Although the demands of existence have not yet been fully developed, we are on the edge of doing so.

What we are to look for is not an explanation of why we must go on to intellectualize; for the root answer is that we can, so we do. Rather, the focus is to be upon what it is that we say we can do here.

The answer is that we manipulate images. Intellection consists of looking to the imaginative ventures which do not work and testing the propriety of these results by looking to discover why they did not work. To answer this "why" is to set out what is true not only of this image but of the whole of existence, and on the more local level what is demanded for the consistency of any existence of this kind. What separates individuals is that, being many, they cannot be the same; and what separates kinds is that for the fullest and most consequential development of some possibilities, other possibilities have to be excluded.

Ideation is the activity of developing the requirements for each kind to be as it is. It is above all an activity, it is not a thing. There is no need to assume that all the kinds in question are natural kinds, perhaps not even that any of them are. All that is necessary is to recognize that a distinctive set of possibilities has no coherence but that given by its own demands. These demands are called "principles," in reference to their rooted standing, and "rules" insofar as they set a framework of boundaries and of possible moves within them. The activity of seeking these boundary conditions for any particular set of possibilities, for a particular kind of being as distinct from a particular individual, can be carried further and made the search for what in turn hedges in these specific principles and rules, namely the conditions which must attain for any existence to be possible at all. The search is itself another category of activity, namely philosophy, itself open to that investigation to be carried out upon itself, but by none other than philosophy itself.

The presumption throughout is that there are demands of existence and of kind, and this in turn enforces the presumption that existence can be identified not just as the actuality but as possibility. This does not put existence off into a mystic container, but it does imply a precondition upon any mode of existence, namely, that individual possibilities require multiplicity one over against another for them to have any meaning as possibilities.

Judgment

The concept is this activity, and the judgment is the completion of that activity. These are the knowledge parallels of the process of life, whereby each struggle to completion can rest there not a moment but must descend. Similarly, having satisfied ourselves that the requirements for existence are present through the act of conceptualizing, we can at most then settle the issue for that instant: at this moment, the conditions are satisfied, and the judgment then is ended, with the process of conceptualizing to be repeated until another time—perhaps immediately thereafter—we judge it successful again, again to fall. In simpler speech, we may answer that this X of this A type now exists; but, though this will never be refutable from that very moment thenceforward, still from then on in the very next instant one must come back to inquire again, "But does it still exist?"

Reasoning

The third stated component of intellection, reasoning, can be better seen now for what it can be. To the extent that it is anything different than imagining or from conceptualization, it can only be the movement from a completed judgment to another, and thus is essentially ex post factum activity. Since the only persistence of the completed judgment lies in the fact that it was true in the past, as soon as it is made, then the only movement out of that which reasoning can undertake is for us to note that the conditions of possibility for that existence involve the conditions of possibility for this other one, in such a way that for that same past moment the other existent can claim also to have been equally necessary, likely, possible or impossible. More often, we mean by reasoning what we experience as we either vary an image or else we decide upon as conditions for possibility being met in conceptualization.

The dive into nothingness with which we live our lives of concept and judgment is made more profound with reasoning. Here we move from what we know, that what we don't yet know.

The contrasting view is that reason is a faculty for presentation, not for discovery; it is useful only to link the new to what was known only after it is discovered or desired, and to make it appear falsely as though this is the way our knowing or acting proceeded in arriving at the new conclusion. The epitome of this viewpoint is that nothing can be known by reason unless it were known analytically, i.e., was already present in its premises, but was just drawn out.

This misconception of reason arises from identifying it with formalizable sets of propositions. But if we appreciate the function that appears fresh with reason, instead, then its impotency falls away. Reasoning goes far beyond reasonability. Important as that function is, to humble our common expectations to the capacities we actually have, still reason is far more noble. Every set of premises opens not simply upon its own backyard of conclusions already fully trapped there, but upon the unfolding realities never yet dreamed, to which they will be relevant, once having appeared.

What links premises to conclusions, especially with that necessity which is said to follow? It is not only that this one application has been herded up inside the corral with other samples (the extensionalist answer); nor that this conclusion has the very same feature as those which link together in the premises (the intensionalist solution). Instead, the premises serve as rungs on a ladder which we can mount to climb out of where we have been settled.

Any set of thoughts will drive us out of our staid position; this is the nature of even one, any speculative observation. The premises which allow us to go further with certainty, in addition, are ones which describe their own process of movement outward. "If . . ., then . . ." is a commitment. It may be erroneous in fact; it is nearly the only place for error, in fact. Only time will tell if we have overlooked anything when inferring; or, if we're lucky, critical reason brought to bear on it will show the error before having to undergo its consequences.

The process does not create its own correctness. Only if what it is about is correct, is coherent to itself when it arrives, will its inference be correct. The set of possibilities from which one claim is privileged as a conclusion do not preexist anywhere. They only come to be when they arrive in the future. But we do nonetheless reach into that future, which is now a nothingness, in order to fetch back its reality in anticipation.

Intellectual Realities

If we do meet, now admitted, these conceptualizings, do they not form the content of our experience? Yes, this is what we are aware of: not a well-formed completion, a duplication in compact form of what the object of knowledge possesses in sloppy form, its essence; but instead the activity and expenditure of energy to bring a set of criteria into play, i.e., to bring them to existence at all, while setting them to the test of our experience. We also experience the judgment, not fleeting as it occurs, but imprinted in its permanence, frequently to our own deception.

To urge that our intellectual operations are concerned with kinds rather than with individuals is to suggest that kinds, while distinguished by the possibilities their respective conditions realize, are unified within; all individuals of the kind are not the same, in this way. What should be noted is that this does not mean that there is anything which they have in common. What it means is that the set of conditions is applied to each. The set of conditions remains unchanged, in some sense. But note that it does not "remain" at all, but is reworked by each application. It includes individual existents but is not limited to them. Above all, even granting that the idea remains the same, still it does not enter in as anything inherent to the makeup of the individual.

Instead, the criteria for discerning the right possibilities set only the boundary conditions, outside of which the type cannot wander, until it changes. They do not determine the makeup of the particular existent. At least, some conceptual rules do not. So possible individuals which are of the same kind may exhibit some features which by reason of proximity, association or whatever attract our attention; but others may well meet the criteria for sameness of kind without exhibiting many or any features which join them. Others may; it depends upon the sort of rule or criteria in question, some of which design a structure, some of which set a fence, some of which dictate moves. The sameness of rules is of one of the two former types, for as was just said these rules are not recognizable by the latter characteristics.

Much the same has to be said of the alleged precision and clarity of intellectual operations, the "clear and distinct idea." Some intellectual operations and resultants are clear and distinct, some are not. Part of the reason it is not possible to give a decisive answer to this is that clarity and precision are different for different purposes. Not every estimation of a possibility requires that one be able to disentangle it from all others not of the type, for some possible ways of existing are entangled ways. And not all ideas must have precisely the full list of their components given, for some ideas concern vagaries which would be denatured by being rendered no longer vague. Of course, if that is the case for some possibility, then it would be inaccurate to call it vague when it kept to its own proper demands, precisely; much better to say that if given further precision, it would be only vaguely accurate.

Intellectual Operations

There is some popularity in finding intellectual equivalents for various sensory or perceptual operations. In particular we could note that intellectual memory seems to be a parallel to sense memory. What would this mean, if it were so? We have seen that sense memory displaces perception from the present and locates it as having occurred earlier. By comparison, intellectual memory would seem to mean that an idea or a judgment or a reasoning process had been done before. This would not mean that an individual would have to have been earlier encountered, and so no purchase upon the past through a past individual is feasible. Instead, it is our own act which would have to be identified now as having occurred earlier, and this act is not concerned with a single individual, but rather with a more broadly applicable set of conditions.

Once having occurred, if a fully formed terminus such as the rejected notion of idea were to be found, it is questionable that the event would have to occur again at all. Lodged somewhere in us, idea would need only to be brought forward again, not reenacted. As it is, any memory of idea or judgment is the remembrance of an act which ceased occurring when it was completed. The only memory trace it could have would be for us to be predisposed to repeat the act, since we had facilitated its exercise by once performing it.

Intellectual memory merges, then, with history. Instead of a collector's memory finding the past in its present remains, by intellectual memory we know the past as leaving no remains but the actions performed out of the conditions its options left remaining. I remember what I never saw, so distant am I from it, but so shot through my present options is it.

To sum up the sequence of human mentality, sensation-perception-memory-imagination-conceptualization-judgment-reasoning seems a sequence in which each gives the following an object to act upon. However, this appearance is deceptive. For only as we move toward the end of this set do the activities come more and more into our experience; we are not even aware of these earlier ones but as moments of the completed whole, moments we do not ever recognize until we are caught in whatever error is possible at the next stage and stand with an incomplete part in our hands. There is no difference in the object of each of these acts: it is existence. But each of the acts is operative in differing ways upon existence, in coming to know it; they would not even be called knowing or mental activity at all but for their phasing into one, judgment. Instead of each earlier one delivering to the successive one a transformed object for yet further processing further down the line, the relation is rather that each further operation renders possible the exercise of the preceding one, an operation which would otherwise have been senseless, impossible or unfocused.

Skill: Bodily and Mental Habit, and Virtue

Repetition is thought of as indispensable to habit; if you keep on doing it, it will become "automatic." But automatism is counterproductive; it unleashes activity at the most inopportune times. What we need is awareness of the proper moment; and so the acquisition no less than the expression of habit could be expected to involve awareness.

What is needed for habit is intelligent presence to our location in the world; what's happening here? No less is presence needed for that habit which leads to good production (skill) and to good action (virtue). The attention to what we are doing distinguishes both from attention to its payoff or usefulness; allowance of its uselessness, even when it is not useless, is the condition for any skilled work, as for any virtuous activity. This is the dimension which slots them among facilitators of leisure.

Mentality and Morality

The directions we have already seen in the movement from the first to the second parts of this book now appears within this second part as well. As bodiliness seems our most evident characteristic, we discovered in attempting an analysis of it that it remained among the least known of our features, only recognized at all as made possible by knowledge or mentality. Too proximate, body was not as well known as the greater distancing mentality gives us. Having seen the same true within the domain of mentality, the relationship will be even more acute in moving from mentality to morality, and from morality to sociality and spirituality.[69]

What emerges from the analysis of mentality, and particularly from the study of conceptualization, is that human mentality is a normative activity. It is not a duplication of what is given it, but is a set of activities which provide the limits of just what can appear to it. These limitations have been heretofore spoken of under the various names of criteria, rules, principles and standards. All of these are evaluative, all involve the knower in an evaluative activity which does not follow after his knowledge but which makes up his knowledge, especially under the principle of non-contradiction. When we add to this what was mentioned but slipped aside, that attention is the directive for such knowing and for whichever set of criteria would be formed to yield up some kind of an object of knowledge, then it is apparent that mentality is inseparably twined into morality, knowing to doing, and to the reasons, motives and purposes of doing.

Beyond even this, we are not at liberty to know falsely; we are not entitled to our own opinion. "That's my opinion" is never a conversation stopper, but an invitation to push beyond it. If it is nearly impossible to express a statement of pure appearance, a product of imagination, this is fostered by the thrust of our language which, in its indicative mood, permits us only to say what is and not what seems. Whether our knowing is a correspondence to what is or a tool of our designs, there are norms of perfection implicit in the very description of knowing. The belief which is held must also be true and be justifiable, or else one's claim to know is emptied of meaning, as Plato's dialogues incessantly point out.[70]

This formal norm of knowing in turn implies a less formal call for personal honesty. If opinion is not self-justifying, then not only must our knowing coincide with what is, but both what we are must coincide with our knowing and our knowing must coincide with what we are. If our habits of behavior rest too long or widely at variance with what we know, then either the world must be restructured psychotically to leave these two compartments hermetically sealed from one another, or else the beliefs must finally give way to be modified in accord with behavior.

Our knowing must coincide with what we are. Our knowing is to become more true, i.e., less false; and we are to become less wrong, less in error. The error arises from saying that what is, is not and that what is not, is. We can avoid error by saying that what is, is and that what is not, is not; we can also avoid error by saying neither what is nor what is not if we do not know. That is to say, we are to become less wrong by recognizing we are more ignorant. We must refuse to say we do know what we do not know.

But there is a less familiar counterpart to this, which fulfils it and is perhaps even more important today: we must refuse to say we do not know what we do know. It is not unusual for us to say we do not know, for the reason that there is more we could know about something. But if there is no more we can know about something than we do know, then we know all we are capable of about it and are deceiving ourselves that there is more. The most usual occasion for our doing this is when we discover that the evidence and proof of one thing, e.g., a constructive operation, does not match up to our evidence and proof of another, e.g., a mathematical theorem. But if the object of knowledge is, in fact, constituted by the rules for making it evident, and differentiated from others by these same rules, then it is unmistakable that these rules of proof themselves differ for each object of knowledge. Different objects demand, and allow, different proof; and to insist on more than its own from any one is just as erroneous as to insist on too little rigor.

Even beyond such objects which demand each their own kind of proof are others which demand and allow no proof, for they are basic to the proof of all others. They cannot be proven at all, and by the same token they cannot be doubted at all, fortunately. We cannot help but know them, i.e., use them in our knowing.[71] As we depend on the fact that something cannot be and not be at the same time even to deny that, so we depend on the ultimacy of sensory experience even to disclaim its validity. The moral demand to know truly involves here especially the call for the humility not to push the human beyond the human.

Games and Rules

Games are constructions which totally define the identity of the elements within them. The elements are defined solely by the game, and entirely by opposition to the other elements in the game; one is not the other. It is the tension defined to exist between them which makes up the game, whether between equipment and player or between player and player.

Because of this feature, the game cannot be understood by starting with the elements and constructing the game by adding together the parts; instead one must start from the interdependent whole and by analysis from that obtain the units. Nonetheless, this same feature of games introduces a characteristic just as essential to it: because the elements are conventionally agreed upon, they remain immutable, and resist all the players' whimsy and even rebelliousness. In this they differ from natural objects and designs, which have a life of their own and alter through time, in turn altering the activities they can be engaged in. All that is required of game pieces is that they remain distinguishable one from another.

The essential feature of definition is given in games by their rules. A rule is a measure of behavior, i.e., a guide to the correctness of past behavior evaluated and future behavior prescribed. Rules differ widely depending on what the behavior is and how it is measured.[72] While "measure" implies some formulation, the formulation is meaningless if no rule right within behavior is present, although such a rule can exist without formulation. This is not to imply that if a rule is not being followed in behavior, then it has no standing as a rule; on the contrary, it is essential to a rule that it be able to be absent in the sense of not being followed. Its presence in this case will be either as a rule setting up and defining the practice at all, or else as a rule for how to do the particular acts well within the practice; clearly the latter "municipal law" is dependent upon the former "constitutional law," for the practice cannot be being engaged in at all unless the former is being observed. That is, if these are not being observed, then one is either doing something badly or doing something else. The fact of experience that by doing something badly enough we can eventually be doing something else indicates, as well, some dependence of constitutive rules upon practice rules. This coincides with the affirmation studied earlier that the perfecting of an activity is required by the very character of that activity.

The two sorts of rules may seem to blur further in that, during many sorts of games with ill-defined rules—or, perhaps, in their complexity indefinable practically—one may commence the activity with no advance instruction possible. The rules constituting it may even be made up as the game progresses. But in every such case it is necessary that someone be able to tell the neophyte at each step that this is or is not right. The beginner may not know, of course, whether he is being shown how to play the game or how to play it well; to keep the (dummy)hand off the table in bridge is not to play at all, to keep hands below the table in poker is not to play properly, to keep the hand below the table in a rapid simple game like "hearts" is not to play well. His training over, however, he will then know the difference; no one will start playing bridge with him, no one will continue playing poker with him, and no one on the "A" team in "hearts" will allow him to play but will let him join the "B" team. Also, to change the first rule makes a different game from bridge, but does not obliterate poker although it alters poker from within, and affects "hearts" not at all. Thus the first consists of regulation, the latter two of regularity; accordingly, only the latter could be discerned adequately from experiencing the activity being carried on or from observing it (although not with certainty, if the rules were not being observed), while the former could not be so learned and would have to be taught either in their formulation or by inhibiting responses.

The mention of inhibitions and the fact that some changes bring about new games serves to point out a significant feature of rules and in turn of the anthropological service of games. Rules, and most clearly the constitutive rules, bring into existence whole new realms of activity by defining practices and their acts. Instead of restricting activity from the scope it would otherwise have had, rules open up activities which were closed to people before because the activities did not even exist; we could not be engaged in them at all unless engaged according to rules and except by reference to rules. Instead of prescriptions and proscriptions being the order of the game, it is permissions which most adequately characterize it. While this is most clear concerning constitutive rules, it is also the case with practice rules. For, while these seem to contract the range of activity and enable us to do nothing we could not already do, they are simply directives on how to perform the constituted activity to our satisfaction and, from a different perspective, how to attain success in reaching the goals in the freshly constituted activity.

This distinction between two sorts of rules (which is not, of course, the only distinction of importance among rules) moves our discussion of game beyond the technical intellectual and into the moral order. Moral rules and legal rules have commonly been considered as restrictive practice rules, except that their "oughtness" cannot be discerned from an examination of the ongoing practices. It is suggested, however, that these are constitutive rules, which nonetheless can be discerned from experience. There are only two metaphysical presumptions which would defeat this possibility: that human existence is not constituted but necessitated; and that human existence is all that there is. Under these assumptions there is no new practice opened up but only a restriction upon a necessarily given practice by moral and legal rules; and there is no alternative practice to engage in if one leaves the given one, viz., being human. If, however, one considers the possibility that human existence is itself freely constituted, i.e., created, then its practice rules are no more restrictive than those which keep one playing cards. And need one keep practicing humanity? There are alternatives, the life forms and non-life forms we have scanned, "beast or god" as Aristotle set our parameters. Although we cannot achieve full success in living such a life, there can be enough moderate success to satisfy. There is no restriction of freedom by moral rules and legal rules any more than by game rules. We may be as sorry at not becoming human as at not playing football; but, as the old saw has it, rules "don't make us do anything; they only make us sorry that we didn't."

Thus far, we have looked at the situation in which the practice is given but the rules are not formulated. The opposite state of affairs is what has provoked "game theory," the mathematical theory of games, also known as "decision theory." This consists of estimating which of alternative courses of behavior should be undertaken upon the inadequate information about starting points, capabilities and goals which the participant has available. One does have some information, however, and this information together with the rule that he will always seek his greatest advantage (the "rationality" rule), form the "rules" of this "game." From here, the course of action is selected upon the directive that, having determined what is the worst possible consequence and the greatest possible gain for each decision, the alternative should be selected which has as good as possible its worst consequence. This is stated alternatively in two principles, the maximin principle (maximize minimum gain) or minimax principle (minimize maximum loss).

There are two sorts of situations for deployment of game theory, where there are other participants (gamelike) and where not. If gamelike each player's optimum strategy, which as "rational" he is presumed to follow, is incorporated as a factor into the others'. This is the case for any "zero-sum" game, i.e., a non-negotiable situation between two parties in which one must win and the other must lose; the win (plus) added to the loss (minus) yields a sum of 0, canceling out the game. If ungamelike, the worst possible consequence, however improbable, is to be the determinant for avoidance.

Problems face each situation: the players may not be rational; or there may be solutions agreeable to both, such that the goals must be questioned if these are unavailable simply because the idol of rationality make them non-negotiable; or the results of choosing to guard against the worst outcome are intuitively unacceptable for many practical decisions, e.g., too taxing for the support population to carry the cost. Besides the evident alternative of leaving game theory behind, the alternative has also been taken of including at least some random element if one is identifiable or else a coefficient of randomization in order to make the decision more rational by taking account of an even worse possible outcome, viz., the failure of the game theory in practice. The reentry of the unformulated wisdom of body and sense which this ploy equates right into the heart of games is closer to the meaning of rationality developed outside game theory in the preceding pages.[73]

Puzzles: Paradoxes and Problem-Solving

A puzzle consists of a situation whose wholeness is incomplete but which nonetheless is known as a whole. The situation is less one which requires deduction from a set of preliminaries to their terminus or conclusion; instead, both conclusion if given, and premises if those are all that is available, are encountered as parts of one whole which is unsatisfactory while interrelated. The dissatisfaction may arise from the interest provoked in the puzzle as a block to further and perhaps necessary movement, or there may be no more reason to undertake it than seeking the sheer satisfaction of attaining wholeness and overcoming obstacles.[74]

Success may be impeded by various sorts of obstacles: by absence of the missing part (jigsaw puzzles), by some obstacle to its inclusion (Chinese ring puzzles),

by simultaneous demands seeming to be mutually exclusive (paradoxes), by incoherence among available parts (riddles) such that the wholeness is taken only
upon faith. The problem or puzzle consists in overcoming the impediment to
success.

The techniques of problem-solving fill psychology textbooks. In general the
technique consists in "divergent thinking" to form a new "gestalt." The gestalt
is the whole which is grasped, a whole which is midway between the whole with
which one begins, which includes the impediment precisely as a lack, and the
whole with which one ends which has no lack. The new gestalt contains tenta-
tive fillers for the missing piece or technique. One way to obtain them is to try
and feel the present pieces as a whole with no lacks and so to manipulate them,
in order that its failure will force itself out in precisely its proper form.
Alternatively, one employs a divergent thinking by trying out solutions which
are admittedly unlikely: putting the pieces in upside down, drawing lines outside the set of given lines and dots, turning the hands that hold the puzzle back-
wards. Again the purpose is to permit the puzzle to impose its own demands;
by relinquishing ours, we can listen to its.

The result is frequently the easiest possible way to use the most prominent
obstacles to success. When they are worked against they are insurmountable; but
when they are but slightly turned so that the direction of their force is altered,
then that force tends to work "against" itself to the solution. The pieces of the
Chinese puzzle slide apart as smoothly as the attacker is thrown by jujitsu, by letting the obstacle work for our ends instead of as an obstacle. Of course, the
"against" of the working is really in accord with the demands of the gestalt; it
was felt as a counterforce because it was being driven against itself in fact.

This is clearly the antithesis of deduction, of "squeezing" out a conclusion
from premises, which Aristotle already recognized as a way of ordering and
demonstrating what we already know rather than of discovering what we do not.
In problem-solving the raw data cannot serve as premises for deduction, for one
does not know what about the data is relevant to serve as data until the solution has been found. However, this can be approximated by letting unworkable
trials exclude dimensions of the data, then forming new gestalts of the remaining data, trying in suggested solutions to this, and starting *da capo* to orchestrate
the puzzle.

The solution to the puzzle is recognized when it appears because it works;
often it has been encountered but not recognized because it has not been tried
to see whether it works. However, unless the solution originally formed part of
a whole from which it was later removed, as happens with puzzles artificially

constructed in their entirety, it may be that not only do all the suggested solutions not work but that there can be no solution to the puzzle. In this case the original whole formed a fully adequate whole with no impediment already, or alternatively it was not truly a whole with this particular impediment. In some sense these come down to the same thing, but the latter explanation gives greater scope to intellectual activity.

For intellectual puzzles are posed as questions, and it is only appropriate for questions to be answerable or it would be unkind to ask them. But questions may fail to be answerable when they have some flaw in structure (syntactics: "Why are for?"), in sense (semantics: "Why are angels round?"), or purpose (pragmatics: "Why aren't angels unhappy?"), when the usefulness of the question has been disguised (e.g., I have pleasure from my bodiliness, and if angels have none, how can they have pleasure as I do, but if so then how can I enjoy my intelligence. . . .). To each of these the proper response is not to answer the question, but instead to point out why it should not have been asked, which is relatively straightforward though often intricate in the first two cases. But in the third, even disguised as the second, there is a real need present in improper guise; and simply to undisguise it does not satisfy the need. In fact, and this is frequently the example, to interpret the philosophical question as not the need for a metaphysician but the need for a psychiatrist or an economist is to solve enigma by wrapping it in obfuscation. This sort of "therapy" is reductionist of felt need to unfelt need; the proper approach would be to solve the puzzle by pointing out the proper philosophical answer and framework for the puzzle stated in categories which derive from an improper philosophical framework. While other therapies may also be necessary, it would be an already inadequate philosophy which judged that there is no such thing as a philosophical need.

In somewhat different terms, this is to say that in some puzzles the answers when offered may not just fail to fit the data but instead may modify the data. And here have we come full circle, to the recognition that correct solutions complete their wholes and create their own problems, rather than the puzzles being created by the absence of the correct solution.

Modeling as Hobby

Toys are of two sorts, those which refer to nothing but themselves, and those which are not identifiable without referring to something else. The former are either repetitious mechanisms or puzzles, both of which are dealt with elsewhere; the latter are models whose making and using constitute hobbies along with collecting.

Models exist in reference to something else; they are models-of. They follow in time the existent to which they refer, in the sense here used; they cannot be identified without further reference, even if that to which they refer is unknown except by means of the model's reference. Deprived of this reference they provoke no interest and offer no pleasure. It is the interest and pleasure from playing with model toys that needs investigation, and this investigation must focus upon the distinctive features of models which follow from their representative character, the relationship between modeled and modeling.

What first seems dominant is the fact that using the model, and especially making it, puts in one's control what otherwise lies outside of it. Making a model as complex or as huge as the modeled is unintelligible. But models have a tendency toward approximating closer and closer the size and complexity of the original; the bigger the doll, airplane or train set, the better, and so also the more it wets, is motorized or whistles. While the modeled serves as a limit upon the possibility of approximation and is in fact never reached without ceasing to model, this dynamic of the modeling activity is to overcome that limit. While the pleasure of control is prominent, then, there is an equally strong push toward exceeding control in the course of expanding it, without which the control achieved and exercised would pale into discontinuance. The perfection of correspondence to a given object instead of an elusive behavioral ideal is satisfying; the model-person is a joy to approximate, but less reassuring and less able to be put down and taken up at will without imposing its own demands.

Less connected with the making and more associated with the using is the range of experience which is opened up by the use of a model. While model airplanes, in this respect at least, often lose the representative experience for adults and merge with the experience of using a kite which has no representative character, the very opposite is true for a child. Flying the model (or kite) is pretending to fly the plane, as entertaining the doll is pretending to entertain the baby, as far as the access to experience is concerned for the child.[75]

Education and Learning

"Scholia" as a word for schooling attaches our concerns for leisure to education more visibly but no more truly than does "paideia" for education. For the latter, too, was conceived both as a whole, and in some of its recognizable parts (music, physical education) as leisurely. (See appendix 1.)

What made classical education leisurely, and not laborious? Theirs like ours was an event of childhood, to be moved beyond; theirs like ours involved the

tedium of learning and the hard work of problem solving. But the classic education was focused toward growing the citizen into city-craft, not the knowledge-
worker into employment. And because the former was the apex of leisure
rather than its antithesis in the latter, education shared continuity with the
leisured features of its adult engagement.[76]

Learning is a business for adults, too, among us; "lifelong learning" is its catch-
word. It may, in fact, be the only leisurely education for us. For, to the extent that
it is not skills enhancement, nor a time-filler for boredom, adult education is a
surrendering into active engagement with a discipline, then an object of contemplation, whether of reality or of constructed simulcra.

PART III
HUMAN MORALITY

· 7 ·

EMOTION

If throughout the study of human mentality the key distinctions on the continuum of knowing emerged largely as a function of our states of ignorance and error, so the overall distinction of knowing and doing will emerge through our sense of failure in action, and of conflict among powers. The distinction is not a popular one, and never was. If in the eyes of Plato's characters, knowledge constitutes virtue, then in the eyes of many contemporary philosophers virtue, whether action or affection, displaces knowledge.

The distinction seems evident in our common appreciation; but once it is thought of in terms of a question such as whether we have any knowledge without desire, then the lines become hazy. Desire and action seem to be based on what is known, they seem to issue in further knowledge, they seem to lead us to seek knowledge among other goals. As will be argued here, the relation is one in which the various actions and drives, which we are covering with the term morality, go beyond the knowledge we have. In addition, morality gives mentality the only meaning which it has, in the same way, for example, as perception does to sensation. Finally, there is a cognitive value to moral states as well.

But first take the following failure as a separation. You want to get to destination X. You know you must take route Y. You start out and take route Z. You err in taking Z and end up on Y. You desire Z because you believe it is the right route. You continue to desire it as Y, both while it is Z and after it becomes

Y again, but you desire it as Y only because you still think it is Z, which is the wrong route. You get to X, saying you took a good route, telling your friends so, who contradict you: no way to X by Z. Here two errors have disoriented your desires from the object of knowledge but not from the object of desire. Nor is this such an uncommon state of affairs; it happens every time we achieve something we want by we-know-not-what means, despite our efforts—as in teaching.

Feelings

The most basic affections have already been seen at the end of the section on bodiliness, viz., our feelings. They have the same character as the primitive forms of knowing: there is no way of disclaiming them, there is no distance between them and ourselves, we are what they are, at that moment. Such a privileged access is uncommon, and it cannot last through the gamut of affective conditions. Yet throughout their range, surprisingly, these states lead their bearers, ourselves, to dispel any criticism of them, since they are so much what we are—a possessiveness not usually felt by us over our knowledge, or at least not normally. This is surprising, because one would have thought that here rather than in our cognitive conditions would the action of norms and criticism have been more at home.

Parallel to the more primitive levels of knowing, we notice that some of the states we call affective are well within our awareness while others are more distant from it. Pleasure and pain, generalized feelings of one's state, feelings-about things (as distinct from feelings-of or feelings-that), desires, temperament, character, freedom and action—as one runs through the list and keeps taking his affective pulse, we sense that the further we go the less we know, ordinarily. Perhaps it is the same as with our cognitive states, that the former derive meaning only from the latter, or perhaps here it is the other way around, or totally different. Nonetheless, the differential presence in our awareness is worth noting at the start.

The whole set of these states can only be described in discourse which begins "It feels like . . ." i.e., A feels like B. Following that, one goes on to cite either a bodily change or else the context of a particular state of affairs which is felt likely to induce that state. That change or situation may not have occurred. We felt what the change would feel like if it occurred. There is some bodily change which has occurred and which parallels the description. But that change is describable only by what it is said to be similar to, and not by what makes it up or what the corresponding object might be. Even the description in terms of surrounding environment does not tell how that environment feels, but only what feelings accompany it.

It would appear, then, that there is nothing very pointed about affections, that they are amorphous and can cover indiscriminately a wide variety of events, whereas the cognition of any event is fitted to that event specifically, not one covering many. The temptation from this fact would be to conclude that emotional states are ill-fitted to be of any value in our contact with reality beyond ourselves.

Why would we want affective states to do anything other than this, however? Isn't our set of cognitive conditions adequate for any contact we would wish to make with reality? Why be disturbed if our feelings do not? Probably the answer lies somewhere in the fact that contact with reality has a privileged status for us, and self-containedness has a necessarily suspect aura. If affections leave us in contact only with ourselves, what would the state of affairs be? It would mean that our contentment, for example, would be ill-matched with whether the situation is one which should content us; the very phrasing here shows that the subject of the emotive phrase is the world and only the object is ourselves. This is probably less worrisome to most of us in an environment temporarily secured from natural threats, than would be the alternative possible condition, that our upset—anxiety, anger, dissatisfaction—would be out of tune with circumstances and would have no way of being rectified. We may, summarily, be in danger and not know it, or be in no danger while dreading it.

The presumption obviously shot through this possibility is that feeling reveals us something about the world which cognition does not. Why else worry that unfelt circumstances would impinge upon us? But why would not our cognitive awareness that this set of conditions is contrary to our good suffice to protect us from them, and vice-versa? Why would we want also affective conditions in touch with reality, in fact why not if possible dispense with all the clutter they bring into our lives entirely?

Two answers suggest themselves: that we might recognize things, but not act upon our recognitions without feeling; and that we enjoy the affection for its own sake. Since, however, our actions are as frequently impeded by the emotions as enforced, the latter seems the stronger reason.

Are we ever without these feeling states? We frequently allege that we feel nothing; but in each such instance we can very well be asked how we feel about that situation, and usually in the course of so investigating we do come up with a feeling state that escaped our notice at first sight.

A note which arises from this circumstance is that feeling states are not always evident to us when we experience them, and that as a result they are open to investigation and not just all here or all absent.

One way to raise the question might be to ask if feelings have eyes. If there is no new information they tell us, and if there is no organ for them being a contact with the world, then it does not seem possible for them to have anything other than a self-satisfying function.

If their function is only self-satisfying, then why should they be disturbed by external events, brought to them by cognition? Granted, this is anthropomorphic: we the persons do the recognizing and the feeling, not faculties of ourselves. Still, the question is apt. It means that there is some relevance of externals to the person as a whole, to which some response on his part is required. Feeling states are involved in response, not the whole of it; nor are they always the cause of the overt physical responses, either. But at least they are a beginning of response.

Why require such a beginning? Why not straight from cognition to action? The easy answer is that affective states render more facile the responses, they expedite them; but firstly this is not always true, even of well-adjusted states, and secondly habits can do the same thing, habits of movement, while affective habits may or may not help. That there should be affective habits at all is remarkable, if feelings are set upon individual situations.

Emotion

Another way into emotional conditions is to inquire whether they are directive of the person or whether the person is directive of them. Surely in origin affective states arise of themselves, i.e., without the apparent intervention of decision and direction by the subject. At the same time, once initiated they are liable to control and direction. Trying to control and direct in some ways seems not to focus affections but to disperse them. If we try to bring them fully into awareness by focusing upon them, or if alternatively we try to concentrate upon them even affectively, e.g., by trying to feel this very vigorously, or finally if one tries to use the feeling state very highhandedly, then in all these circumstances the affection dissipates instead of being directed as wished. One way of directing them, however, is to arrange an environment such that they are more likely to be induced; while not so much directing them as ensuring that they persist, the attempt to suppress them has proven the most effective way to retain them, for everyone from ascetics of the desert to cool men of the world. One must work around them, baby them, rather than taking on any sort of frontal confrontation.

Perhaps the answer to the external relations of feelings is that there is a great disparity between the traditional appetites, concupiscible and irascible, than has long been thought. If the former are directed upon the present already attained and the latter upon the future to be apprehended or escaped, then there is a clear breakup between the self-containment and the worldly presence of the emotive states. They are an influence upon the world, rather than the Sartrean notions of passion, a negativing of the world; the undergoing of passion will be touched shortly.

However, even the concupiscible states are related to the environment, since they are not mere notations of how I am, but objectively oriented perspectives of how things are with me, although with no thrust to influence that state of affairs. Whether they are for the stimulation of the irascible, or vice-versa, is moot; one might think that the only reason to be active externally is to achieve internal peace, but it seems no less likely that the only reason for internal peace is to indicate whether or not external action is required.

Nonetheless, concupiscible states are clearly related to the world not just to know it but to change it. They do not affect it directly, but "lead" us as the agents to do so. How is their relationship structured? We can put both negative and positive concupiscible emotions under the heading of desire. We may note that desire is the source of unhappiness for Hindu and Buddhist, and for a Schopenhauerian school among Western philosophers; and that being rid of both happiness and unhappiness is the way to the most desirable human state: peace, the peace of non-individuality; seeking only happiness, apart from upset and unhappiness, would be impossible, since they are in function of one another—lack of one must be the inducement of the other. The reason why this is so is that desire makes us subject to something other than ourselves and so enslaves us, makes us dependent, as said the Stoics, slave Epictetus and emperor Marcus Aurelius. More profoundly, the reason is that desire is acknowledgement of a lack, something needed; any lack; in turn, is associated with our being individuals, one thing rather than another, and so lacking what the other is and has. The spatiality of existence shows up here, with individual outside of individual in his being, even if not a spatially separate individual, as perhaps spirits are not.

If desire arises from a lack, then if it is appropriate to us it means that a two-sided relationship emerges: a deficiency on our part, and a satisfying counterpart beyond us, or a threatening one. In some ways this reduces back to the same situation all over again: how does feeling offer anything new over and above the cognition of need? At this point the important thing to notice is that it would be improper to exist emotionally dependent upon the world only if I do not exist factually dependent upon the world with no needs, only if I am complete. In such a condition, of course, not only would feeling and desire be irrelevant but also action and knowledge; such is, in fact, the Hindu position.

Desire is relationship to the absent good or the absent evil, absent in the sense that it can be alienated, whereas it may be very present proximally. The present evil and good are the focus of concupiscible emotions, present in the sense that they now are effective upon our lives, they are conjoined to our way of life, they are us. So as said above, these are concerned with what we are in ourselves. However, not excluded is that how we are in ourselves is to be estimated by our setting in the world; so even the concupiscible emotions are not without a worldly relevance.

It keeps seeming completely beside the point so to describe in cognitive form the emotions we feel. There seems something so obvious about them that it need not be said, that is necessarily overlooked when it is said. It is not that they are purely private and inaccessible to the public; but rather they are alternative modes of expression, which announce not what they are but that they are. Announcing that they are is sufficient; no one is in doubt how we feel once it is announced that we so feel by gesture, etc.; it misses the point then to inquire why we so feel.

Passion

All degrees of affective states—feelings, emotions, passions—are experienced as deeply us, but not us. For we experience them as something which we undergo, as though there was another agent taking us under control. Perhaps this is the reason for the ascesis regarding emotions on the one hand, and for exclusion of them on the other. But if we notice that cognitive states, too, have this characteristic, that we have to undergo them to experience them, then this does not seem like such a serious problem with feeling states. No more do we say that we *do* our emotions than that we *do* our knowing. We feel as we know, and each of them is too close to us for it to be something we undertake as a project.

So the features of passion, whose distinguishing feature seems to be that it overwhelms us and takes over, is not peculiar to it alone. Everywhere in affective states we encounter this. Is there any difference in the way passion overcomes us from emotion, and feeling states generally from cognitive? We know the feeling of being overcome with emotion, and also of being overcome with passion. Usually the first is used when we retain the sense of where we are going and act accordingly despite the emotion, whereas the latter seems to be used when we blot out any other paths of behavior and surrender to the direction of the passion; the feeling of the latter is of an exploded head and bursting veins.

The fact that we can follow the lead of passion is noteworthy. Now could it lead us if it were not cognitive? Indeed, in following it we may not notice anything but the object of our passion; but we do notice that. We are not unaware of the object of passion; but we can say "No" to it, and once past that point there seems no turning back. The passion abates with the conclusion of our action. There is nothing in itself right or wrong about this event. Instead, it is again only the judgment of where to let it be exercised that determines the evaluation we make about it. The evaluation arises, then, not from the exercise but from the focus, from something cognitively evaluated.

The proper mode of exercise, then, would seem to be that we can follow emotion and submit to passion, that we can use them for the driving force of our action. All that is needed is that they be directed aright. And the direction aright is not to be done by long deliberation and cognitive manipulation, for as seen this will likely abate the passion or emotion and empty its driving force. Rather, the direction is to have been exercised in advance, in such a way that in the emotional or passionate circumstance we may use the affection as itself our guide. As a factual dimension of our human being, affective states' function is not to be obliterated by any other dimension of our being: why trust cognition any more than passion? Both have their criterion elsewhere, in reality; and both can miss it.

That reality criterion is perhaps no better apprehended by the one than by the other, but differently by each. If the world exists in such a manner that it is there to be known, it also exists in a manner such that it contains demands for change, of us or of it, demands which are apprehended by our passions and emotions, that is, grasped by them and responded to, as our knowledge responds to its being there. The world, and ourselves as part of it, is no static given, but rather it calls by what it is for our action upon it in order to become what it can. If we have seen that normative dimensions are profoundly rooted within cognition, so within affection there are worldly and factual dimensions; the fact is that the world wants change.

Cognition can be contemplation, then, only to the extent we are uncertain, incomplete. When we know, and regarding anything we know, the reality is one which demands alteration, not contemplation. Contemplation is adequately leisure only to the unsure man, i.e., one who is humble about some things and not hubris-ridden over everything.

This is the semi-cognitive condition of affection, one which seems solely cognitive only when expressed cognitively, in writing as herein. The world calls upon us for change, and that change is frequently enough on our own side a lack, the call by the world for us to unite with it and to use it. When we activate this, it loses its skewed cognitive feature and becomes what it is, affective. We cannot well express cognitively what is not set apart and cognitive; but just as we must respond affectively to what we know, so we must know what we feel.

Humor

As the giant in an old Kenneth Roberts novel said, "When King Laugh come, he come and don't knock." Laughter is compulsive, the more so the more containment is placed upon it: the more it seems inappropriate, the more inappropriate seems the situation in which it cannot be released. However, if laughter is our habitual or second-nature way of having humor, humor is its separable foundation; one can have humor without laughing and one can have laughing without humor, even if the height of each coincides.

It seems more relevant to speak of humor, the emotional rising and bubbling, in the context of leisure than other context, simply because it is probably more closely associated with the states of happiness that figure prominently in any image of leisure. The traces of humor and its sources are so vast, as well as its expressions, that it could be silly to try and do more than pick up a few strands of commonly employed treatment of humor.

Probably the primary mode of explaining humor has been to find in it the perception of incongruity. The incongruity may be within some presented and created context, or it may be an incongruity in the lived context. While every event can be seen as incongruous, and be a source for humor, only some emerge because only regarding some is the incongruity not incongruous to notice. When it becomes possible to have humor, one is already in a leisure situation, where the seriousness of life is seen to be improper unless it is a seriousness over what life is, viz., a set of incongruities provoking humor. Thus a joke about a recently deceased loved one may be a trigger for tears following the laughter and emerging out of it; for the emotional person has made possible the recognition of his loss as it truly is by providing it an emotional setting. On the contrary, the high seriousness of funeral services is less an attempt to give the occasion its emotional due than it is an attempt to stifle fitting emotion and permit the sufferers to make their way successfully through the honor given to the dead.

Play and Seriousness

For an event to rouse emotion it must strike us as somewhat important, i.e., must strike us at all; we would not even notice it otherwise. If it is important enough to notice, then it is something worth being serious about. And what we are serious about seems the antithesis of what we are playful about; surely these are the first antonyms for each other any of us would suggest. Yet play rouses high emotion in us, and play may be something we are serious about. The alternative ways to resolve this seem to consist either in relinquishing the value of one or the other, play or seriousness, or else in finding an acceptable relationship between the attitudes and objects of each.

This is the problem which J. Huizinga set himself in his book, *Homo Ludens*, which set the terms for this discussion.[77] Subtitled *A Study of the Play Element in Culture*, the study looks for play as a constitutive feature of every serious cultural phenomenon (language, contest, law, war, knowing, poetry, myth, philosophy, art), and not simply as a distinct cultural phenomenon. The formal characteristics of play are summed up from his study as:

> "A free activity standing quite consciously outside "ordinary" life as being "not serious," but at the same time absorbing the player intensely and utterly. It is an activity connected with no material interest, and no profit can be gained by it. It proceeds within its own proper boundaries of time and space according to fixed rules and in an orderly manner. It promotes the formation of social groupings which tend to surround themselves with secrecy and to stress their difference from the common world by disguise or other means." (p. 13)

As anglophones, we may have a privileged entry, as Huizinga finds no other languages that produce the concept of "fun" central to his concept of play. Play appears under two aspects: "as a contest *for* something, or a representation *of* something," i.e., dis-play; it is these which penetrate every cultural phenomenon. Huizinga's judgment upon his contemporary prewar Western world was that play in all its kinds of cultural phenomena had lost its formal characteristics by becoming serious: functional, dispassionate, boundless, commonplace. "Play becomes business"; but the realm preserving playfulness is the heartland of seriousness, as "business becomes play" and takes on those same formal characteristics (p. 200). Science, as well, preserves the spirit by its modeling; the argument is the same as T. Kuhn's account of scientific revolutions through a playful juggling of heuristic frameworks. Only moral concerns are worthy of seriousness (p. 210), and only concern with the ultimate provides the touchstone whereby to determine what is of him and what is of ourselves and thus never absolutely conclusive (p. 213).

Seriousness would, on that view, consist in a partial perspective assuming total importance by displacing all alternative and complementary perspectives. One can be serious only in making a big thing out of a little thing, *mons gemuit et parturit ridiculus mus.* Seriousness would be the enemy of emotion, allowing no value to any affective response except what fostered means-to-end relationships. Play, on the other hand, by its conscious partialness could allow events to assume an affectively provocative importance precisely because they were not so important as to demand exclusion of distracting attendants. This is, perhaps, where Huizinga's thesis is not fully developed by himself; for his swipes at Puritanism throughout the book for its high moral seriousness do not keep his own view of the high seriousness of moral concerns from falling into small-case puritanism. His thesis itself, however, does not demand this. For the touchstone of the ultimate must make it clear that our concern even with the ultimate and the morality of drawing near him is also never absolutely conclusive. Since we may know as much or as little of our morality as of our art or law or war or business, we need not set it beyond the play sphere.

It is not a noisome tautology, then, to say that nothing is sacred because everything is sacred, since the middle term is being used in different senses. Nothing is beyond emotional response to us, because everything is related in myriad ways to its creator. The pleasure of being serious may have to be foregone as a spurious emotion, as really a judgment of the consummate importance of the experiencer. Instead, it would be replaced by the more authentic and object-oriented emotions, of joy in our identity among other persons, of thrill in our accomplishment and competence, of fear at the threat to life and well-being, of giddiness and ticklishness in our pleasures. What will be absent is the devaluation of these as not fully up to the dignity of ourselves.

To this point, the option among the initial alternatives is to drop either play or seriousness. As though proving Huizinga's thesis about Huizinga himself, first, and then about the foregoing comments, J. Ehrmann rebuked Huizinga with the critiques by R. Caillois in *Man, Play and Games*,[78] that *Homo Ludens* is both too attentive to controlled play (*ludus*) over spontaneous play (*paidia*) and to competition and representation (*agon, mimesis*) over change and vertigo (*alea, ilinx*); and also too imprecise in distinguishing the realm of dream-gratuitousness-nobility-imagination-play from that of consciousness-utility-instinct-reality-seriousness. But then with "*Homo Ludens* Revisited" in *Game, Play and Literature*,[79] Ehrmann discovers both Huizinga and Caillois to hold the rationalist view that these realms are separated at all. Both set play as a function of ("a variation, a commentary *on*, an interpretation, or a reproduction *of*") reality and also of culture, taking the latter terms as given and not questionable. Ehrmann finds these equally questionable as play and finds play, therefore, no less primary and more truly penetrating reality and culture by constituting them. Even beyond the bare recognition he finds in them that the very gratuitousness of play is useful, although without it life would remain life, only serious, dull, ordinary, Ehrmann goes on to recognize that if play is truly foundational it cannot be limited to only the situation where basic needs have already been satisfied, as says Caillois: "The hungry man does not play." If so,

> Must we conclude that to play "well" one must be neither too rich nor too poor? Being too rich prevents enjoyment of play—for play is no longer a complement to the needs of ordinary life. Being too poor, too hungry, as Caillois puts it, creates a threshhold behind which these needs totally occupy the mind, and since not even the essential ones can be satisfied, there is surely no room for a complement. (p. 47, n. 7)

Instead, however,

> The hungry man *beguiles* hunger, and thereby plays. . . . If play as the capacity for symbolization and ritualization is consubstantial with culture, it cannot fail to be present whenever there is culture. . . . Whether their stomachs are full or empty, men play because they are men. (pp. 45–46)

A proof of the flaw in Huizinga's argument is that it should not be possible on his own thesis for civilization to become less play-like: "indeed, if play is essential to culture, civilization should become, not less and less play-like, but constantly and consistently more so." (p. 51)

In turn, however, Ehrmann falls prey to his own critique. If "to define play is *at the same time.* and *in the same movement* to define reality and to define culture" (p. 55), and this only because they *are* the same, then it is not possible for a culture to separate them. To suggest that revolution is needed (p. 54) in order to have this separation called into question, is to presume that they have been separated and need healing. But if the thesis that play is foundational to reality (life) and culture is truly meant, revolution is unnecessary because separation is impossible; otherwise revolution would be the serious event imposed to heal the breach of unserious play and serious necessity. Ehrmann no more lives up to the fullness of his thesis than he finds Huizinga and Caillois do to their same one.[80]

In the light of this thesis, we might reintroduce the seriousness of life, not as a counterpoint to play-feelings but as one emotion among others which is elicited when our attention is directed upon our activities in a certain way. This would be when, proving it by living out the finitude which would have led us theoretically to exclude seriousness, we experience the confinement of vision which makes our present activity look ultimate. But this is the very same viewpoint which we saw

Huizinga described for play earlier. And if, truthfully, we do examine the feelings of seriousness which we experience in the "serious business of life," it appears as less frequently the case that we are overcome by the sense of usefulness or of indispensability of our activity, i.e., that it is important for something other than itself. Instead, it is more a sense of our own importance which derives support from identifying with the business; the noble and objective reasons are useful, and sometimes even true, for sustaining this impact in a manner respectable before the public, but the use to which we put those reasons is not identical with them. If the reasons collapse, only slowly does our own sense of worth seemingly dependent upon them follow them, although eventually it certainly does.[81]

The picture seems rather to be that serious business has the same role as does good play: the emotion of seriousness accompanies either because we can throw ourselves into it, lose the sense of catering to our isolated preferences and identify with a public at large. If play and real life are distinct, they are not so on the basis of any sense of seriousness; nor do they differ, if the Huizinga-Ehrmann thesis is correct, on the basis of any distinction between play and real life, i.e., something that *is* serious whether or not it is felt to be.[82]

Friendship and Love[83]

Friendship and love are "hard work," not something to "sit back leisurely" and enjoy. Nothing could point up better the misconceptions regarding these topics. For these activities are indifferent to the time of work, yet are among the most treasured events in life. They are free from necessity; the most necessitous pressure, from death, is what defines them by its absence. For we would risk our lives for our friends and beloveds, if necessary. We want to do good things for them, so they will prosper and be good persons, that is, become the most fully human that they can be.

· 8 ·

CHARACTER

Since we have to trust affective states when they occur, we must have the safe-guard that they are decent leaders. Between feeling affections and being led by affections, there is a gap which makes possible a failure to be led aright. Yet as said one cannot begin to question himself at the moment of the event. It is for this reason that the affections one undergoes do not function either in isolation nor in cognition, but must function as features of an affective habit. This is what is known as "temperament" with reference to how we are disposed to experience affections, and "character" when added to this are the habits of cognition and action. We shall use the two terms indiscriminately.

How does an affective habit, and then a complex totality of affective habits, arise? There is no problem bringing it about. The last paragraph may have implied that this was something we must create where it does not exist, but it never does not exist, perhaps only existing as we would rather not have it. All have temperament and character, although particularly the latter term is used not just descriptively of any such condition but only of the most desirable conditions.

The status these affective habits have is that of a disposition vis-à-vis action, "making" it easier to act and thus likely that we will act in one way rather than in another. Once formed, it has the possibility not only for coinciding with what we do know, but even for revealing to us something of what the situation contains which we had not cognitively recognized, by the response we feel now to old situations.

There are two things, then, to be dealt with immediately: what the habits of affection are; and what their disposing action is.

Temperament

It is easy to conceive, or misconceive, of habits when what we are concerned with are bodily limbs and neurological responses. There it seems that habit is an alteration in the tracks of synapses, development of new channels, deepened and joined, adhesion of constantly joined cells, breakdown of surface resistance to cell firings, and so on. Habits of knowledge can take on much the same appearance, as many sayings point up dependence of study upon physique: Germans insist upon *Sitzfleisch* as an essential ingredient of scholarship, and closer to home some say that the mind can only absorb what the rear end can endure. But habits of affection seem another thing entirely. How does one get at the feelings to practice with them, and to train them?

The chemico-physiological model of habit is, however, no more applicable to affections than to behavior and cognition. For both movement and knowledge are ways of being, not a block and tackle, pulleys and ropes; and so is affection. As pointed out, neither of the former can be trained by direct approach to the mechanisms, nor ever by mere repeated performance, although these can assist the habit formation. They may do the same here. If affection is eminently a bodily condition, so much so that the theorists of emotions are inclined to identify emotion with a bodily condition solely, then it is liable to such chemical and behavioral modification. But just as attention is required for both other habituations to be effective, so also more than such modification is required here.

Affective habituation or character training is promoted by numerous sources, including necessity, judgment and one's sense of loss or lack. Perhaps most important, however, is the presentation of possible ways of development. Each finds before him abstract ideals of wholeness in emotional health, but these remain ineffectual until that becomes a real possibility in the person of another noble character. Once it is revealed as not just noble, but likely and possible, lived and real, then one can know his own humanity in a new way. Hero-worship is all to the good, for only thereby do there arise patterns of behavior which can be imitated not just locomotively but with an end of performing the deeds with the feelings the other does. The bodily import of emotion being two-directional, such intentional behavior can induce the corresponding emotional conditions.

The escape, however, is to simply admire the noble figure. When he is isolated, and not the norm of life, then it is difficult to do otherwise. Then his temperament becomes a goal out of reach, and one which we can no longer feel a responsibility to emulate. While Sartre is surely correct that we can escape responsibility for ourselves by blaming our temperaments, it is equally an escape to relinquish any cultivation of temperament as an obstructive block, and to place heroes on a pedestal instead of emulating them.

This function, however, is only of use in conjunction with other sources of temperament. Of particular note is the above mentioned sense of incompleteness, of unworthiness. This acts as a constant monitor upon emulation of nobility, bringing us first to the recognition that the virtue is not yet ours but another's and, then when it has become ours, to an ease with it such that no longer does it maintain the exclusively high standing it did in the other as model; seen as a habit of myself, it is worth more than its lack, but is insufficient of itself to bring me the completeness which would make control of emotion no longer necessary.

The relation of affective habits to action in advance, and to emotions in isolation behind, now needs treatment. What has been stressed so far indicates that temperament and in turn character is associated with behavior. Two situations of association need to be considered, one in which temperament necessitates behavior and another in which it does not. The first is a condition and not a cause, for the necessitation occurs only if nothing else impedes the exercise; there is a standing order for object-oriented behavior in the case of such or such circumstances. But even this can be assimilated to the second case, since it is the standing order that is the cause of behavior, not the temperament. So much more important is the second case in which temperament or affective habits are not the cause of behavior, but only one condition for it.

Temperament is a disposing cause of the emotion, and either directly or in turn a disposing cause of the action. This differs from an efficient cause which is necessary but not sufficient for the activity, and also from the efficient cause plus the set of requisite conditions which, by definition, are necessary and sufficient either for the activity or for the emotion. To give this the name of disposing cause, or "disposition" as a synonym for "temperament," is to say no more than this: that it is neither necessary nor sufficient but facilitating. Emotion can well occur in the absence of corresponding temperament, and may fail to occur with it; even more true is this of the activity pursuant to it.

But what is added by disposition is that the emotions are more likely to occur; and if the temperament has been sought out, then the emotions are in accord with what the person sees as his proper relation to the world. In turn, then, the experienced emotions can be given moderate trust as a guide for orienting one's activity and for determining his perceptions.

Mood

Mood is often confused with temperament, on the ground that each seems to be associated with a long-term emotional state. But while emotion is responsive to situations, and temperament is the habit of response to situation of the relevant sort, mood is not responsive to situations at all or at best is a lessened responsiveness. That is to say, instead of emotionalizing experience, mood de-emotionalizes it.

Mood is affective in that it can only be described in the "feels-like" rhetoric noted earlier; it does not offer further data on reality any more than the other affective conditions. But unlike them it also impedes direct cognition and cognition through emotional responses. Mood is on the one hand an excess of temperament, a set of controlling conditions which so monitor our relationship with reality that everything is screened for only one relevant affective dynamism; and on the other hand it is more conversant with cognitive states, in that something akin to a judgment has been made in advance of experience. Mood is considerably more attached to physiological conditions than either emotion or temperament, related to exciting or depressive chemical balance and muscular tensions. It is more likely to be thought of as an emotion than is temperament; for like emotion it is a content of experience, whereas only the emotions and not the habit of emotions (temperament) is experienced. As so confused, mood is considerably more resistant to being dealt with than it might otherwise be, for we resist parting with it not only through the inertia due to low energy levels, but also because it seems identified with our person due to its endurance.

The cognitive value or, better, the reality value which mood may have is that the very fact of its presence manifests a condition of subject or object which demands change as inducing mood, as inducing an otherwise unprofitable condition. Unlike emotion's differential focus toward appropriation or alienation of the emotionalized events, the sources of mood do not form the object and content of mood, and so need to be dug out. Especially is this true of what is called "the mood of the times." Also unlike emotion is the fact that the sources and objects of emotion are differentially to be preserved or expunged, while the sources of mood are uniformly to be expunged. In this respect mood is to affection what error is to cognition; and as error is related to cognition, it is to be altered by affective resources alone—the very uniformity of the moody emotional life turns one from it, such that discipline is required to keep one in a mood for a long time as much as to wrench one from it short term. The person's world must be completely restructured for this to be possible.

Temperament is found irrelevant to mood, in that any temperament may endure any mood. Only with complete restructuring of experience is temperament displaced and replaced by mood; cognition and activity are still not caused by its emotional flatness and lack of affect, but may well be necessitated due to the refusal to take up certain activities or to see certain things. It is here that the grounds of unconsciousness on the one hand and self-deception on the other arise, the inability and the refusal to recognize the grounds of our action.

Neither temperament nor drives make up an unconscious. The habits which constitute temperament are not within the range of which we are aware; but neither can they be brought within this range in any useful sense—the temperament does not form part of what we feel or perceive, but rather is a structuring and bulwarking of our feelings. It is reached as a condition for what we do feel or perceive. However, neither do our drives constitute what could be called an unconscious, since we are far from unaware of them. Taking for granted that we have a drive for whatever we are capable of doing, since the drive is the fact that it is difficult for us not to exercise a capability when the conditions and objects are available, we are aware of as much as we are aware we can do, and we have out of attention only those of which we are unaware. They are subconscious, outside awareness, but by no means unconscious, inaccessible to awareness. Temperament is too inaccessible and drives too accessible to constitute an unconscious. Neither are drives are identifiable as instincts, i.e., untrainable movements toward behavior.

But what frequently does escape us is only the intricacy with which drives interweave with one another, impeding and reinforcing each other since we cannot do everything at once. The place at which they obscure one another is where they seem to take on a life of their own, losing the perspective which is essential throughout this study, that everything given a name as a dimension is a mode of action of the whole person, and even more that each of the named dimensions is not self-subsistent but is "covered" by a yet more human dimension until the entirety of the whole person, the whole community and the whole creation has been involved.

The independent life which is taken on by affections is associated with the experience of moods as described above. Within the context of a mood, e.g., guilt feelings, the color cast upon events appears to arise from the events rather than from the person facing them. Instead of knowing himself as affected in his emotional and thus cognitional relations, he sees the event as being such as leads him to be so affected. His own standing does not appear; what appears is solely the object or event, upon which his own standing has been made dependent. It seems only appropriate to be affected in the relevant way by such an event as this, though the event is such only by reason of how it is allowed to confront us.

While this may seem like an overly simple description of self-deception, we face the same problem as in explaining error of a more objective type. That is, the difference between ignorance and error is that in the latter something is indeed being known but it is not what is thought to be known. What is the locus of the known object, which is not the object mistakenly known? Similarly, here our affections are responding to a circumstance we encounter; and if that which confronts us is not of the relevant sort our mood requires, then how do we go about locating that relevant sort? Or how is this one recolored to type? One does not know or even feel that this is going on, so it is necessary to locate what he does but does not know he does in whatever obscures his emotions, viz., his moods.

This has had an ascetical aura, cutting off one functioning of the affections. Instead, it should be seen as isolating the eccentric space of moods, such that they can be used to advantage during persistence, which both rectifies them and in short order disintegrates them.

Psychological Games: Self-Deception, Shame and Guilt

The "games people play" that was a reference point for popular psychology has its more profound paradigm in dealing with the unconscious during more traditional therapy.[84] Reaching the unconscious is by definition a puzzle-solving, and a deciphering of symbols, because what makes the unconscious what it is, is that it cannot be reached by conscious thought; all one can do is to identify its effects in the behavior that is available for observation during conscious states. This substitute or "similacrum" needs interpretation just as a poem or a riddle does. Not by intensity of focus and attention alone, but by alternating that with release and distention, does an answer appear. Therapy involves both states, so leisure becomes a component of recovery, truly leisure since manipulative holding to the simulacrum does not get the job done.

It is a short step to suggesting that getting psychotherapy is leisure, as reflected in its treatment of neurotics but its helplessness before the desperate but confident needs of psychotics. This status is popularized as the roles which visible people play toward each other, rather than each toward his own unconscious. Trivializing self-awareness into role-playing does allow, however, for opening an appreciation of guilt feelings. When linked to a role that one plays toward another, who is the guilt-demander, it becomes clear that guilt feelings can be dispensed with, while leaving guilt unaffected. Guilt is the way I stand before some others, whether I feel that way or not. The distinction puts me in touch with dimensions of myself not exhausted by my behavior, although not separate from it.

In turn, this becomes the precondition for standing before myself, and the affect of having that intimacy exposed to others. While the latter is called shame, the former is called dignity, which is untouched by others' failure to honor it, unless I allow their neglect to displace my presence to myself, and so my dignity beyond any acts of leisure or work.

· 9 ·

FREEDOM

The movement into the possibility of unconsciousness and self-deception points toward the classical problems of freedom and determination in human action. In the immediate context of the preceding discussion the issue will be handled directly, then the relationships with affective conditions will be explored, to be returned to, again, but more adequately, as we move to discussion of human action and personhood.

Determinism

The issue of freedom would probably not arise at all, even as a claim, except for the counter claim. In the sequence we have been following, there is no causal necessitating of one human dimension upon another, nor of the world upon any, but rather there is an agent, with powers leading back to that agent, at large in a world which gives room for their exercise and thereby defines or limits each of the exercises to the materials under action. In this there is no claim to freedom, nor any to necessity.

The claim for necessity in all this arises chiefly from two sources: the mistaken pulley-and-ropes model of human physiology and chemistry, and thus of human cognition and affection; and the accurate recognition that in similar circumstances the same person will act similarly or, taking the sociologist's perspective now instead of the psychologist's, that in similar circumstances most people will act similarly. The equipment for dealing with both have been of offered already, the first from unity and the second from habit and motivation.

It would appear that we can do nothing other than what we do manage to do, if what we do would have happened by itself but instead requires some occurrence to bring it about. If it is the case that no energy is added to the world system but in fact some is lost from its free form by entropy, then it will not be the case that some event may happen without having energy communicated to it from another part of the system. That is, it is often put, nothing happens without being caused. The further argument is made that cause means only one thing, namely, an event which precedes another event with a regularity flawed only by contributing conditions being absent. Of course, in turn the same restrictions upon its occurrence apply also to the earlier event, the cause, and so on indefinitely. The upshot is obvious: nothing happens unless it is made to happen, and what makes it happen was made itself to happen; since there is no gap up to the present occurrence, each present occurrence must happen just as it does. There could be no more concise way of stating what necessity means, except to turn the statement negative by saying that nothing could have happened differently than it did. Human acts are included.

The case seems overpowering, but its flaws point up not just the logical weakness of the claims but also the total miscomprehension of human being as thus far described. First, the energetic claim overlooks the point, otherwise almost axiomatic, that energy transfer can and usually does occur with a change of form; especially so is this when the transfer is occurring across vital lines, from inanimate, rather than just from mechanical to chemical or radial. The sense in which the food consumed or the solar energy assimilated determines either the type of activity or its specific object is quite obscure; brains may work better on protein, muscles on irons, but neither implies that a theorem will be solved rather than a football kicked. Another way of putting this is that even if the questionable premise that there is no energy input to the closed system of the universe is admitted, this still says nothing regarding the possible transfer from one energy system to another, with the other's exercise thereof in no way able to be associated with the exercise of the first communicating it.

This should in turn point up the flaw in the notion of cause that is used to specify the energy package transferred. The likeness between cause and effect is much more slim than is implied in the classical example of billiard balls clicking one another into motion. The one event preceding another obscures the fact that the experienced event is seldom the cause, precisely; the pains of scientific work come about in trying to isolate which aspect of the whole event is the causal factor. To suggest then that some particular happenings are causes of human activities is asking more than the natural sciences can ask of themselves.

Overall, the claim of determinism confuses what has happened with what has not yet happened. Once it occurs, human activity cannot be otherwise (though we shall see some reservations upon this); but until its occurrence this restriction does not apply. The preceding events precede the activity in question; however, this is nothing but a statement of sequence, not of causality. This is the confusion in moving from the positive statement of determination (everything must be as it is), which is reasonable, to the negative statement of determinism (nothing could have been other than it is), into which is imported the subjunctive past reference which is not contained in the affirmative.

The second approach, being statistical, is more popular but probably less convincing than the first. The immediate response is that statistical averages of populations cannot be fastened onto any single person in the sociologist's purview, nor onto any single act in the psychologist's. And the second most immediate response is that there simply are too many shifts which individual persons make in their way of life for such prediction to have force beyond advertising and censuses. Once beyond the limitations of statistical discourse, the claim that it is known in advance what persons will do suffers from the same faults as the theological argument for determinism, that since God knows all in advance it must happen. For the theological argument makes of God someone who knows the future through its causes now present; whereas the divine foreknowledge is not a knowledge of the future but of the present, the whole of existence to which omniscience is at once present.

The more interesting and profitable way into this second argument, based on like modes of behavior in like circumstances, is to approach it in terms of habit. It would be surprising if, the more emotionally habituated we are—and thus, we shall argue, the more free we are—the more regular would not our behavior become. For this, however, to be taken as the basis for the claim that the behavior could not have been other than it was, misses the point that habits are made and not born. And thus can be unmade, and frequently are unmade with (repetition of) individual acts counter to them, individual acts of a sort which under the hypothesis should not be possible. Habit or disposition and also emotions function as disposing causes, not as determining causes. They leave open the question of whether there can be determining causes for human action; but none have been supplied to point.

The final possibility would be that mood would serve this purpose, that the self-deception practiced under the influence of the unconscious would supply such a determining cause. For if we act under the drive of what we do not even recognize, how can we be said to be open to alternative stimuli? It is not a complete rebuttal of this to say that only what we take as a stimulus is a stimulus, that there are no stimuli by nature for us. For, although true, and while it is admitted that we make the unconscious factors into our stimulus, still the point is added that we cannot help doing so, since we do not know we do.

The argument is a potent one and seems irrefutable. And indeed it is irrefutable, since it alleges factors to be present in all behavior which have been located in some behavior, factors which we cannot get hold of to deny. But for that very same reason the argument is also unprovable. The occasional factors are hypothesized, not discovered, to be present in all behavior because upon their occasional discovery they are identified according to a theory of human nature which begins with the presumption of determinism; and so the factors can and must be projected into all other behavior, thereby proving the presumption circularly. It cannot be taken for granted that the mislogic of the theory falsifies it; but it certainly does not prove it. Whether or not we can allow our ignorance, for that is what it is, definitionally so in fact, about such factors to be replaced by an affirmation of them depends upon a different argument entirely, as follows.

Liberty

Until now we have been concerned to point out merely that freedom in human activity is not impossible according to the claims advanced for determinism; for, as noted at the start, aside from those claims it would not occur to us to doubt our free self-determination. What we must now attempt, since the issue has been raised, is a proof that free self-determination is not only possible but necessary. Even if unsuccessful, we would not be aghast, for there are no reasons to doubt our freedom, while the whole institutional structure of the culture shouts it to us; but such a proof would be reassuring.[85]

In addition, the proof that freedom is necessary will have the advantage of linking the not yet closely enough twined sections on mentality and morality since it returns to the descriptions of knowledge. In sum, we must act freely because we know the way we do know. That the notion of freedom has not been defined is no problem here; as we have seen the sense of the term change through each counter-argument, so the argument itself will provide its own sense.

Whatever is proven is what we mean by freedom, and we would suggest that this is a sufficiently powerful meaning to cover any special demands.

What we have seen in regard to cognition is that the various phases of knowing snowball and peak in intellection. The objects of knowing move from the individual to the possible individual, and thence to the possibility of such individuals, and finally to the possibility of individual existents at all. Each succeeding phase offers the framework into which the preceding is built, and these are the same structures as pertain to the objects known, since there developed no need to distinguish some inner object from an outer object.

Just now we have noted the movement of appetite from the emotions and desires regarding particular events, to habit or temperament concerned with all such events in appropriate circumstances. The final step remaining to be made is to note that this in turn requires an initial acceptance of all events and objects in their very being, in the fact of their availability. Specification out of this by emotion cannot occur but from an initially accepted realm of possible existences. Just as any object which stalled knowing and impeded the movement to intellection was suspect, so is any which stalls affections or appetite.

And the features which made appetite distinctive until this point are culminated here. At each stage, appetite for the object has exceeded knowledge of that object. In desiring the particulars, the strength of appetite could be measured by how far beyond what was known as desirable would that desire go. Would it be sufficiently driving to attract to the individual object not just in the fashion that it was known to be desirable but, in order to appropriate that dimension, on to the object as it existed, undesirable as well as desirable, warts and all? Sometimes it would, sometimes not; but the point of importance is that it could. Knowledge in some sense reaches beyond its present, for in reasoning some further dimensions are latent which are all ready to be activated; but one could only say these are latently in knowledge. But when affectionate humans go after the object of appetite, part of our hedging is quite clearly to see whether we can get what we want without what we do not want; and, because the unknown may be something we do not want, to see if we can get what we want also without what lies beyond our estimate of the object's desirability. If our desire is strong enough, then even if we cannot do this we take it anyway. Our appetite has gone beyond our knowledge, reaching to the existence independent of our knowing. Although our knowing, too, reaches to that existence, the knowing only reaches it, the knowing does not clutch it.

When appetite, then, extends in due course within any appetitive circumstance to the possibility of existing at all, it extends to it as fully as does knowing, and more fully. Appetite must so extend for this is its necessary logical condition-ing, just as knowledge must so extend; the best we can do, in denying it, it to pretend that it does not and to pull ourselves apart in the process of pulling apart our cognitions and pulling apart our appetites.

This puts us in position for returning to our focus upon freedom. If our appetite is inescapably trained on existence in its wholeness, then any particu-lar object of appetite is desirable for just this reason that it is within the whole; any particular object is also inadequate to exhaust appetite for just this reason that it does not exhaust the whole of existence we are trained upon. Every object of appetite, then calls for a hesitation before it, to determine whether our desire is sufficiently powerful in regard to it to take on the inadequacy inherent in its particularity, as the price for the features known desirable. We may or may not go ahead; but closing off this pause, non-temporal as it may be, can only be done by exercise of that same potentiality. As explained in regard to mood, we are able to block our free exercise only by exercising that same freedom, although so exer-cising the freedom will not only block its present exercise on a particular but will contribute to habitual impedance to freedom and its near loss.

There is no way, then, that the exercise of our appetite cannot be free: free-dom is necessary to human activity. The promised sense of freedom stands out from this: freedom is the availability of an alternative response to every avail-able object of appetite; just as logic is not two-valued but multi-valued, so here the apparent two-valued morality is simplified to overlook the various degrees of acceptance or rejection between the polar possibilities. Nothing is lost by this, however, for those details depend on this conclusion.

Further consequences follow from this notion of freedom, first regarding habit and then regarding responsibility, and finally commitment. Out of these a morality based on freedom can arise.

Will

In advance, however, we must restore the classical term to its place. The will is the faculty with the traditional status of making choices among intellectual objects. We have refrained from using the term until now, however, in order to integrate the activity of willing into the affective and appetitive continuum, to attach willing to desire and to temperament as their precondition, instead of leaving it eccentrically introduced as a correlate of an equally detached intellec-tual event, the judgment of existence. It now should be safe to introduce the term "will," and to note that the freedom discussed is a freedom of will, the freedom of our capacity to exercise choice not just among intellectual objects but among all objects. However, contrary to some points of the tradition, freedom of choice while not implying freedom in every sense does imply freedom of choice in every circumstance and in every exercise of will. It is sometimes contended that the will acting concupiscibly is a direct action with no mediating deliberation, which only enters with irascible activity. This seems untrue, for the attraction of will to the existence it is shown, is an attraction to the whole of existence only through the mediating particular, so that there is as much activity open with the contentment or dissatisfaction in the present reality as in the absent and possible reality.

Regarding habit, it should now be apparent that habit and freedom are not opposed but are tightly joined. The regularity with which habitual action is performed appears as an obstacle to freedom only when freedom is conceived as a privilege for the erratic. But there is no reason why freedom as described should not be quite regular; it remains to be seen just what will constitute a morality of freedom. To this point, however, it has become clear that the habituated temperament developed from emotion and passion is a step upon the route which both in the existence of appetite and in the reasoning process which follows its windings leads to the will, and to its characteristic exercise in freedom. In the light of this, the question left open earlier in discussing the likelihood of unconscious factors is now closed. These motivations toward choice may be as real as any others; that is not a claim which needs to be settled. But real if they are, they supply only grounds whereupon a particular object becomes desirable, without in any way closing off the manner in which, because it remains particular, the object must also appear partial and so potentially undesirable.

Regarding responsibility, no one can disclaim from his free choice those features of the chosen which are undesirable to him. It is its native mode of operation for affection to go beyond knowledge; since the weighing of desirable to undesirable is part of the consideration involved in any exercise of free choice, the unknown has already been weighed precisely as an unknown and has either been accepted with the whole or rejected along with it. One's commitment is not something he makes over and above his choice, but something which inescapably accompanies it. He has cast himself into the future in the company of the object chosen, for better or worse. Because appetite clutches the object in its reality, the person exercising it is himself "clutchable," to employ a word growing more popular in this context in discussions of legal accountability of the insane. If one is deprived of the outcome of his choice, he is deprived of his choice and so of his freedom, since the outcome is what he has chosen.

Regarding morality, it now becomes possible to use the very freedom which is the location for morality as itself the criterion of morality, In attempting to judge how one should choose to act, the basic consideration has to be that we must choose to act in such a way that we keep open the possibility of continuing to act, in such a way that our choice does not destroy the faculties for acting. Since choice is the star faculty in question, we are to choose freely in such a way that we continue to be able to choose -freely. That is, we must place our bets on particulars in such a way that no one of them or no type of them comes to cover the entire field of vision, appearing to exhaust the desirability of existence, seeming to have nowhere wherein it permits something else worthwhile and so itself includes something undesirable. Perhaps this is done brutally by closing the eyes; it remains a feature of faculties that they are powers, operating intermittently and not constantly. More frequently, totalizing vision is done by assimilating every mode of being to one single mode of being, reducing all hills and valleys in existence to the plain, to the narrow backyard. Then choosing the local is choosing the universal. One mechanism for doing this has been described as moods.

Action

As decided at the end of the section upon mentality, the truth of knowing is not so much a true correspondence of subject to object as it is a trueness of aim. The rules which any object of knowing determine are rules dependent upon the use to which the knowledge is to be put. What meaning our knowledge has, then, is a function of what action we perform; from the apparent independence knowledge has, we find it now subordinated under affection and the exercise of appetite. If without knowledge appetite is deaf and blind, without affection knowledge is crippled and mute, as well as lonely.

An example which brings home both the dependence of knowledge and appetite upon action for their meaning also consolidates the reality value of them both. We might ask ourselves whether we could choose any and everything. At first we would tend to answer "yes" in the light of the recent notes on freedom, once we had set up some obvious conditions such as that we could not choose everything at once, or after the choice had been made. But our ability to do things much more stringently limits our capacity both to know and desire.[86]

We might, for example, ask not just whether we could choose but whether we could even desire to fly. Upon the history since Kitty Hawk the answer would seem obvious. But note that what we tried to do there was to make some approximation to what flying is, acknowledging in advance that we could not do the relevant act itself. We build the flying machine because we know we cannot do what we know as flying, i.e., what the birds and bees do. Having developed aerodynamic principles we may make the substitute activity even more apt for our own ends, if not for a bird's; but this still does not place us within the bird's frame of reference toward flying. What it would have been like is given in the standup comic's banality that he's just flown in from Los Angeles, and his arms are so tired. Even this is not really what we had wanted to do, for the comparison of arms and wings ends directly one looks to function, the: prime consideration here; they have nothing in common but that they sometimes both stick out.

Nor is our yearning to fly any entry into what is being done by the bird we envy. The most we can do to approach the bird is to begin with our own experiences, of running across an open field or swimming into the middle of a lake out of sight of the shores, and then to look upon yet another field of activity belonging elsewhere and transfer what we had done to what we would do though we know we cannot. One has entered further only into our own activities, not into the bird's.

We cannot join him because we do not know *what* he is doing. We do not know this, because we do not know *how to* do this. Anything from which we are excluded by lack of ability is something we cannot wish to do; and this applies equally well to activities that we do not yet know how to do or which we are no longer able to do, even though at some time there arises or might arise the capability for us doing them.

From action, then, comes not only the fact of meaning in knowledge and affection, depending on how the knowledge is used and what appetite is trained upon, but the very possibility for meaning, without which both knowledge and appetite are senseless. To put it differently, knowledge and affection only appear as something not identical with their deployment when one does not know what to use it for or, when tried, it misfires. Then, just as sensation shows up naked in the instances when perception fails, so do knowledge and emotion for the first time appear as something in their own right, apart from action, when action fails. If this is the case regarding the meaningfulness of action, then we are given some pause in assuming the traditional phraseology of will as a commanding faculty and intellect as a directing faculty, respectively commanding and directing the bodily movements and indirectly the voluntary nervous system. Another way of stating this is that action is behavior plus intent (or reasons or motives), or behavior caused by some other state of the agent. Understandably one is reluctant to identify the actions of the human being with sheer behavior, understood as what is observable movement; too many interjections of both external force (e.g., having my arm lifted) and internal force (e.g., my arm raising after being pressed against a wall, or my shielding my face from a mosquito and striking another person's eyeglasses) are available concerning which we would not say that we performed the action of arm-raising or of battery. How sufficient is this mode of explanation for how it does happen is doubtful, however.

If the cognitive and appetitive input to action are distinct events which bring about the bodily movement, then the same question arises regarding them as themselves actions: what caused them, and so on indefinitely. Further, the way in which they are joined as cause to the bodily movements or behavior as effects is, under the hypothesis of their distinction, impossible to visualize; no available points of contact are given. This problem is insoluble, whether the alleged causes are motives, reasons or choices, any of them known as the "intent" joined to behavior. Further, one would have to expand his Galilean notion of the natural states of the bodily system in a Newtonian way. Actions include omissions as well as commissions, i.e., absence of bodily movement as well as its presence, and include partial relative omission in misfeasance as well as total omission in nonfeasance. For the intent to cause the absence of movement, one would have to conceive the bodily system as being as fully in motion as at rest, so that the intent could cause rest as well as motion. No problems arise with this conception, of course; but it lies on the outside of the hypothesis. Finally, to return to base, the inseparability of intent from action shows that we do not know what we are going to do, in detail, until we commence it. Rather than a mass servility to executive and administrative activity, body's wisdom and cleverness at how to go about things is the very condition for cognition and appetition to have meaning.

In addition to this, it is not quite proper to locate the key features of action in intelligence and will. The shading into them of cognitive and appetitive activities preliminarily glimpsed is so borderless that the presence of perception and emotion to an activity must be sufficient to identify it as human action.

To try, then, and determine what distinguishes human action from what up until now we have been careful to call activities, behavior or inchoate actions, we must look for the distinguishing features in the two ex post facto termini of knowledge and affection: rule-following, and responsibility. These are human actions: activity which the agent will describe as activity of some sort, i.e., not as helter-skelter business but as governed by the criteria for that kind of activity; and activity which the agent will claim himself responsible for, or which adequately insightful others will so claim for him. It is difficult to say more about them, because these are the constituting factors. We can speak of what they are directed towards, and will do so; but this is to pin down the types which fall under them, not the features by which we identify them. In fact, what can be the possible ends is a function of what the actions are, not vice-versa.

However, taking this step may be a delaying tactic useful in letting us catch our breath before going on. Overall, human action can be directed toward nothing other than the accomplishment of the action or can be directed toward something other than the fact of performance. In the first case the action is complete as soon as it is undertaken, while in the second that action is complete when the goal is reached for which one is taking responsibility, and whose rule-structure he is undertaking or creating; even though the second is incomplete action until that goal is reached, an act can be said to have been performed even before reaching it, the person has acted.

For action of the first sort to occur, there must be available some activity which not only may but also must be confined to itself, which has nothing new arise from it except itself. For even some form of permanent record of the action would be a product, something produced in its performance. Some endeavors come to mind, in particular the activities associated with bodiliness, which have no terminal point at least finally, but which must be continually redone over again. If they are not continued, the life process ends.

But at this rate all human action should be of the same sort. For throughout this we have struggled not to give priority of status to any "higher" activity, but to look upon all as equally emerging from human capability, no more and no less, since all of them culminate not in themselves but at a supreme covering norm of cognition and appetition, in the human action we are now studying. To each activity corresponds an object: food to nutrition, offspring to reproduction, sensory existence to sensation, etc. It is not only later activities which have an object. And the mode of correspondence is much alike, as well; for we were at pains to stress that food only becomes food in the eating, the visible in its being seen, etc.

Action of the first sort, then , would have to have for its object nothing but itself, be what is called reflexive or reflective. It must turn back upon itself, not in advance of it for there is yet nothing to turn upon, but in the course of it moment for moment, such that what is now being done is what it is being done upon, and the following moment is concerned not with the preceding but with its simultaneous doing. The question may be made vague by considering that the activity as a whole is concerned with the type of the activity; but this does miss the point, and clearly falls apart when the prescription just preceding is laid out as an alternative to it.

Turning to the second sort of action, concerned with a final point other than the self-contained performance of the action, the status of this product is equally problematic, surprisingly. For no more than the action itself does this product exist in advance to form the object we are intent upon. The object does not exist until after the performance, and prior to this it can only be present in intention, in image. By now it should be clear that this status is not the comfort we would like, however; image and in turn the intellectual possibility for an existent exists as nothing fully formed but as a set of procedures which one can pursue bit by bit. In pursuing them he may well discover that the procedures lead where he did not anticipate, and he will either abandon them and seek another set or will follow to the end. The rules are not just a feature of the subject's knowing; nothing has that status, in fact, we have seen. They are possibilities as constitutive of the knower as of his anticipated product, and so as real for both; if he is to be reckoned with, so are they. The action directed to product, however, is in league with the rules for the product and not just those for the agent. As such the agent must subserve them, and acknowledge their imposition upon him, whether or not he recognizes that he does so.

Action of either sort requires that an object be available which is not due to the agent, but which is dependent upon the agent's action; which is independent of the agent, but not of the agent's doing; which is not prior to the action, but is made possible and determinate by what is prior to the action.

Play: Rules

Play of the many sorts we have considered usually has prominent rules which pertain to it. Whether they are found in rulebooks or are assumed in the practice of play, they bound the activity of the participants. For play also, then, to give the sense of freedom and unrestrictedness which it does, seems paradoxical. To penetrate it we have to consider whether there is a particular kind of rule which gives the sense of freedom, and others which do not.[87]

The first solution is that rules which imprison do not originate from me whereas those which free stem from myself. Prime examples of the latter are occupational rules, legal rules, social rules, moral rules; to these might be added the restrictions upon capabilities from environment and our own individuality. These seem imposed from without, whereas the others seem to come from within. However, since the rules of play can also be felt as restricting my activity, they too on occasion appear with the externality of the others. For them also to free, these latter must have the feature that they are not disconnected from our activity at all. That is, in order to be playing in a particular manner, to be about a particular game, I must be engaged in something rather than something else; and the distinction and exclusion while inseparable from my freedom in play, bind me down to it. I could not be playing this, unless I were unable to play that, while I am about the first. The same goes for simply the activity of playing as such; even if we accept the doubtful proposition that one can simply play without playing something in particular, this play which one is engaged in is the source of particular sensations and enjoyments only because it is not something other than play. Again, the limitation off from that other feels like an imposition.

If this is the case about the antithesis of servitude, about play, then the assumption that the servitude of the other activities stems from their being rule-bound must be reexamined. Since the rules in much play also come from other than the players, it is no different from imposed rules. And since, on the other hand, we have a role in the formation of many of the other sorts of rules—legal, moral, social—the difference seems to disintegrate from this side as well.

One new approach is to claim this: that if I disapprove of the rules of a game then I need not play the game, whereas if I disapprove of institutions with rules of the alternative sorts I must still continue within that institution; I cannot go along one way while the rules run along beside me on their own route. There are, of course, some immediately apparent alternatives to this oppression, however; and they come down to this, that I am unable to escape social, moral and legal rules only if I refuse to pay the cost. If I wish not to have what resignation to those rules brings, at least, quite apart from observance of them, then I need not live with them.

The issue in philosophical terms is the modern question of the categorical imperative, facing the classical question of the priority of will or intellect. Kant, the clearest expositor of the modern position, had already solved to his satisfaction the classical question, by putting will in the forefront. In turn, his solution was that the categorical imperative, viz., "act in such a way that your action may be a rule for the action of all other persons," was a forceful reality. One could not deny it without denying his own humanity, as this is defined not just for an individual but for the species which the categorical imperative enables to exist; and the act of denying it was impossible without the implicit affirmation of it. To deny the freedom given by the categorical imperative, I must exercise that same freedom differently understood. This is the crux, whether the freedom could be differently understood, in particular whether logic and intelligence must follow when will acts or whether understanding makes possible the reality of will.

The classical exposition, whether in Plato's *Euthyphro* on holiness, or in the writings of Aquinas and Scotus about the love of God, set the question this way: is what is good (loveable, holy) good in itself or is it good because of something else (e.g., because it is chosen by the good being, whether God or the prudent man)? The answer hinges on why the good-making source is good-making, i.e., good; this demands some sort of stop-rule, which allows one point to be final. The answer differs insofar as the choice either way depends on the presumption that the faculties could be at odds with one another.

Our solution, as would be apparent from foregoing discussions, is that the faculties entrain each other and that conflict arises out of the relationships among their objects rather than between faculties. Some objects of exercise are inconsistent with others; those selected are done in the unity of human action. It is possible, then, to act independently; in doing so, one cuts the ground from under his own action because of destroying in principle the possibility for his action, some sort or another of institution based on the rules refused; but one is able so to act. He is being illogical and alienated; but he can be these. It is just that he must be both together. If this were not a possibility for him, then there would be no possibility of him being rule-abiding, either.

In terms of the question of play and its rule-boundedness, definition and limitation is present everywhere; but the definitions are to be made by us, everywhere. In some areas the consequences of making them are less severe, in fact beneficent; in others, they are morbid. The first we call play, the latter seriousness. But there is no difference between them in structure.

Play: Details

There is often felt to be a conflict between the performance of some activity and the details which go into it. It may be impossible for one even to separate them; a child may not know how to hurry up, because he has not yet learned just what details can be skipped and how to cut corners, the various strategies. For most of us, however, there is not only a distinction but a conflict between them; our lives seem to be wrapped up in details, to the exclusion of the value in the activity. In order to do one simple thing, a half dozen preconditioning activities must be taken care of first. The same is as true of play as of any other dimension of life, but some of the features of play make it easier to see how detail fits into human life, and these may be extendable to other lived domains.

Nothing in play happens accidentally. Everything that is done is in accord with rules: either the game requires or excludes the activity; or the manner of carrying it out is in accord with the style of the player, his own habitual way of performing the game most easily and effectively, his game habits which may or may not be those of his life. His sideshow of personal traits and needs are in the context of the game no more than ways to facilitate playing the game better or worse; they lead him more readily to winning or losing, or simply to being part of the play, if that is the kind of play it is.

In life much the same occurs; the personal traits and habits facilitate the passage into the structure of human existence. Nothing is outside of it, everything is part of the development. What cannot be left aside is done in one way or another, and that way brings the human existence to something new; what can be left aside either is or is not, and keeping or sloughing it, too, will be what the man has made of himself. No detail is outside of it; for whether it is one that could be left aside or not, it contributes to the human project, because it contributes or detracts from the subordinate projects within.

Dramatizing as Virtue

In order for any virtue, or habit perfecting a faculty, to be developed, one must be able to train himself, to develop the habit. Since this requires practice and the practice can be no mere repetition but a direction of the being upon the whole way of life, then one must be able to cast himself into the way of life that the virtue undertakes. He must do this long before the virtue is acquired, i.e., he must act in a way which is not his own. He must, in a different sense of the word, act; he becomes an actor living out a role not proper to him but one which the acting is intended to make proper. Unlike the stage where one's attention is directed toward the way of life of someone else and takes it on as one which would be a possibility for himself, in acquiring virtue one's attention is directed toward the way of life possible for himself and makes that possibility real. It does not remain a concretized possibility as for an actor, but becomes an actualized possibility, i.e., no possibility at all.[88]

Mimesis: Representative Gesture

Plato excluded the dramatists from his youthful republic for their lies, since imitations were not as good as the real thing; other aestheticians have insisted that art build the future, not imitate the past. The attempt to mirror, reflect, represent reality has been decried for its perversity; we might consider whether it is possible at all, and in the light of this figure out just what representation is and how it should be looked upon as leisure activity.

Imitation or representation looks like an attempt to offer what the reality imitated offers. Obviously only a starting point, this cannot be an offer of everything, for selection is made. It is not the offering of what will deceive the viewer; few artists or the public consider it a virtue if the craftsman deceives them into thinking an object is really present. It may be good for a laugh only, not to recognize that "this is not a pipe." Obviously he excludes some unpleasantries: no flies buzz, even if flies are pictured buzzing around the bowl. When tragedy stuns us from the artwork, we are stunned at the artwork; at least not directly but only in retrospect could the work bring about this relationship to possible event. Excluding essentials which do not contribute to an overall achievement, is what is at stake. Every representation is such an action. This is not just a desideratum but a necessity.

The impression is, however, not what is done but what may be hoped. What is done is to establish a relationship between pieces of material—paint, stone, metal, ink, wood, sounds, movements, etc. The relationship of pieces forms a surface whose depth is to be ignored. Attention to the surface is an abstraction which allows reference to be made to some object, whose depth is accordingly ignored as well in order to make the reference possible. Even the intent of portraying the principles of the object (conceptual art) rather than its surface must work in terms of surface, both that of the object and that of the artwork. Even if surrender is made of the attempt to represent an object in this way, and attention is given to representing the way in which art represents, one remains in the same context. Cues must be provided to know that this is what is being attempted, cues which give one understanding prior to entry into the object's details, and cues which are dependent on a particular social environment to be read.

This is a complicated claim, and the reality is no less complicated. Recognition of imitation is not to be taken for granted, when most people fail now and then to see a representation as a representation, and some people fail at all times to know that this is what art objects purport to do. In order to see this artistic reality, one must expect it. Otherwise, one can see constructions only as that, constructions; if his first question is not what does it do, then surely it must be what to do with it—hang it on the wall, throw something at it, cover something over with it, hang something on it, or one of the more commonplace purposes. In each case, what one has is an action of intelligence and will with movement, an action on the same basis as every other action. As with other action, one is to be expected to say what to do with such a thing in front of me, and then I shall either do that or something else with it. Coming full circle, representation is one among these purposes. If I am supposed to see a reference to something, I can expect to be told; and if I am not to see one, I can expect not to be told, but rather to be told what else it purports to be. Of course, as whatever else it is the object cannot be expected to be given the conditions of existence which a representation would, but ones fitting it or fitting an audience's confusion by it.

The same gesture can be made whether one is talking about metaphysics or about motors. While the discourse about carburetors differs considerably from that about causality, the same movement occurring in both contexts expresses something in either. The temptation would be to say that there is something underground in existence, some thread of correspondences that is referred to in the two ostensibly diverse subjects.

The temptation can be overcome by recognizing that the very same is true of words, that used in different contexts they mean different things, or have different meanings. Can the comparison be extended in any other ways?[89]

In principle there should be no problem; whatever can be said should be able to be whistled, too, or expressed in any other manner. Although we have left aside a language theory in which anything could be substituted for anything else since all words just stand in place of the object referred to, still it should be possible to use gestures to convey all that language does. Or so it seems. For the problem arises chiefly in the physical properties of the two media; there are more things that can be done with speech than with gesture. So while there seems no reasons why language cannot do everything that gesture can do, there are some limitations upon gesture in becoming as meaningful as language.

Language is possible because of the myriad uses of a small number of meaningless components. The components are some two or three dozen and they can be arranged in any order. Using them in different orders is to use them for doing different things. Bodily gesture has surely as large a number of components, in fact there are many more. The order among them can be equally diverse, and the fact that many gestures can be emitted simultaneously should add immensely to the merely sequential orderings of vocal speech. The fact that the sensible media are different does not affect the number of possible uses, even though it does alter the universe of meaning within which each can occur; but in principle this is no different than the difference between the meaning universes of written and spoken speech.

Artistic Models as Preconceptions

To the extent that the model for art or artisanship consists of an existent to which approximation is sought, the executed work is a model-of what preceded it. What is being sought, instead, here is the model-for what will follow it. The difference lies in the fact that although the model-for does precede the activity in some sense, it is as much a creation as is the product of the artistic activity, and therefore in another and more basic sense does not precede it but also follows from it, or better is within it. More formally, being a model-of and being a model-for are not symmetrical: what is a model-of has been preceded by a model-for, but what is a model-for may not distinctively precede what is a model-of it.[90]

With this status, the model for a work of art is not imitated, it is not representative. The maquette of the plastic artist is part of the completed work, even though none of the lines, pipes or casts form part of the materials of the finished piece. The same is true of its imaginative model: this is not a picture-in-the-head which is then imitated, as the existent represented by it is. It is not itself a representation of anything else, but a composition of possibilities incomplete until acted upon. The acting upon such a "conception" is so integrally a part of its formation that at each step of execution this model is reformed to mesh with what are no longer fully imagined possibilities but now partly real possibilities which have narrowed the possible range of activity.

Work and Work-Ethic, Idleness and Job

Work ethic is a combination of directions and satisfactions, the directions being to remain busily involved in some sort of productive service, and the satisfaction being to feel justified and competent from doing so. "Justified" is the right word, for this leads to the famous sense of salvation on the part of religious persons doing good deeds. Work ethic is the antithesis of leisure and recreation when it becomes compulsion, when the need for reinforcement by this one sort of satisfaction excludes the allowance for any other sort of satisfaction.[91]

Work ethic is the precondition for leisure and recreation, however, insofar as these latter gain identity only by being distinguished from the demands of work. If we do not see that we have a boundary where we must stop working in order to refresh, we cannot achieve appropriate recreation; if we do not see that our activities involve more than just working and the recovery from or preparation for working, we will not experience leisure.

The work ethic helps define the boundaries of work from the inside, by carving out when it is that we can experience the rewarding satisfactions from working. Even secularized, at its best it will also allow for discriminations between effective activity and the ineffectual "spinning our wheels" from which satisfaction does not follow. In the degeneracy of a compulsion, work ethic validates every and only vigorous activity, usually repetitive since the candidates allowable for the activity are limited in their variety.

The "ethical" dimension of work ethic appears in its demanding modality, as well as its habitual presence. Distinguishing humane norm from psychological compulsion, and virtuous facilitation from repetitive demand, helps point up the true character of the leisure in real ethics or morality, and the slavery of this pseudo-ethic.

PART IV
HUMAN SOCIALITY

· 1 0 ·

PERSON

Bodiliness, mentality, morality—the direction these have brought us, most proximately through the demands of freedom and action, is to personhood. Man as individual is not others; but as person man is himself. By now it may be looking as though, of course, personhood is the first obvious thing about humans; but "by now" is after considerable thinking through of the more factually striking features. Personhood may in fact be the root condition for all the others, and more concretely real than they were; but it is not the first thing to cross our minds about humans.

We have run upon personhood because action left us facing upon ourselves and upon the world; directed toward actions by ruled possibilities, we have at every stage had to speak of our attention being focused upon some object. We have had to speak, as of something we knew about, of awareness and consciousness as these penetrated every phase of our movement. It is these categories which introduce us into discourse upon person.

Throughout each of the partial studies above, it has been stressed that man as a whole acts. There is no action of body, of mind, of appetite independently of the whole; each exercise is man exercising himself in some fashion. The proper discourse to this point would have been adverbial ("man mentally") rather than nominal discourse ("man's mind") which easy speech has suggested to us. It is this agent who is and does all these functions, but who is more than them by reason of recognizing himself as their agent, that we must call person. We persons turn not a face towards the objects of our faculties, but turn our being as a whole; this is our attention, not another faculty over the previous ones.

Identity

This self-recognition has made for most of the problems about personhood. It might seem to designate the person as a root, center and source of activity, activities which then are envisioned to surround the real self as do the rays of a halo. Were such the case, then Hume's critique would be not only true to experience but also telling; for as he observes we do never come upon ourselves bare, unclothed by activities of our powers, and bearing the resemblance not to any special self but rather to only the likeness of our powers' objects. The self discovered as a content of experience cannot have a unity to it, cannot have an identity separate from its operations and the likeness of their objects; it can at best have the unity of a bundle of these separate events, and then the self and so the person may as well be dispensed with entirely as unnecessary complications.

This would be the proper conclusion to what we know of ourselves if we were expecting something in experience other than the contents of experience. But the selves we are, the referents of the word "I" spoken by each of us, are not expected to appear in the way other things appear, and not to appear at all apart from the activities. How appear, then, if neither as them nor as other than them? The response is to point out the misconception taken for granted in the Humean attack, namely, that the activities themselves appear without the person, as contents to which the person would have to be added. Instead the activities themselves appear not as bare contents but as personal activities. The self and agent does not appear alongside them. Nor do we appear as what makes them appear. Rather, self is as far out of the picture's contents as possible; the more unsubjectivized the knowledge or the appetite or action, the better. Person appears only as the scene for appearances; and person does not appear as this until reflection. The reflection adds nothing to the content, it only recognizes that it is content. That is to say, person is recognized in judgment and by the string of judgments in reasoning, not in image or percept or concept. Even this is inaccurate, for not even in judgment does person appear, but in action. Knowledge being only a function, it cannot be adequate to deliver the whole: the existence of person must come straightforwardly, not mediated through faculties, if we are to have person aright. And this is equivalent to saying that we do not have person aright.

The self found in reflection is mediated through the experiences and activities, but is not among them. Self is, as it were, active on the other side of them, as already having acted to bring them about. This self we can know. But we can only know it in this way. Self is not clearly before us, and we can only reach to it at a distance. Were it otherwise, that we could know our active selves as just what they are now, those acting selves, then the contents and the occurrences of our activities would have to be equally one with us for them not to mediate us to ourselves. We would all be one together. Such has been the sometimes notion of the cosmic god, the pantheist god; but this is not even the personal God, much less anything we can identify as ourselves, as we would have to be able to under the hypothesis.

We are, as Hume acknowledged, aware of a lengthy series of experiences, including a constantly accompanying bodily state which alters less rapidly than other ones. This memory, however, does no more than Hume knew it did: it allows us to associate out of habit and inertia many things together to make up not a synchronous bundle of self, but a diachronous bundle of self. The temporal continuity which is of importance for locating the only self we would find worth talking about is the duration which is given in advance with the commitment of every free act, and which is then filled out as the promise is kept, to accept what we have become as our own work, and to better or alter it. This commitment does not bind together what is disparate, but instead gives an announcement of what is persistently unitary throughout the promise.

The awareness, attention or consciousness cannot be spoken of as continuing throughout and characterizing personhood; for many states of self render this impossible.[92] How self relates to their discontinuity, however, is by acceptance of the mode of existence brought by oneself. If consciousness is intermittent, then that is the human way; as other activities, consciousness is an exercise of personhood. And person faces upon all the modes of human life, including those which render it ineffectual, and absent, such as unconsciousness (not to be confused with the unconscious).

Interpersonality

Person has been identified over against the activities we perform, and in terms of the commitments our actions make for us. But is there nothing more acute that such persons as we are can know of ourselves, nothing more apt to our singularity? The relationship each of us cannot get beyond between our *I* and our *me*, between the knowing and the known self, and the inability to identify the two in other than a judgment which mediates their identity, points toward other relations which bear revelation of the person.

In all respects person is open upon the world, in body and mind, desire and action; he is not privately locked away, and he cannot help manifesting himself. It is for this reason that there is no appropriating of persons, with the consequent ability to dispose of them; for their alienation or their being thrown open upon the world is already accomplished once and for all. To alter this would mean to have no more person. Thus the one side of personal dignity.

The other side is that the freedom in action of persons cannot be known without being manifested. There is such a wide variety of possible meanings which an action could have, that there is simply no way of knowing what it means unless one is told. This parallels the condition of imagination, in that there as well the rules invoked are not discernible from the work in progress, but must during the process be taken from the creator, and sometimes even after the completion if the rules are foreign enough to our own. The meaning which person gives his trek by free commitments is not able to be known but by being told.

Yet what one is told in this revelation can only be communicated in a way peculiar to and referent to only one event of personhood, our own. What occurs, instead, is that the references are made to comprehensibilities, the cognitive side of possibilities, rooted in the various actions men do in fact undertake, insofar as they face a world setting common conditions upon them. If we persons were unable to make relationship with this we could not make any sense even to ourselves. That is, we are accessible to ourselves only in the same way that we are accessible to others, only by the same commonness.

By the same token, we persons are unavailable to ourselves without the means of self-knowledge provided by the surrounding meaning context, one which we receive not directly from the world since it is not just possibilities of the world, but from our human group since the possibilities are ones for men facing the world. We do not know ourselves but by reference to others' modes of knowing persons. Therein we find solidified, in authority and in institution at the limit, the dignity of man as person and the contexts for pursuing it.

This does not mean that we persons are just what we are told we are by our fellowmen: we are not a reflection of what they tell us. For how would they know? If in principle all persons were to be known to ourselves only by being told just what we are, there would be none who had the insight into what any person was, into what our needs to be informatively dependent on others were, and so none would take up the task of going about distributing personhood. Wherever there would be such an attempt, there must be some who do not require it, and who therefore represent what person is but who are so treating others for designs apart from their personhood.[93]

Consciousness: Attention and Awareness

In each of the activities or dispositions of persons there has been the need to select an object or focus from among a variety. This variety has not been encountered in the same way that the one selected is met by the activity or disposition. Instead, such an operation would seem to be dependent upon that more basic operation of selecting an object or focus: since the normal encounter is singly focused, and since the focus is a selection from many, that manifold must be present in a way other than the normal encounter; and the selecting itself must also be an activity distinct from that encounter. The presence of that manifold is discussed earlier, in principle and as the possibility of the whole under the titles of judgment and of freedom, and in actuality and concretely under the studies of senses and of emotions. In only some of the senses (viz., sight and, in a reduced fashion, touch) is there a manifold given altogether, such that selection must be made; therein we are related to many possible objects not as general possibilities of the faculty, but as really available at once here and now.[94]

Of course, the manifold does not come without gradations: we are always already involved more into one portion than another, though we may shift from it, still within the exercise of the same faculty. Thus the selection is more proximate than the "vision" of the manifold, and it is this "attention" which wants discussion.

Attention is the name of an activity, rather than only a readiness for some other activity, since performing many other activities already requires attention. It characterizes some other activity, adverbially as it were, since that other activity can be done with greater or less attention; however the activity cannot be performed without any attention at all. By reason of attention having degrees, which parallel the degrees of respect, [95] attending may become an activity in its own right, which we exercise by doing other things, as being attentive by passing the potatoes. It is this secondary sense of attention which is ultimately primary, for it is the personal history of our experiences forcing something upon our attention which in maturity has fostered an openness to possible manifolds.

We respect the whole of reality with the whole of our person; we turn our whole person in anticipation of the whole reality to be encountered in the myriad ways of our distinct faculties. We have actively prepared to respond, rather than attention being either pure activity or pure disposition.[96]

Attention exercises our human wholeness as persons, and is the best glimpse of our selves; it is a global relationship to reality prior to any localized ones. But it also shows our human condition of health: the attention is available to us only as the modification upon the activities of our various faculties. As persons we are the infinity and the nothingness Pascal found in us.

Sexuality

Person's singleness in identity and conjointness in multiplicity, is expressed most succinctly by sexuality. To some extent there is little difference in its effect from various other multiplicities available for carriers of human existence: variations in size and intelligence, differences of wealth and status, oppositions of party and creed, uniqueness in culture or race—all present the problem of explaining the manyness of what is single, human being, from the essentialist point of view or the singleness of what is manifold, human individuality, from an existentialist viewpoint. There is no novelty in the problem over simply explaining how the many individuals are somehow one; how we are one or how multiple is expressed in different terms in each case, taking various positions along the spectrum from undivided unity to disconnected multiplicity. In each case the problem is the classical and continued one of "the problem of universals."

But sexuality is a key relation among these, for several reasons. First, it is more deeply rooted in all our personal dimensions than the others. Being short or being smart are highly confined characteristics to group persons and divide them; any broader dimensions they may have, such as impact on social standing or personal integration, can only be considered as effects, and effects only under peculiar conditions, rather than essentially tied up with that dimension. On the other hand, the various social dimensions above mentioned are equally confined; for, although they may more clearly bind people, they less clearly discriminate them. While "poor people are not just rich people without money," their unification goes less deep and their alienation seems less serious and less important even when it is serious. Both these other polarities are less founded organically or socially.

Perhaps distinctiveness by race is closest to distinctions between sexes; it, too, penetrates every dimension of the existence of the person existing racially, from what is distinctly organic to what is screamingly societal. But the difference in impact might, perhaps, be shown by the fact that people will define themselves racially only when another race exists nearby, in a unified stand-ing and in an important position, and will neglect even to think of this other-wise; whereas each person defines personhood for itself at least partly in sexual terms even in the complete absence of the other sex.

The comparison with race introduces a second distinctiveness to our sexual multiplicity. For all the other multiplicities of people have the structure of a continuum from a least to a most; any characterization of a person in their terms consists simply in locating that person at some point or another in the spectrum, with many other locations "above" and "below" that person, if we were to model the spectrum vertically. One is more or less tall, wise, rich, author-itative; a major problem for cultures, creeds and parties is to define themselves with sufficient sharpness that they can appear distinct from others, with a con-stant difficulty of how to classify persons who stand along the blurred edges of the grouping and whether or not to integrate a practice which seems more char-acteristic of some other grouping.

This is less true of races; for, although the grossly apparent skin colorings blur almost indiscriminably, there is a composite of anatomical, chemical and genetic differences which identify it, together with their psychological socio-logical and operational counterparts. Even more strongly rooted and sharp are sexual differences in these domains. This is not to claim that they cannot be modified, for being aberrant; surely psychological, sociological and functional differences are open to alteration, may cry to be altered, and frequently differ from one sexual setting to another.

Similarly, it is highly possible to alter chemical and hormonal differences, purposely or accidentally; since these are simply matters of comparative bal-ances, each of which characteristic balances include all the components of the other, the balance can be shifted to its alternate by addition and subtraction, stimulation or suppression of these chemicals and hormones. Also, primary and secondary anatomical differences can be exchanged in sexual surgery; already not too uncommon in the anatomy of external genitals, one would be reluc-tant to exclude the possibility for transformation even of internal organs, as by transplantation. By the same token, the change of genetic composition by genetic surgery seems not too distant, obliterating even this most ultimate dis-crimination. Thus, the existence of persons who stand by birth in a sexual no-man's-land, who are anatomically bisexual or psychologically homosexual, becomes more comprehensible, on the basis of present technology; as we can understand airplanes better when we learn to build them, we can comprehend sexual aberrants better when we learn to mold them.

But this possibility of obliterating sexual lines misses the point. While the lines between other classifications do not exist but can be drawn, sexual lines exist without our input but can be undrawn; and even then they cannot be erased but only crossed. Quite apart from the moral propriety of crossing them (or, perhaps in some cases, of not crossing them), the anatomical and genetic lines stand by themselves; not simply a characterization reached by averaging the dominant features of those who bear them, as are the characterizations of "Caucasian," "short," "Ugandan," "Jewish" and "socio-economic middle class," sexual classifications instead stand, however few or many bear them. They result from observation, not manipulation.

This focuses down yet further onto a third distinctive feature of sexual variety among people: that it is a very sparse variety. As a result of being continua, the distinctions upon most of the bases above can be innumerable; and while not so structured, perhaps, racial differences seem to provide some half dozen alternatives on their own base.[97] But the striking feature of our sexuality is that it is not just a polarity, but a bipolarity; there are only two sexes. Again, it is not difficult to generate further sexes, imaginatively: genitals on the knees, as some insects, shaped like flatirons; hormones of yet further composition; different genetic compositions, on the model of the "criminal" extra X-gene. But, again, there are not such. And it seems impossible to fit them into our sexual scheme: gelded eunuchs have often been fitted among us, but precisely as non-sexual in role and function. A triple or quadruple sexuality seems out of the question for persons.

The alternative would seem to be a single sexuality, although the meaning of the term "sexuality" would have a problematic suspension; "a redefinition of the identity of the sexes within a new image of man" (E.H.Erikson), even overlooking the factual obstacles to definition, appears difficult. We could approach it as a possibility by inquiring what personhood and its relational necessities would be like in that condition, that there were only one "sex." Some small model communities consisting of one sex are available, temporarily or permanently absent from members of the other sex: prisoners, soldiers, religious, members of sports teams, children in separate schools, workers on a location. Each is established for a special and limited purpose, so that the persons therein can devote themselves to that purpose without expenditure of energy and attention elsewhere. Its economy requires redistribution of sexual roles within the one sex; this may or may not involve activation of both roles in genital intimacy. The other sex's impact is usually felt by its absence, the only slackening in this occurring when members are enmeshed in their private devotions there.[98]

Perhaps the dominant feature is the blandness of the atmosphere, its boredom; persons are indistinguishable in terms of the common purpose; they distinguish themselves, instead, not even in terms of the characterizations treated above but in terms of even more minute and artificial distinctions, who prefers a yellow handled screwdriver or a red covered book over a green; the consequence is that persons in their individual personhood are not recognized at all but only their "nasty, brutish and short" operations.

This is, perhaps, the suggestion that is needed to explicate personal sexuality, and to present probably the most suggestive characteristic of sexual sharing. While other distinctions among persons repel them from others, the sexual distinction attracts them to each other. Those of different races, statuses, physiques do not take the greatest pleasure in each other's company, but seek their own; the decision to reach out to other groups and recognize the fulfillment they can bring is initially an act of faith rather than a spontaneous response, and always is somewhat stilted. At the extreme of timidity and laziness and blindness, it becomes discrimination in the popular sense. But however unvirtuous we may be, this does not stand in the way of our sexual attraction to each other.

Again associated with the bipolarity of our sexuality, we are not only attracted sexily but are forced upon the other sex: there are so few alternatives to it to choose our preference from among, and there are so many members of the given alternative. Our bipolar sexuality is in fact, and can be conjectured to be, the gift of being, a means of seeing other persons. Individual personhood, and thus our own, is difficult of access, as we saw; it is more difficult than ever when the individuals are seen not as persons at all but as "shorties," "kikes," "niggers," "papists," "losers," "exploiters" solely. But the attraction of sex brings us together, and to ourselves, not only in the falsifiable public domain but in the hidden and so unhideable domain of our bodily privacy and needs. We can be penetrated here only with continued association, for we exist across temporal spread; the association of procreation with such a continued association is not accidental, for if only here is it possible to generate our own personhood along with the other person's, only here is it fitting to expect further personhood to be fostered.

If the obvious feature of sexual intercourse has been out of sight until now, this is the reason; for by itself it gives no hint of its meaning nor of its role. Surely it is not the sole locus of sexuality, which instead penetrates the very breathing of the sexual person; nor is it essential to sexual communication and affection, although we shall see intercourse as its natural lovemaking; nor is it essential to procreation, or even very efficient. On the first of these last points, generation *in vitro*, including synthesis of the sexes' contributions, has not

been impossible to successfully conclude for human being as well as lower animate life. On the second, it is a shock to read B.Hocking summarize in *Biology:
The Ultimate Science* this fact:

> Sex is usually regarded as subserving reproduction and increase in numbers; in point
> of fact, because it takes two individuals instead of one, because fertilization is a fusion
> process, sex is antagonistic to reproduction. For the sheer production of numbers, both
> simple division and budding are more efficient.

Thus intercourse is also possible outside of reproductive conditions, and even
in non-sexual ones, such as the intercourse possible between at least one pair
of homosexual partners, using organs not sexually specific at all.

Our sexuality, on the other hand, as a meeting of persons and perhaps an
indispensable vehicle for seeing others as persons rather than mere individuals,
is modeled in sexual intercourse. There we are forced into meeting the other as
person: the giving which makes up intercourse becomes, in a longitudinal perspective, the source and crown of both forgiving and thanksgiving, the truly personal experiences which respectively are the release and the ecstasy which make
up leisure.

These features of sexuality and sexual intercourse—our bipolar facilitation of
the personal universe—have not been missed by any of the major traditions. The
Hellenized Hebrew translation describes the creation of the male's helpmate as of
one "like unto him," a translation in terms of the matching of universals puts it;
but in the literal Hebrew it is as one "face to face" with him, meeting him in image
and senses and brain, and excluding the depersonalization of meeting the person
only obliquely, offhandedly, as an individual in the sodomy shared by homosexual
encounter in imitation of non-human primate intercourse.

This notion is met in somewhat weakened form in the storytelling of later
Jewish *haggadah*: "The woman destined to become the true companion of man
was taken from Adam's body, for 'only when like is joined to like is the union
indissoluble'. The creation of woman from man was possible because Adam
originally had two faces, which were separated at the birth of Eve." This turn-
around, *volte face*, is unnecessary in the Greek and Indian histories:

> Primitive man was round. . . . After the division of the two parts of man, each desiring
> his other half, came together and threw their arms about each other, eager to grow into
> one. (Aristophanes (not Socrates), in Plato's *Symposium*)
>
> A man who is lonely feels no delight. . . . He then made himself to fall into
> two. . . . "We two are each of us like half a shell." Therefore the void which was there,
> was filled with his wife. (*Brhihadaranyaka Upanishad*)

The Chinese version while less detailed is yet more powerful on the location of the personal universe in sexuality and sexual intercourse: "The passionate union of Yin and Yang and the copulation of husband and wife is the eternal rule of the universe" (Chuang-tzu).

Pets

As any other activity, pet-keeping may be done "for fun or profit"; and as in any other activity there is no reason questioning why those who do it for profit do it, since even their profit is dependent on the clients doing it for fun. There are numerous theses propounded about why people live with domesticated animals which by only the most stretched imagination can be called useful. Substitution is perhaps their most common element, but this is inadequate because, even if true, it does not deal with how and why animals can substitute for other human beings.[99]

The master feeds, walks, trains, curries, protects and breeds his animal, fish, bird or reptile. The animal lives with him, follows him, gives him affection and plays with him. In many ways that is the relationship to a child. The owner has no requirement to continue this treatment, however, other than his own pleasure; nonetheless few masters dispose of their pet when this care becomes burdensome—their wives or mothers take it over. The animal almost unfailingly recognizes the master, and experiences none of the extremes of moods which the owner himself does. It does not seem to be a question of the master knowing his own dignity and power as over against the dumb beast, for it seems that the more he so feels the less accurate is the feeling. Man is not the only animate species to have hangers-on from other species, but among other species the relationships purely parasitic on one part and a form of ranching on the other. Perhaps the satisfaction comes partly from this being an acknowledgment of human responsibility for all things. And perhaps additionally the pet calls in a diminished form for all the sorts of attention another human person does, and that it is the diminishment which makes it possible to gain satisfaction from taking it on—acting and seeing oneself act humanly, but only acting it, reducing to our earlier analysis of acting.

Care

The spectacular advent of care to the rank of moral criterion in the past few decades implies its kinship with obligation, and clouds its role as leisure activity. While care spreads across the spectrum of activities—from merely non-neglect to a people-centered way of carrying out tasks, to a non-penal way of approaching supervisory roles and a gender-sensitive mindset for every encounter—its core locale remains in the care for the disabled. Sick or deprived or injured, infant or elderly, the recipient has need of help in order to achieve her fuller humanness. But the protocols which license an approach as "caring" may best be seen in the burgeoning limit-case of care, the Alzheimer caregiver. Here the crucial injunction to "share your client's world" can be carried out most fully. For that world is both totally different from the one apparently surrounding them, but is also thoroughly malleable. Space and time, tasks and relations are not what they seem. It seems to her: the city is Newark, not Montreal where we are; so we can go for a walk in Old Newark. It is breakfast time and the start of the day at 3:00 in the morning; so we'll take a brief snack, and then talk our way through an entire day, all in five or ten minutes, until we've reached bedtime again, by 3:15. I'm my client's brother, not son; so I'll act brotherly for the time being. The service of softening my client's fear at her confusion also becomes a trip beyond reality for me as well. My careful entering her stage so as not to disconnect its props more than they are, ensures that for me too the confines of the present are momentarily lifted, and the painful enforced leisure is realized. I gain a brief glimpse of how friable the rigid boundaries are upon my human potentialities.

Encounter and Intimacy

The subject hardly starts here, and certain doesn't end here. Humans' sexuality provides much of the energy for our experience, from cellular masculinity or femaleness to mystic transport in only the male or only the female mode. What is narrowly of concern from the spectrum of sexuality in the context of community and leisure is the core set of distinctions constituting gender once and for all.

Differentness is how men and women's leisurely humanness is played out by their living around sexual intercourse. Not that sexual congress is immune to unleisurely distortion. Since lovemaking can express the full range of human involvements, it can be done for the sake of business, productive or reproductive, even when not as a business. It can be the best way to manipulate and confine, rather than to liberate and foster. It can be tortured into mere pleasure-seeking, though not successfully for long, since pleasure has too hazy a structure to be made an objective.

But in its experience lovemaking is able to refresh and to free. Of few other actions is the bromide recited, "Even bad sex is good sex." Being one flesh is more than the metaphor from one religion; it is a metaphysics of pure secularity. Excitement from initial frisson to foreplay, through arousal of organs to orgasmic climax, into the satisfaction of post-coital tenderness and perhaps re-arousal, no one prefers not to have the experience. Something usually goes awry. But enough always remains for maturing lovers to laugh and learn. The community of diversity in sexual intercourse breaks open the ghetto of sameness of kind, into the openness to fellow humans in their singular multiplicity. Sex makes the mingling with others not only useful, but has capability to serve as end in itself, in turn modeling the possibility for all our other relations.

Each party's total time at sex play is spent far more in pleasuring the other party, up to the point where increasing the other's pleasure further requires allowing the other to pleasure oneself. This turn-about is the mutuality definitional of community, for that is what constitutes it, not the solution of prisoners' dilemmas and solving coordination problems.

· 11 ·

COMMUNITY

Rather than looking to the others as mirror, it is as though we were to look through them as a medium of vision in order to see ourselves. Not by comparison with them any more than by reflection in them do we know ourselves as persons, wise and free in our bodies, but each with a peculiar and singular knowledge; the only comparisons are for partial purposes, necessary as they may be. What we see, of course, looking through them is the bridgework of possibilities and openings to action which our knowledge content has to be, and the commitments in responsibility that every step brings us.

Human persons being object-focused and energy-intensive, there is no question but that they require a breakup of effort in order to cover the full range of human possibility. Person is an eccentric term as a singular, by content having the plural meaning of "people." And as the interaction is essential among individual persons for human action to occur, knowledge of persons and love of persons, so too multiplicity in personal action is inescapable if the whole of man is to be fertilized by each of his possibilities.

What is called the division of labor, then, is something required for human personhood prior to the specialized economic demands which particularize it to these and those divisions. Diversity of sexes, ages, races, cultures and nations, as well as in turn of occupations, is as inescapable to personhood as the multiplicity of individual persons. Appearing to others in the guise of my sex or occupation (taken in the sense of some energy-expenditure of facultative operation) has none of the disfavor attached in humanistic literature to roles. Instead, it is unavoidable. The disfavor, instead, attaches to the separation of roles from personhood and attachment to the objects, including techniques, involved in that role. The solution is clearly not to abandon roles or to become morose that they are inescapable, for that they are, but to lead them back into conscious relation to personhood lest they fly off on eccentric trails of their own. Just as the various components of human faculties, the partiality of roles only appears in their failure, when they cease to mesh intimately with other roles.

Etiquette

Etiquette is associated with the leisured life, by being made the image and preoccupation of the leisured classes. Aside from the factual falsity of the image, due to the rushed life of these classes and the percentage of boors among them as well as the politeness expected by unleisured classes from each other, the proper relationship might be that this makes life more leisured for others. As the activity of etiquette is practiced, it differs considerably from the standing it has in books of etiquette. There, of necessity, it appears as the rules which restrict the natural behavior of people. In practice these rules are merely generalizations from the way polite people do behave. As they are found in people's behavior, they are not a constant check upon natural ways of acting, for there is nothing more natural about acting boorishly than acting politely; both are trained, rather than there being a pool of natural responses which is either released or covered over. Only in borderline situations does one have to think of rules. Not only do the responses of etiquette emerge naturally, but they also serve functions which could not otherwise be served. In the West, it may be possible to compliment a stew directly but not a pretty face without embarrassing the recipient and leaving him unknowing what to say; so one does not belch but says how good it is, and one does not say how pretty but how the people stopped and looked. In the East, a stew may be something to be eaten and not spoken, and a pretty face something approached for action with no verbal response expected; so one belches at the good stew and lavishes direct compliments upon the pretty face. Although directly contrary behavior, both sets of etiquette are selections at critical points of one out of two contrary alternatives; and the selection is made in accord with other mutually reinforcing selections. No one who shares such a system misunderstands the responses, or misreads them for the behavior which participants would engage in were the system absent. Just as the framework is for an effect, so it can be and is broken in order better to achieve that effect.

Language Game

For the central action of personhood and sociality, speaking, the model has been proposed of language games. Language is compared to a game, so that it may be more accurately comprehended. The way in which this model begins to be developed is first by noting what misconceptions of language can arise apart from it.

The primary misconception is one we have seen throughout the study of cognition, that knowledge and thus language are tracing paper laid over reality, through which we trace the outlines and as much of the detail as will come through. Every line in language duplicates an edge in reality, every point is referent to a corner, every color represents a surface and its qualities. The words, sentences and descriptions in language duplicate reality by jointly representing it and severally referring to it. In this light, interrogative, exclamatory and imperative discourse, subjunctive and conditional speech are deviant from the model, but basically they are explicable within it; they are more like the tonalities in which indicative discourse can be issued. Present and future tenses are secondary in reference, for each of them depends upon the past tense, in which we encountered the objects and events traced in the others. Adjectives, adverbs and verbs are degenerate nouns, nouns used in a secondary way so as not to interfere with the main thrust of the discourse, while prepositions, conjunctions and exclamations are nowhere, being equivalent only to the conditions of the atmosphere or at best to rhythmical modulations to the speech proper. Foreign languages are inter-translatable word for word, or at worst description for description, since each puts into its imitation the duplications of the very same universe. Speech is a selection from among this store of what is available ready to be said in language.

This does not seem too ribald a statement of what our language is all about; we feel it very familiar, and run upon it every day. But consider what is involved in it. Above all, there is an obstacle put between us and reality, so that the only way we can know reality is through it at best and perhaps even only know it as a replacement for reality. Since under this hypothesis reality does not force language into existence, then this substitute for reality is an animal of our own creation; one is *locked* into his own *humean* being, since this is all we know. Secondly, even if this were the way we know reality, what would be known through it would not be a reality of the sort that could be known through it. For the reality known is not one of atomized bits and pieces with no bonds between them possessing any reality. Instead the world known is one sculpted into myriad interlocking and inter-defining shapes, with qualities given as much by the environmental setting as by the separate owner, caused as much by the continuing conditions of its existence as by the prior events.

The further dimensions of this world known in fact, which could not be known either under the hypothesis, are determined from a third observation, that the role held by language other than first-person singular present indicative declarations of existence is highly suspect; there is too much weight to language for such a minute part of the parsing to carry. Nor is there any reason for making it do so, apart from the need to sustain the given model. The obvious solution would be to change the model.

The replacing model would have to be one which allowed knowledge of existence rather than its substitute, one which recognized the interpenetration of existence while explaining the breakage of reality into words, and one which made as much sense of all modes of discourse as of the single privileged assertion. This is done by pointing up how language is not something additional to knowledge but is instead as much as we do know, at least with a certain kind of knowledge; that recognizes the purposefulness of language which selects out points in the stream of existence and carves them loose into words; and that makes assertions one particular kind of purpose among the other kinds which determine other modes of discourse. The old way of seeing speech was one goal among others which could be held, and more or less successfully realized; but by no means does this single mode determine all that is and can be, nor all that is and can be said.

The other model has been called a "language game"; it takes game as the model for language. Besides expressing an important dimension of the philosophy of man, it also aids in our local purpose of seeking how leisure and recreation, and so games, fit into human existence. We play our games by using things in a particular way; that way of using them is what gives them their meaning in the game. Rope has a variety of possibilities; it only takes on meaning in jump-rope when it is used to jump over, in prizefights when it bounds the ring, etc. A figurine may be a pretty knick-knack, but only becomes a rook when it is so used in a chess game, and then it need not be anything that could be used as a knick-knack at all but only a piece of cardboard distinguishable from others, or even the number and letter used to identify it in email and journal chess. A gesture may be a way to shoo flies, but when it is used in a portrayal of a passionate character on stage then it takes on a meaning. The possibility of use gives the world the possibility of meaning in games; the actuality of being so used gives it that meaning in actuality. At this point it need not be decided whether reality lacks meaning outside of games, for that will depend on whether it ever can be located outside of language; and under the hypothesis we could not know whether it did so, since we could not recognize it without giving it some meaning and the meaning arises in game. However, when it is said that reality has no meaning apart from use, what is meant is that the features of reality have no meaning except to discriminate portions of reality one from another, and that thus discriminated each feature is characterized in terms of what it is not. Its description is not the opposite of the description of what it is not, but says only that it is not something else; for what it is not is, of course, described in terms of it not being the first. The features are not recognizable except as differentiae; under the game hypothesis, as moves in the game.

Given what meaning is and how it is acquired, one and the same, we can consider the circumstances surrounding these events (which of course acquire their meaning in a similar way). When we do not know how to play a game, or what something means nor therefore where it is, what we do is to ask for instruction in the game which often is given in terms of watching the game, or else we may simply watch to begin with as our learning procedure. When formulated rules are given us, then at least our comprehension is determined by whether we can make proper use of them. And even when we play without comparing our activity to a set of rules, although there may be no rules for what we cannot do, there surely are rules for what we do do, distinguishing it from what we do not do; these will, in turn, constitute rules for what we cannot do, unless of course we change them by doing the excluded. The only difference of this from games in the formally constituted sense is that in them this is done in advance, although even there one frequently meets up against alternatives which are neither explicitly permitted nor explicitly denied by the rules, and then one acts one way or another, thereby establishing rules for future moves.

For the novice onlooker, the regularities of the game cannot alone tell him of the rules and thus the meaning; rubbing one's nose before each jump, move or response may or may not be part of the game, even if it is done with regularity by one or some of the players. When given a place, he may find that this is not the way to play, i.e., not the way to continue from where the earlier players left off. This will then be left out of his repertoire. This trial and error is an essential part of the test of learning, but not an essential part of the learning; for one may well introduce all of the correct and none of the extraneous uses into his game, and usually does so for simpler games, as he usually gets most things right even in complex games. The rules and meaning are not equivalent to the regular behavior, but there is little regularity to the behavior apart from them; so while not constituting the rule, regularity is a good sign of it. Of course, to determine what is a regularity, what is done the same, demands a preliminary reference to a relevant context, e.g., that the persons observed are playing a game at all. In turn, this will be determined over against yet further regularities, in turn treated the same way, until one comes full (hermeneutical) circle to systems of meaning which inter-define one another, rather than to independent and ultimate elements on which gradually all purposes are defined.

Purpose begins to separate off as a key factor, but we should beware of this appearance, as it is the start for one of the many ways of easing back imperceptibly into the tit-for-tat, representation-for-reality model. Purpose indeed is important, and it is not equivalent to merely the way in which something is done; many regularities occur purposelessly. But neither is purpose equivalent to the image held in mind of the final product to be achieved; it is not a replacement for something else, not even in advance before the other, the reality, is available. This would be, as said, a covert way to smuggle back in representationalism. Instead, what purpose is, is the using of some sound or object in a particular way; that way consists in the self-awareness, i.e., recognition of cognitive and affective openness, before possibilities dependent on nothing other than oneself.

In this condition it is possible to orient oneself in one direction rather than in another, not simply in view of an object either immediately in contact or grasped though at a distance, but in the recognition that it is sufficiently absent for any surrogate to put in its place, or need to be. People, who are open upon reality, act in terms of contemporaneous absences rather than of future presences. As we move towards what will be a future presence of some terminus to our action, we discover the bounds upon each sort of existence as we try unsuccessfully and blindly to push past them; rebounding from them, we move on within, and by such fits and starts orient our action so that finally the end appears.

The description of language has become a description of human activity, human being and the human world. This is perhaps the best way to take the claim that language is a distinctively human feature, that one cannot understand it without understanding man, and that in turn the exercise of it is the exercise of specifically human existence. In this light, the disclaimer that instead of language having to be understood in terms of game, games have to be understood in terms of language, can be taken up. The disclaimer is correct, and what it disclaims is also correct; different but analogous senses have been put upon game. In the disclaimer, "game" is used to pick out a limited dimension of human activity, something which one does and ceases doing; in the claim, "game" is used to pick out features of the limited domain and to project them in turn upon a screen of existence, and discover that they fit there, too. The games we play are limited; the language we speak is more comprehensive; and the features accessible to us in games and extrapolated to existence are yet more comprehensive, ultimately so, and warrant the name "game" in turn. Games are understood in terms of language, language is understood in terms of the features of game, and these features are concretely present more visibly in game.[100]

Conversation

If partiality is the way of our knowing, then the acquisition of knowledge must consist in the multiplicity of parts being brought together. The viewpoints of one person, his opening onto existence, are inadequate and must be supplemented by the viewpoints of other persons. Rather than just received and assimilated, each viewpoint and the observations from it need to be tested in terms of the other available ones; such is at every stage of knowledge the mode of correction. And as it is rewarding for its own sake there, so also is it rewarding for its own sake here.

What we are speaking of is, of course, socializing and conversation as a kind of leisure. Just being with friends in speech and in silence is worthwhile to us; while with only infrequently met friends one naturally seeks to mediate our relationship through speech, on the other hand with persistently present friends we can find the same sort of reward in their company quite apart from our conversation together. While with those less close there is a testing of our worth in conversation and a judgment made upon this, with close friends the testing goes on as an attempt to open up our common world without any advantage being gained and lost by the participants with respect to each other. Some persons seem to have the ability to relate in this way to everyone they encounter.

Conversation need not be forcefully focused upon a truth set off from our details, not upon the principles underlying some multiplicity. We do not need to get past the small talk in order to test what we have seen. Instead, everything we say contains its principles instead of them lying outside in our serious talk; and the context from which what we say makes sense is not something we know fully well, such that we can tell our companion just what it is that he should attend to in order to know where we are. We are not sure just what gives our knowledge the meaning it has for us, even while having no doubts about its meaningfulness. Anyone interested in more than just getting rid of us will pick up more shortly the key interpretants in our existence than we could hope to select them out for him. The fact of what we do select, in fact, is more illustrative than the content of what we select.

If we move toward the expression of feelings of great importance to us, or of beliefs which involve more of ourselves, the only manner of doing this is to induce the other to help us bring this out. If it is simply volunteered we feel too doubtful of its authenticity as being too much under our control for it to be what we control ourselves towards achieving. We must induce the other to elicit, for his prying would be threatening to us if he came at us strongly on his own. This backing and filling is what takes up most of the conversation time, finding out whether the other is really someone we want to induce to elicit from us what is most important to us.

An attempt can be made to shortcut this and to approach a conversation with the anticipation on the part of everyone that this will be a trusting gathering. Even here, the trust does not begin to generate at first; until it does, there is the ping-pong of trying each other out. With the first revelation a new phase is entered; people know this can be a beginning, since whoever threw himself on the mercy of the group would be ill-advised to harm others in it. The advantage of having a minority in the group who are under great pressure or who are not fully balanced emotionally is that their concerns lie brimming out, because there is no more threat in giving them than in keeping them anymore. The majority of the group can not be such, however, or no support to receive this can be generated but only a set of one-sided outpourings with no concern for what is said by others, i.e., the sort of group which is the antithesis of what was anticipated.

Reading

When we consider reading today, we mean by it something quite different from what it meant through the middle ages when reading was carried out aloud. When now we recreate with leisure-time reading, we are doing an isolated act with materials meant for such an isolated act. Our recreation in fact consists more in the wrapping up of ourselves in the reading than in what is read; the reading matter is just that, fodder that will suffice to carry us off from the burden of carrying around our separate personal responsibility. Whatever will allow this is good reading material, whether we judge it worthwhile on other grounds or not; it is unfortunately true that most people's absorption is not a sure sign of value, while those whose absorption would be a good sign are seldom absorbed but remain astutely critical.[101]

Contest

In contest one pits his own condition against the condition of other persons or things. He appears only in the one way, as a performer in the contest, and his whole being is tied up into that. He is made totally public, since the criteria on which he judges his worth alone are being replaced by ones which others can judge, too. He parts from depth and enters into publicity in contest. This is the source of the pain of separation he experiences upon entering the contest, the roiling stomach, the shaky hands, the feeling of nakedness. It is also the source of the utter contentment which follows completion of the contest; for the winner is confirmed in a way which he could never confirm himself, by reason of having put himself forward for testing against public criteria, and the loser knows that because the contest is over it is not his depth (he is "out of his depth"), which he can never part with, and so the importance of contest is to be judged only relative.[102]

Competition

Competition is in low esteem, as proven not only by the journalistic scuttlebutt of non-sports writers but by such institutions as the former Sports Institute at Esalen Institute, concerned to develop the meditative state of mind and body in the athlete. The cries against the dehumanizing character of competition arise out of the negation below self-identity for the loser and the euphoria beyond self-identity for the winner. Competititon on the field is taken to be the image of competition in the office, market and factory, an imposition of alien standards upon an activity and the manipulation of those standards for personal profit and exploitation.

Contrary to the Esalen approach of accepting this critique from the start and centering in upon the Cinderella sports for training, those in which the sportsman performs alone (but still in view of records abstractly given), we shall look directly at sports admitted to be competitive and try to see just what is involved in them. Two aspects present themselves for consideration, in their relation to human identity: the relation of individual to his team, since all team sports are competitive even though not all competitive sports involve teams; and the relation of individual to opponent, whether team or individual.

"Team" has certainly been a concept abused by its employment for families, whose unity it degrades, and for companies, whose unity it bloats and hyperbolizes. The unity of team is temporary and it is narrow, unlike family; and it is freely created and leisurely, unlike the company. The individual player's action is subordinated to that of the team, even the outstanding heroic action of performers who realize the team's objectives on condition of the rest of the team's submersion. "There's no 'i' in 'team'." Each individual has a role to play, and failure to uphold one's end of the role will affect the success of the whole team. He is free to exercise imagination and creativity only within the confines of his role.

Whether this condition is one which eats at the fiber of personhood is doubtful. It is by no means assured that the solo performer is any more fully a person than the team performer. Vanity is no more sure a road to openness than is servility. But the team player is miscast as servile. He has associated himself freely, and so continues; he frequently has input to the direction of the team; he has a relatively wide range of creativity within his role. It is possible for one to subordinate all his initiative to the team purpose; but that sort of player is of little use to the team, which must be carried by players and cannot afford to carry any of them. Only overextension of team ideology beyond the narrow confines of the sporting purpose, into influence upon other domains of responsibility, is the source of team degeneracy.

On the other hand, it has been urged that competitiveness is unable to be redeemed by any sort of attitudes; it is foreign to human betterment in itself. The claim does not discount the drive to better oneself, but only to do it on the scale of others. It makes for a vicious, unforgiving, cruel person, one who at the very least is uptight, untrusting and always on the lookout for an advantage lest another take advantage of him: any means—cheap, immoral, treasonous—will be apt for the end of success, success defined by the failure of the other in comparison to oneself.

That this is possible is surely undeniable, although the proof by practice in the business world is questionable; few athletes can make it there, few who make it there are athletes, and the overall pussyfooting and servility which makes decision more and more impossible in the business organization and threatens the commercial community bears little resemblance to the stereotypical nineteenth century robber baron, who after all had had little time to be formed on the playing fields. Perhaps military life is a better vehicle; but here again the most vicious recent stars have been born losers who never entered the competition rather than those who entered and either won or lost.

This factual approach, however, is insufficient to design an acceptable structure of principles for competition. To begin, first, it is not possible to surrender the goal of winning; this is integral to the successful performance of the sportsman's play, for doing well will be doing either better or worse than the other. Next, it is not possible to surrender the other, the opponent, if the sport is to be played at all: only against resistance can the perfection of this activity be realized. Working within these parameters, competition would be destructive if it were to orient the activity solely towards its end; in this case, it would be productive and not leisure. To keep the winning as a criterion of perfection, but to maintain the activity as an end in itself, would seem the appropriate way to play sports.

The parameters themselves may be in question: why continue competitive sports at all? Why make winning over another the criterion of perfection at all? Isn't reaching one's own full potential all that is important? While all this may be true, the supposition underlying them is that some human activity is such that self-reference is all that lies in it. This is not true. The confirmation in competitive sport is a confirmation that is objective and cannot be subject to the illusions possible to one's self-knowledge. It has become clear the extent of reliance upon others for fulfillment and even the beginnings of self-knowledge. It would be curious if human activity should at this point in sport change this structure. Competitive sport is the escape from the solipsism that threatens the self-contained athlete.

Volunteer Service to Group

You could not pay them enough. Pay them at all, and they'd stop. Just cover their costs. Whether coaches of all breeds, or helpers to the handicapped, from Habitat for Humanity to Firefighters at Ground Zero, the only way to recruit and keep volunteers is for them not to be paid, but appreciated. What could be more definitional of leisure? The volunteer's service is a secondary objective; while again she would not be active without a worthwhile outcome or aspiration, that is only a condition without which the volunteering would not go on. The condition through which, however, the activity is constituted is its leisureliness. Better here than elsewhere is the essence of leisure shown, not incompatible with stress and panic in execution, nor with competition and strategy to succeed, but reduced to the sheer being-with other persons in their need for you. Payment has been tried; it is why the "gift" of life in U.K.'s blood system thrived, while the pay-for-pints exchange in the U.S.A. collapsed.

Politics

You'd think that politics was nothing but financing dams and trading favors for votes. But we have only ourselves to thank for making politics such a tawdry work-a-day affair of groups' competing self-interests. If we had refused to let people in politics do no more than feed us and protect us, to keep us alive, then our imagination would not be so stilted.

For the character of politics is far different, not to do the things we should be doing for ourselves, but to do the actions we can only do together. Those are not only eating and fighting together, servicing the humanity which already exists, but acting into the future which none of us are yet. We can create this only together, for it is our new grouped selves, not the old self to be reproduced, or the one we figured out how to produce beforehand. Now such prediction is useless, for our very taking consideration together, and how it will occur, makes up the object of our considerations. Whether those be the considerations of school committees or of legislators, of block parents or of judges, makes no difference to its importance as a leisure moment in human being.

PART V
HUMAN SPIRITUALITY

· 1 2 ·

TRANSCENDENCE

By reason of the need to start somewhere, we began with human bodiliness, with the inescapable impression given that this was a distinct figuration cut off from and preliminary to mentality, morality and now sociality. As much as possible, this inescapable impression was fought both within that section by a rhetoric of human bodiliness rather than of body, and in subsequent sections by never departing from bodily dependence and interpenetration. Arriving now at the apparent contrary of bodiliness, human spirituality, a corresponding misconception threatens; it shall be belayed by basing all assertions upon what has already been said, and by using a rhetoric of human spirituality rather than of human spirit or soul. While one may well harbor the notion of spirits as nonbodily but still singularly existent realities as one dimension of the relations relevant to human spirituality, that could never be our condition as humans; so it seems not worth the misconception to work for ease of diction with "spirit" and "soul" as terms.

Whatever our spirituality is, it must be a mode of existence for person to which we are propelled by our body, mind, appetite, action, personhood and community, particularly the last. If community has been essential to the deepening and realization of human personal singularity, spirituality must be essential to deepening of our existence in its bodily and communal dimensions. What hints to us of it is the bodily cosmic relevancy, the intellectual and willful relationship to all reality, the commitment beyond our present in action, the identity of self-containedness and publicness of our person and community. Throughout all of these is the interplay between an increasing differentiation between and distance from one existence to another on the one hand, and an integration all the more fast and binding made possible by this on the other. Human spirituality must, whatever else it is and does, carry out this dynamism, extending it to a limit. Little other meaning for spirituality has ever been proposed; and our alleged spiritual characteristics are introduced as presumed necessary to do this.[103]

Immortality: Nothingness

Extending human temporality to its limits, we broach immortality. A time dependent on space began us, quickly transformed by the biological rhythms. Time measured as a duration of perceived events gave way to the time-chunks determined by our projects and purposes. Memory of the things we have known took on the appearance of a subspecies of the history and tradition of our reality we had never encountered. Our personhood and community appeared as dependent upon the commitments made in free and responsible rule-bound action. Time has become first measured more by, and then even constituted by, our own humanity. At an extremity this would mean that instead of a humanity oppressed by time, we have a humanhood which brings about the time that unceasingly continues as the context of human life. At the apparent cut-off point of human time, then, viz., in death, there is no reason for more than a boundary to be reached, a boundary within humanity rather than one terminating it.

The simplest mode of transcending our ordinary life is to make it go on longer than it appears to. That is, when we appear to die, this is only to appear no more, or among those to whom we have appeared. That is hardly unlikely, for no evidence runs against it, and much runs for it. None against, for not only has this book's audience never experienced its own end of being, it has never experienced anyone else's, either. That sounds insultingly dismissive; but it changes none of our painful experience of death and our grieving at it; all of that continues to have its force and meaning for we who remain.

While much of our grieving is for ourselves, left without the departed, let us assume some at least is for him. Our experience of his dying is profound; it manifests that an event of major importance is happening in his life. That much we know. Why would we infer from that, his "entry" into non-existing, the end of his existing? It may be similar to his going away, and not being seen anymore.

Is our grieving, then, a failure of imagination, at not letting ourselves see past the absence from sight, an adult return to early childhood's incapacity?

That doesn't seem true, because we know of his decay after death with certainty, even if we seldom witness it. Doesn't that prove that the person we knew is not only gone, but no longer exists? The most it could prove is that our deceased cannot exist as fully as he did any longer. His presence was always a bodily one to us, and now we have seen bodily things that can be him no longer. As we have seen already many times, the body he was long ago is not the body he was recently, with not just partial changes but total ones. Nonetheless, now he is no body at all, for the one we saw decay was laid down not with a simultaneous replacement, but with no successor.

Why say that? His body we knew was never the piece of meat and bone we saw decay. He was the animated body, indistinguishable from the passion and fantasy, the viewpoints and thoughtfulness, we saw him live, and that we've seen earlier. We've never seen *that* body decay. Well, neither did we see him do them without it. So with its demise, they demise, and he too. Too fast; all that we can conclude is that he can't do some of them, can't do any as well, and misses whatever he's missing. Never did he do them, while among us, automatically, any more than he did them with thoroughgoing recognition. Just because his total being is crippled now is no reason to conclude the rest is not in existence.

Given the possibility of our continued existence after death, are there any grounds also to infer its necessity? The most striking is the human movement, at all levels, into nothingness. To focus only upon the intellectual level, our least impressive capacity of conceptualization is already so far beyond the things which exist, that it would be impossible if it were only a collection of those. Thinking of the characteristics of a group of individuals provides the opening for innumerable others to be added. It encompasses them just as they are, too; for as with those already in existence, the way in which each holds the common character is unique to it.

This is only heightened when we drive judgment and its native correspondent of choice, beyond the given perception to the wholeness of the being; and reasoning, along with moral commitment, to embrace in advance all the history of the world to come. The conclusions yet to be drawn but already required, the follow-through on commitments made, now have no correspondent in the present, but have already moved us on to live where we do not yet exist.

This is where we already dwell. Non-being propagates in our lives and populates them. And we live it. No surprise, then, to find that here is where we are, still, when we have done our dying away from others' presents. This is one last step, beyond even commitment and conclusion, which brings us into the domain that is proper to us. Immortality culminates what we are, by transcending the different refusals to become it.

Immortality: Fulfillment

That we no longer experience beyond that point those who have passed it is no more of a problem than that we continue believing that our hand continues to exist when it is out of sight, once we have learned past the four-month old stage. Nor does the evident corruption of bodily composition present an insurmountable obstacle, although it surely is a provocative puzzlement. For at every turn thus far we have found bodiliness to take on new dimensions which it lacked in a more partial perspective, dimensions which not only extended the partial but, when we had absolutized that partial condition, appeared to disintegrate it. When this is what we have done with bodily moldering, it is no wonder that the new bodiliness would not only be problematic but scandalous from the old viewpoint. But what is any more scandalous here than the relationship of our incorporated bodies of moral and legal personality, or the two-in-one-flesh body of sexual encounter, to the pedestrian part-outside-of-part bodiliness of primitive materiality?

Death bears with other negativities or undesirables involved in our normal exercise the features of self-recovery. One would not die if he could avoid it, as one would not err if he could avoid it without too high a cost. But just as the faculties lead us toward error, in either a cognitive or affective sense, only because they must be able to do so in order to make trueness in either sense possible, and just as they therefore have the wherewithal to be self-corrective, so dying is an action which is the only way, under given circumstances, to certain accomplishments. Our faculties may well be first brought into play simultaneously with their first misdirection and malfeasance, but continued exercise is both the corrective of the flaw and dependent upon it. It would be foolish to deny that our facultative exercises are fragmented in fact; this is, indeed, what made it even possible for us to structure our study as it has been. But the study of them has shown conclusively that, fragmented in fact, they are not fragmented in principle but rather operate with a drive towards completeness and reintegration.

We operate, then, with our faculties in the drive toward completeness punctuated with corrections of faculties by the same faculties, wrenching themselves around in confusion and vertigo. What is done for a faculty by itself is done for life as a whole by itself. There is a point of completeness whereat further integration cannot be achieved by piecemeal continuance and conversion. At this point, some wrenching of and by the lived existence as a whole, which we call death, can alone mature us further. As at every earlier stage, the movement out is not so much in the light of a fully visible future end stage, but rather in terms of a present structured demand for alteration. This is the mode of presence of the ideal to us, we have seen. Of those who are not ready to take this advantage of death, there can be only the greatest ignorance of what happens. For some who are still being carried by the community, that will suffice. Of others who careen into death in splinters of personhood, only destruction or frustration seems possible.

Together with this dynamism of our powers, is the accompanying movement towards an integration of greater universality and greater singularity. Initially the distinctiveness of objects consists in them lying placidly outside one another, not being able to be merged, in utter contempt of our functioning with them. Any one could be replaced by any other, or then by another of the same kind. As our facultative analysis matured, the movement was towards an individuality residing in differentiation of function, each function harmonized with another; replacement could be made insofar as another individual could fill the same function. Then, as our personhood became one of free commitments and revelations thereof which no other person could make for us, the singularity of our existence became tied to the irreplaceable route, to which our action gives common existence, of access to the structures or rule-binding of existence as a whole. However we do or fail to do, we are indispensable, in the singularity of our accomplishments and thus of our whole being right back to our bodiliness.

The singularity of our persons in a complete way would have to be community in which the being of the common whole is no threat to us but rather an insurance of our personhoods. The tasks it would lay before us would be an unending, knowing and loving penetration of the object which always lies beyond us insofar as it can never be fully brought within grasp and exhausted, although it lies in the closest proximity to us and penetration of us. The object is itself nothing other than knowing and loving community incorporated into one, marked off from us only by the fact that it gives and saves our existence and not vice-versa.

Sacrament and Ritual

Have we nothing to look forward to, then? Is this the best there is, is this all there is? And haven't we lost something? If not, then why do we yearn for it so much? No one wants polyanna reassurances and vapidness to displace the hard and reliable realities of our experience.

It's like yodeling. In touching octaves above his singing voice, the yodeler doesn't strain toward somewhere else, by retracing a tacit scale of some twenty-four tones. He would be completely incapable of singing those pitches. They lie beyond his vocal range. Instead the yodeler simply turns to notes which lie right beside the one's he's singing. It is almost an imaginative change, from climbing a vertical scale to reach what is distant, to turning to what's lying right alongside his pitches. But not only imaginative, for they are there in fact to be executed, whereas they weren't there, for his capacities, in any other way.

Similarly the world we yearn for in leisure transcends our problematic world not by being different and distant from it, but by revealing itself as what it is once we understand this is the way it is, and look for it. "Wishing won't make it so"; but knowing shows it already is.

Leisure: Past Eden? Future Utopia? Present Paradise?

Why seek after a life of leisure that is lost in the distant past: Why strive for one yet to be achieved in a receding future? The very yearning stands in the way of the access, for the character of desire is always the absence of what is desired. In order for leisure to be available at all, it must be available at all times in the present, right now. (See Appendix II.)

And that is what our studies have led us to see that it is. Human wholeness is implicit, folded into every exercise that we glimpse at first in a partial way. Human fulfillment is bound into every achievement, once the role for struggle and competition is glimpsed aright. This is not an abandonment to our attitudes, letting it be alright if we feel alright; for what has appeared is the complete objectivity of our attitudes. The world can only appear concerned for and cooperative with us because it exists that way.

NOTES

1. Linda Duxbury, Chris Higgins, *The 2001 National Work-Life Conflict Study* (Ottawa: Health Canada, 2002).

2. Thomas Anderson, "Technology and the Decline of Leisure," *American Catholic Philosophical Quarterly* 70 (Supp, 1996) 1.

3. Vintila Mihailescu, "Signification of the Anthropology of Play as 'Method'," *Philosophie et Logique* 26 (1982) 57.

4. Gilbert Boss, "Jeu et philosophie," *Revue de Metaphysique et de Morale* 84 (1979) 93; Charles Stephen Byrun, "Philosophy as Play," *Man and World* 8 (1975) 315; R. T. Allen, "Leisure: The Purpose of Life and the Nature of Philosophy," in *The Philosophy of Leisure*, ed. Tom Winnifrith, Cyril Barrett (New York: St. Martine's Press, 1989), 20.

5. See on conflicting totalities my "Problematic of Violence: Theological, Philosophical, Economic," *Religious Humanism* 9 (1975) 150.

6. Socrates, at least, is represented as living out his maxim, "I am wise because know that I do not know."

7. Frederick F. Fost, "Playful Illusion: The Making of Worlds in Advaita Vedanta," *Philosophy East and West* 48 (1999), 3; L. Stafford Betty, "Aurobindo's Concept of Lila and the Problem of Evil," *International Philosophical Quarterly* 16 (1976), 315; Charles Hartshorne, "Theism in Asian and Western Thought," *Philosophy East and West* 28 (1978), 401.

8. "Time is a child at play, moving pawns; the royalty of a child." (Heraclitus, Fragment 52) The literature on this view in modern philosophy is extensive. OVERVIEW. W. Ritzel, "Review of *Der Begriff des Spiels* . . .," *Kantstudien* 59 (1968) 487; J.L. Esposito, "Play and Possibility," *Philosophy Today* 18 (1974) 137.

 SCHILLER AND HEGEL. Eva Schaper, "Towards the Aesthetic: A Journey with Friedrich Schiller," *British Journal of Aesthetics* 25 (1985), 153; H. Pauly, "Aesthetic Decadence Today Viewed in the Light of Schiller's Three Impulses [Play, Art, Life]," *Journal of Aesthetics and Art Criticism* 31 (1972–3), 365; V. A. Howard, "Schiller: A Letter on Aesthetic Education to a Later Age," *Journal of Aesthetic Education* 20 (1986), 8; Y. Blanchard, "Travail et téléologie chez Hegel chez Lukacs," *Dialogue* 9 (1970) 168.

 NIETZSCHE. L.M. Hinman, "Nietzsche's Philosophy of Play," *Philosophy Today* 18 (1974) 106; S. Byrun, "Concept of Child's Play in Nietzsche," *Kinesis* 6 (1974) 125. André-Jean Voelke,

"La métaphore heraclitenne du jeu dans les premiers écrits de Nietzsche," *Diotima* 17 (1989), 91. Richard Perkins, "The Genius and the Better Player: Superman and the Elements of Play," *International Studies in Philosophy* 15 (1983), 13; Manfred Kerkhoff, "Juego y Reuino del Nino (Nietzsche y Heraclito)," *Dialogos* 17 (1982), 17.

MARX. G.A. Cohen, "Marx's Dialectic of Labor," *Philosophy and Public Affairs* 3 (1974) 235; H. Marcuse, "Philosophical Foundations of the Concept of Labor" (1933), *Telos* (1973), 2; Ruth Kinna, "William Morris: Art, Work, Leisure [Marx], "*Journal of the History of Ideas* 61 (2000), 483.

SARTRE AND EXISTENTIALISM. R. Netzky, "Playful Freedom: Sartre's Ontology Reappraised," *Philosophy Today* 18 (1974) 125; H. Slusher, *Man, Sport and Existence* (Lea and Febiger, 1967); Linda Bell, "Loser Wins: Play in a Sartrean Ethics of Authenticity," in *Phenomenology in a Pluralistic Context*, ed. William McBride (Albany: SUNY, 1983), 5, and her *Sartre's Ethics of Authenticity* (Tuscaloosa: U. Alabama Press, 1989); Antonio Gutierrez-Pozo, "Metafora e ironia, claves de la razon vital" [Ortega], *Daimon* 20 (2000), 107–123; Randolph Feezell, "Play and the Absurd," [Camus] *Philosophy Today* 28 (1984), 319; Brian Rigby, "French Intellectuals and Leisure: The Case of Emmanuel Mounier," in *The Philosophy of Leisure*, ed. Tom Winnifrith (New York: St. Martin's Press, 1989), 160.

HEIDEGGER AND GADAMER. J.D. Caputo, "Being, Ground and Play in Heidegger," *Man and World* 1 (1970) 26. Jerald Wallulis, *The Hermeneutics of Life History* [Gadamer] (Illinois: Northwestern U.P. 1990); Alexander Aichele, "Gadamers platonistische Aesthetik: Kunst und Spiel in 'Wahrheit und Methode' ," *Prima Philosophia* 12 (1999), 3–18; Hans-Georg Gadamer et al., *The Relevance of the Beautiful and Other Essays*, tr. Nicholas Walker (Cambridge U.P., 1986); Richard Detsch, "A Non-Subjectivist Concept of Play—Gadamer and Heidegger versus Rilke and Nietzsche," *Philosophy Today* 29 (1985). Jeff Mitscherling, "Hegelian Elements in Gadamer's Notions of Application and Play," *Man and World* 25 (1992), 61.

PHENOMENOLOGICAL AND HERMENEUTICAL. E. Fink, "Oasis of Happiness: Toward an Ontology of Play," *Philosophy Today* 18 (1974) 147, and in *Game, Play and Literature*, ed. Ehrmann (Beacon, 1969); D.E. Krell, "Toward an Ontology of Play: Eugen Fink's Notion of Spiel," *Research in Phenomenology* 2 (1972) 63; Serge Meitinger, "Eugen Fink: du jeu et de l'origine ou le prime-saut," in *Eugen Fink: actes du Colloque de Cerisy-la-Salle 23–30 juillet*, ed. Natalie Depraz (Amsterdam: Rodopi, 1997); Kostas Axelos, "Planetary Interlude," in *Game, Play and Literature* (*Yale French Studies* 41 (1969) 6); K. Axelos, "Play of the Whole of Wholes" [in Czech], Filosoficky Casopis (1990), 605, concerning his *Horizons du monde* (Paris: Editions de Minuit, 1974); James S. Hans, "Hermeneutics, Play, Deconstruction," *Philosophy Today* 24 (1980) 299.

PRAGMATIST. J. Feibleman, "The Leisurely Attitude" [in C.S. Pierce], *Humanitas* 7 (1972: *The Leisurely Attitude*) 279; Michael L. Raposa, "Art, Religion and Musement," *Journal of Aesthetics and Art Criticism* 42 (1984) 427.

Ambivalent about a Continental tradition generally, see: Drew A. Hyland, *The Question of Play* (Lanham MD: University Press of America, 1984), and his " 'And That is the Best Part of Us': Human Being and Play," *Journal of the Philosophy of Sport* 4 (1977), 36. Also Wesley E. Cooper, "The Metaphysics of Leisure," *Philosophy in Context* 19 (1989), 59.

9. "We are unleisurely in order to have leisure." (N.E. X, 1176b) The most widely used aristoteleanism in this context is: S. DeGrazia, *Of Time, Work and Leisure* (1964), e.g. as applied by his "Political Pliancy and the Loss of Leisure in Universities," in *Education and Values*, ed.

Douglas Sloan (New York: Teachers College Press, 1980), 147. A Maslowian version of the same is: J. Farina, "Toward a Philosophy of Leisure," *Convergences* 2 (1969) 14. Several of the Thomistic views, infra, have been embarrassed by their Aristotelean base: Mihai I. Spariosu, *God of Many Names: Play, Poetry, and Power in Hellenic Thought from Homer to Aristotle* (Durham: Duke U.P., 1991); Joseph Owens, "Aristotle on Leisure," *Canadian Journal of Philosophy* 16 (1981) 713. See appendix 1.

10. "Man has been constructed as a companion in play for god, and this is the finest thing about him; thus every man and woman ought to pass through life in this role: playing at the finest and noblest of plays—to the complete inversion of current understanding." (*Laws* VII, 803) See: G. Ardley, "The Role of Play in the Philosophy of Plato," *Philosophy* 42 (1967) 226; J.F. O'Leary, "*Schole* and Plato's Work Ethic," *Journal of Leisure Research* 5 (1973) 46; Harold Alderman et al., "The Ballard Retrospective," *Southern Journal of Philosophy* 19 (1981) 293; Bernard Freydberg, *The Play of the Platonic Dialogues* (New York: Lang, 1997). This is the attitude also of S. Kierkegaard, especially in his *Concept of Irony*; see V. Sechi, "Art, Language, Creativity and Kierkegaard," *Humanitas* 5 (1969: *Personality and Play*) 81.

11. "Be at leisure and know that I am God." (Psalm 65: 11) "Wisdom is always at play, playing through the whole world." (Proverbs 8: 30) See: G. Soell et al., "Sport in Theological Perspective," *The Scientific View of Sport* (Munich, 1972); T.F. Green, *Work, Leisure and the American Schools* (Random House, 1968); R. Lee, *Religion and Leisure in America* (Abingdon, 1961), and his "From Holydays to Holidays," *National Forum* 62 (1982), 29. More thomistic is Josef Pieper's *Leisure : The Basis of Culture*, tr. Gerald Malsbary (Mentor, 1952); Roger Scruton's introduction to the re-edition commemorating the fiftieth anniversary of the work's first appearance in Germany includes a retrospective of past reviews since the first English edition in 1952 (South Bend IN: St Augustine's Press, 1998). Also: M.D. Chenu, *Theology of Work* (Regnery, 1963); Y. Simon, *Work, Culture and Society* (Fordham, 1971); H. Rahner, *Man at Play* (Herder, 1972); R. Burke, "Work and Play,"*Ethics* 82 (1971–2) 33; J. Lacroix, "The Concept of Work," *Cross Currents* 4 (1954) 230; F. Wilhelmsen, "Work and Leisure," *Triumph* (1969) 11; J.U. Lewis, "Leisure, Wonder and Awe: An Introduction of Joseph Pieper," *Philosophy Today* 17 (1973) 197.

12. This creative activity is not the utter mystery it seemed when it made its appearance in revealed tradition; it is resolved, but only in another revealed mystery, that of trinity. The creative activity in which God makes world existence is exemplified in the internal activity of God, wherein Father generates Son as his self-knowledge and the wafting of their boundless love institutes Spirit. Acquaintance with trinity is God known primarily in redemptive activity, since the incarnation by which salvation is executed is also the crown of creation, showing that creative activity is for the sake of joining into love with God. The explosive activity interior to trinity is glimpsed not only in some six days of easy-going creation but in thirty years and three hours of agonized redemption, the contact with existence and the center of existence which constitutes leisure wherein it is reinterpreted. Nothing is lost but new dimensions are exposed. This summarizes some of the views in the next note.

13. Several recently competing conceptions of leisure are catalogued by J.F. Murphy as the outline for his anthology of *Concepts of Leisure: Philosophical Implications* (Prentice-Hall, 1974), and by M. Kaplan. in the second chapter of his study on *Leisure: Theory and Policy* (John Wiley, 1975; 2d ed. Madison NJ: Fairleigh Dickinson U.P., 1991), prior to each developing a further model purported to subsume the others.

230   PHILOSOPHY OF MAN AT RECREATION AND LEISURE

14. A. Portmann, *Animal Forms and Patterns: A Study of the Appearance of Animals* (Faber, 1952), initiates this penetration by pointing to the indistinguishability of inner organs, as against the varieties of external appearance coordinated with behavior.

15. Louis Marin, *Utopics: Spatial Play*, tr. Robert A. Vollrath (Atlantic Highlands NJ: Humanities Press, 1984).

16. R. Bruce Kelsey, "The Actor's Representation: Gesture Play, and Language," *Philosophy and Literature* 8 (1984) 67.

17. H.S. Slusher highlights surfing differently in *Man, Sport and Existence* (Lea and Febiger, 1967), p. 179, as a human engagement in nothingness. See Bell supra for Sartre's version.

18. Robert J. Paddick, "What Makes Physical Activity Physical?" *Journal of the Philosophy of Sport* 11 (1975) 12.

19. Abel B. Franco, "Duration and Motion in a (Cartesian) World which is Created Anew 'At Each Moment' by an Immutable and Free God," *Critica* 33 (2001) 19.

20. Compare DeGrazia, op.cit, ch. VIII, and Green, op.cit., ch.3. Also: Maurice Roche, "Lived Time, Leisure and Retirement," in *The Philosophy of Leisure*, ed. Winnifrith, 54.; Sean Sayers, "Work, Leisure and Human Needs," ibid., 34.

21. W.M.Brody, "The Clock Manifesto," *Interdisciplinary Perspectives on Time*, p. 895.

22. S.B. Linder, *The Harried Leisure Class* (Columbia, 1970), reversing T. Veblen's classical *Theory of the Leisure Class*. See "Luxury" next chapter.

23. In "The Biological Fabric of Time," in *Interdisciplinary Perspectives of Time* (*Annals N.Y. Academy of Science* 38, Feb. 1967), 440 at p. 443, Roland Fischer reproduces Descartes' "exponential life spiral of time," scaling lived time as a continuity of increasingly rapid adaptive events, viz., of evolution, of learning, of perception, and of hallucination and dreaming.

24. This is not to deny that in order to assume this non-problematic stance the problems that have been raised may not need therapy, as is effectively given by J.N. Deeley and R.J. Nogar in *The Problem of Evolution: A Study of the Philosophical Repercussions of Evolutionary Science* (Appleton-Century-Crofts, 1973).

25. M. Montessori treads the sensitive line between functionalism and play in children, as in L.M. Savary, *Man: His World and His Work* (Paulist, 1967) 53. Also: Nancy J. Nersessian, "Child's Play," *Philosophy of Science* 63 (1996), 542; Jan van Gils, "Children Playing and Children Doing Philosophy: Why are They Both So Interesting?," *Thinking* 12 (1995), 2.

26. See J.N. Hattiangadi, "Mind and the Origin of Language;" *Philosophy Forum* 11 (1973) 81; also L. Hockett, "The Origin of Speech," *Scientific American* (Sept., 1960: *The Human Species*) 89.

27. H.F.Blum, "The Concepts of Energy and Entropy in Biology" in *Interdisciplinary Perspectives of Time*, p. 894, cautions against relating too closely the expenditure in entropy and the replenishment of energy, since the concepts are not used at the same level, one at a molecular or submicroscopic level and the other at the molar or experiential level. So at the level of our lived experience we must consider our bodily energy as replenishable and continuation of our bodily existence as normal. At this level we are not out of step with the universe; all appears stablized, and not enslaved to galloping disintegration under the inexorable second law of thermodynamics. We are not dissuaded from efforts toward better order, toward a "negentropy" of increasing energy. Also: Ruth Caspar, "A Time to Work, A Time to Play," *Listening* 16 (1981), 18.

28. H. Arendt, The Human Condition (Chicago, 1958), ch. 33. Also: Jay S. Shivers, *Leisure and Recreation Concepts: A Critical Analysis* (Boston: Allyn and Bacon 1981.

29. See, in *Work and Leisure: A Contemporary Social Problem* (College and University Press, 1963), ed. E.O. Smigel: Dubin, "Central Life Interests of Industrial Workers"; Orzack, "Central Life Interests of Professionals."

30. See H. Jonas, *The Phenomenon of Life: Toward a Philosophical Biology* (Harper and Row, 1966), Third Essay, Section VIII.

31. See: H. Johnstone, "Toward a Philosophy of Sleep," *Philosophy and Phenomenological Research* 34 (1973) 73; and F.J.J. Buytendijk, *Prolegomena to an Anthropological Physiology* (Duquesne, 1974), Part B on "Exemplary Modes of Being Man" (Being-Awake, -Asleep, -Tired, -Hungry, -Thirsty, -Labile, -Emotional).

32. See H. Arendt, *The Human Condition* (Chicago, 1958) Part III and passim, for the powerful insights which govern any discussion of the issue; also the approximation and summary in T.F .Green, *Work, Leisure and the American Schools* (Random House, 1968), and W.E. May, "*Animal laborans* and *Homo faber*," *Thomist* 36 (1972) 626.

33. C. Reich, "The Greening of America," *The New Yorker* (Sept. 1970); H.Marcuse, *Eros and Civilization: A Philosophical Inquiry into Freud* (Beacon, 1955); H. Fingarette, "All Play and No Work," *Humanitas* 5 (1969, no.1: *Personality and Play*) 5.

34. Contrast, on Veblen, Frank L. Fennell, "So Runs the World Away: Playtime in Modern America," *Listening* 16 (1981) 5; and John Patrick Duiggins, *Thorstein Velen: Theorist of the Leisure Class* (Princeton U.P., 1999)

35. See the debate among: J. Zernan, "Organized Labor v. 'The Revolt Against Work' ," *Telos* 21 (1974) 194; D. Looman, "Unorganized History and Organized Labor: A Reply to Zernan," *Telos* 22 (1975) 165; J. Alt, "Work, Culture and Crisis: A Reply to Zernan and Looman," *Telos* 22 (1975) 168. Contrast: Francis Hearn, "Toward a Critical Theory of Play," *Telos* 30 (1977) 145.

36. See F.Perroux, *Economie et société: Contrainte-échange-don* (P.U.F., 1963).

37. On our self-regulatory systems, see Buytendijk, op. cit., Part C; and also the works of M. Merleau-Ponty, especially *The Structure of Behavior*.

38. Israel Scheffler, "Reference and Play," *Journal of Aesthetics and Art Criticism* 50 (1992), 211; John Fizer, "Reflection on the 'Arche, Hyle' and the Existential Mode of the Work of Poetic Creation," *Dialectics and Humanism* 5 (1978) 13.

39. P. Weiss, *Sport: A Philosophic Inquiry* (Southern Illinois University, 1969), p.73: "[G]ymnastics can be counted as a sport, while exercise and calisthenics cannot. They merely get men into good shape; sport extends a man into the world about to make him a larger, more effective man." This "extensional" sense of equipment complementing our "horizonal" sense above is the bulk of the suggestions throughout M. McLuhan, *Understanding Media: The Extensions of Man* (McGraw-Hill, 1964). Also: Paul Grimley Kuntz, "Paul Weiss: What is a Philosophy of Sports?" *Philosophy Today* 20 (1976) 170; Randolph M. Feezell, "Sport: Pursuit of Bodily Excellence of Play, An Examination of Paul Weiss' Account of Sport," *Modern Schoolman* 58 (1981) 257.

40. The idealist and the existentialist positions are developed, respectively, by P Weiss, op.cit., ch. 1 and 15, and by H. Slusher, op.cit., ch. 5. David L. Roochnik, "Play and Sport," *Journal of the Philosophy of Sport* 11 (1975) 36, contributes to this discussion.

41. A theological perspective would add that praeternatural gifts of instantaneous locomotion, of unpained endurance in contact with matter, and of unimpeded alertness and communication are perfections which belong(ed) to us, but which we do not have and which can only be pursued for the future.

42. See D.Wrong, "The Meaning of Work in Western Culture," *Humanitas* 7 (1971, No. 2: *Work and Human Development*) 215.

43. H. Jonas, op.cit., Essay Four: "To Move and To Feel: On the Animal Soul," notes that this is why no spatiality is perceived between the irritant and the living body.

44. Buytendijk, op.cit., Part C again.

45. This triadic relationship of sense—A holding B for C—is analogy of improper proportionality; it ceded to the four-place relationship of intellect—A:B::C:D—called analogy of proper proportionality.

46. This is what is meant by defining human being as "tool-making" rather than just "tool-using"; for the design and not the use is all that requires a purpose conceptualized in advance rather than a trial-and-error fall into the manipulation.

47. More at length, see D.G. Gordon, *The New Literacy* (Toronto, 1971), ch.2.

48. Much of this study is indebted to the insights of: H .Jonas, *The Phenomenon of Life* (Harper and Row, 1966), esp. his Sixth Essay on "The Nobility of Sight"; D .Idhe, *Sense and Sensation* (Duquesne, 1973); M. McLuhan and H. Parker, *Through the Vanishing Point* (Harper and Row, 1968); and J. Macmurray, *The Self As Agent* (Faber, 1966), ch. 5, on "The Perception of the Other."

49. If we had experience only of hearing it would be possible to design some concepts but not others; of course, this is not literally true for we would not recognize the concepts unless we had something to set them over against.

50. The irony of this emphasis in some students of mass media is that this "tribalization" is accomplished by electronic circuitry—which is of course not the audial medium but a visual one, despite contrary characteristics in visual experience.

51. H. Jonas' conclusion here that "mind has gone where vision has pointed" suggests that if this is true it is terribly incomplete and that it may not even be true, in the light of the whole other alternative which hearing yields us. The study of touch is undertaken here, as by Jonas, to heal our wholeness between these.

52. Steven Barbone, "Schlick on Aesthetics," *Indian Philosophical Quarterly* 24 (1997), 105; Wang Zhaowen, *Art Appreciation as Recreation in Contemporary Chinese Aesthetics* (New York: Lang, 1995); Timothy M. B. O'Callaghan, "Sensibility and Recreational Appreciation," *Journal of Aesthetic Education* 22 (1988) 25.

53. Since A. Montagu, *Touching: The Human Significance of the Skin* (Columbia, 1971).

54. This still remains a sensory need, however. This is exemplified by the Balinese response when questioned on their art, as recited several times in M. McLuhan and H. Parker's *Through the Vanishing Point*: "We do all things as well as we can. It is not that they have no art, but that art has subsumed daily need."

55. This is the leisure structure on Maslowian model of J. Farina, "Toward a Philosophy of Leisure," *Converences* 2 (1964) 14.

56. See I. Shaw, "The Girls in Their Summer Dresses," *The New Yorker* (1939).

57. A curiosity of the Montreal transit system are signs from the company encouraging social contact among passengers, but doing so because "The buses belong to you" in a public system, as though that were the condition for contact occurring.

58. Steven Galt Crowell, "Sport as Spectacle and as Play: Nietzschean Reflections," *International Studies in Philosophy* 30 (1998), 109; S. K. Wertz, "Beauty in Play: Aesthetics for Athletes," *Southwest Philosophical Studies* 2 (1977) 77.

59. E.g., a suggestion for remedying the deficiencies of film over drama: C. Koch, "Cinema, Discours, Evenement," *Revue d'esthetique* 26 (1973) 173.

60. Marvin Henberg, "Wilderness as Playground," *Environmental Ethics* 6 (1984) 251

61. J. Kuehl, "Imagining and Perceiving," *Philosophy and Phenomenological Research* 31 (1971–72) 212 at p. 223.

62. D. Idhe, "Auditory Imagination" in his *Sense and Significance* (Duquesne, 1973).

63. M.-D. Phillippe, "*Phantasia* in the Philosophy of Aristotle," *Thomist* 35(1971) 1.

64. J. Piaget and Binhelder insist in *L'image mentale chez l'enfant* (P.U.F., 1966) that image is an imitation of perception, not its residue. Shifting in perception is from incompleteness, in imagination from the license given by demands for action. Similarly, perceptual *schemes* allow generalization by selection of common features from a series of events, while imaginative *schemata* are active purposes allowing any presentation of schemes at all. Imagination introduces new operations over perception, and any similarities stem from common sensorimotor sources (pp. 1, 30-1, 440).

65. Larry W. Smolucha, Francine C. Smolucha, "Creativity as a Maturation of Symbolic Play," *Journal of Aesthetic Education* 18 (1984) 113; Janusz Kuczynski, "Play as Negation and Creation of the World," *Dialectics and Humanism* 11 (1984), 137; Josef Fruchtl, "Playful Self Control" [Czech], *Filosoficky Casopis* 43 (1995), 828.

66. Pierre Laszlo, "Playing with Molecular Models," *Hyle* 6 (2000), 85; Jose-Luis Suarez-Rodriquez, "El juego de la logica," *Dialogo Filosofico* 9 (1993), 385; Mihai I. Spariosu, *Dionysius Reborn: Play and the Aesthetic Dimension in Modern Philosophical and Scientific Discourse* (Ithaca NY: Cornell U.P., 1989). More formally, Edward F. McClennen, "Some Formal Problems with the Von Neumann and Morgenstern Theory of Two-Person, Zero-Sum Games, I: The Direct Proof," *Theory and Decision* 7 (1976) 1.

67. *Commentarium in Boethii de Trinitate*, V and VI, translated and edited by A.Maurer as The Division and Method of the Sciences (Toronto: Pontifical Institute of Medieval Studies, 1953).

68. The response more apt in metaphysics than in anthropology is that an individual's existence is not the same as its essence; and since the former can only be reached by judgment, as much act as is existence, then the attempt to do anything short of judgment and to end with something more static must end up with essence.

69. Anthony J. Celano, "Play and the Theory of Basic Human Goods," *American Philosophical Quarterly* (1991), 137.

70. See E. Husserl, *Formal and Transcendental Logic*, "Introduction"; and J. Habermas, *Knowledge and Interest.*; and E.Gettier's famous negative answer to Plato's question, "Is Justified True Belief Knowledge?" *Analysis* 23 (1963).

71. L. Wittgenstein, *On Certainty*.

72. The breadth of the concept of "rule" is surveyed in: D.S. Shwayder, *The Stratification of Behaviour* (1965), 233–280; M. Black, "Notes on the Meaning of Rule', *Theoria* 195 107–12; Bernard Suits, "Tricky Triad: Games, Play, and Sports" *Journal of the Philosophy of Sport* 15 (1988) 1, replying to Klaus V. Meier, "Triad Trickery: Playing with Sport and Games," ibid., 11; M. W. Rowe, "The Definition of Game," *Philosophy* 67 (1992), 467; Bernard Suits, "Appendix I Words on Play," *Journal of the Philosophy of Sport* 4 (1977) 117; Johan VanBenthem, "Computation Versus Play as a Paradigm for Cognition," *Acta Philosophica Fennica* 49 (1990) 236; Philip Lawton, "Sport and the American Spirit : Michael Novak's Theology of Culture, " *Philosophy Today* 20 (1976), 196. Few take the point of view developed below.

73. J.Milnor "Games against Nature" in *Decision Processes*, ed. R. Thrall (1954), offers some alternative remedies to game theory.

74. Wu Kuang-Ming, "On Playing With Arguments," *Southwest Philosophical Studies* 7 (1982) 58.

75. Robert I. Williams, "Play and the Concept of Farce," *Philosophy and Literature* 12 (1988) 58.

76. Kingsley Price, "On Education as a Species of Play," *Educational Theory* 27 (1977) 253, with Ignacio L. Gotz, "Response to Price's 'On Education as a Species of Play'," Ibid. 28 (1978) 241; Ignacio L. Gotz, "Play in the Classroom: Blessing or Curse?" *Educational Forum* (Wisc.) 41 (1977) 329; Sebastian DeGrazia, "Political Pliancy and the Loss of Leisure in Universities," in *Education and Values*, ed. Douglas Sloan (New York: Teachers College Press, 1980), 147.

77. Kathy and Phil Lewis make their English translation (Beacon, 1955) from Jacques Ehrmann's French translation of Huizinga's Dutch original (1938); the Lewises point up some illustrative conceptual variations between these at p. 34.

78. Free Press, 1961.

79. Beacon Press, 1969.

80. This seems also to answer J. Farina's Maslowian Aristoteleanism in "Toward a Philosophy of Leisure," *Convergences* 2 (1969), 14.

81. An extended application of these three authors' conclusions that the word "mere" cannot be attached to the word "play" is made by K. Blake in *Play, Games and Sport in The Literary Works of Lewis* Carroll (Cornell, 1974), with excellent summaries of the psychotherapeutic, literary and stochastic theories of play. But despite her agreement with them and her critique of E. Sewell for separating play and seriousness, Blake illustrates the difficulty of being consistent in the thesis, when she follows the Reverend in judging that " 'live' is just 'evil' spelled backward" (*Sylvia and Bruno Concluded*, II, pp.11–12). As she says: "There are two dangers in play. One is that it is purely self-motivated and self-gratifying, unrelated to extrinsic claims, which cuts it off from the stablizing laws of work and duty. The other is that is it selfish, as eating is, as a matter of pleasure in exerting one's own power, and can often, naturally enough, turn destructive" (p. 210), as a balance of opposites, not a reintegration.

82. The debate is continued in terms set by Huizinga: Rupprecht Dull, "Das Spiel mit der Freiheit im Spiel," *Conceptus* 30 (1997), 199; R. Scott Kretchmar, " 'Qualitative Distinctions' in Play," in *Die Aktualitat der Sportphilosophie*, ed. Gunter Gebauer (Sankt Augustin: Academia, 1993); John Darling, "Is Play Serious?" *Journal of Philosophy of Education* 17 (1983); Paul G. Kuntz, "Serious Play: An Absurdity or a Paradox that Integrates Life?" *Listening* 16 (1981) 68; Richard J. Burke, "Taking Play Seriously," Ibid. 56; Robert Anchor, "History and Play: Johan Huizinga and his Critics," *History and Theory* 17 (1978) 63.

83. Maria Lugones, "Playfulness, 'World'-Travelling, and Loving Perception," *Hypatia* 2 (1987) 3.

84. As the transactional analysis of Eric Berne's *Games People Play* (New York: Grove Press, 1964) moves *Beyond Games and Scripts* (Grove, 1976) in Ian Stewart's "View from 2001," concluding his *Eric Berne* (London: Sage, 1992).

85. John Neulinger, "The Right to Leisure," *National Forum* 62 (1982) 28.

86. Nathan Rotenstreich, *Reflection and Action* (Boston: Nijhoff, 1985).

87. David Aspin, "Ethical Aspects of Sport and Games, and Physical Education," *Proceedings of the Philosophy of Education Society of Great Britain* 9 (1975), 49; Christina M. Bellon, "At Play in the State of Nature: Assessing Social Contract Theory Through Role Play," *Teaching Philosophy* 24 (2001), 315; Rudolph M. Feezell, "Play, Freedom and Sport," *Philosophy Today* 25 (1981), 166.

88. Lesley Wright, "The Distinction Between Play and Intrinsically Worthwhile Activities," *Journal of Philosophy of Education* 19 (1985), 65.

89. Wittgenstein was turned from his early theory of language and led to include it only within a broader perspective by having a colleague ask him how well that early theory could be whistled.

90. Eliot Deutsch, "Causality and Creativity," *International Philosophcial Quarterly* 18 (1978) 19.

91. Robert Rimmer, "The Play Ethic," *Free Inquiry* 3 (1983) 11; Evan Simpson, "Life As Work," *Listening* 16 (1981) 31; Mark Okrent, "Work, Play and Technology," *Philosophical Forum* (Boston) 10 (1979) 321; Lawrence M. Hinman, "On Work and Play: Overcoming a Dichotomy," *Man and World* 8 (1975) 327; Pieter DuToit, "World, Leisure and a Meaningful Life," in *Life, World and Meaning*, ed. A. P. Roux (Pretoria: University of South Africa, 1990); Elizabeth Telfer, "Leisure," in *Moral Philosophy and Contemporary Problems*, ed J.D.G. Evans (Cambridge U.P., 1987), 151, and "Leisure," *Philosophy* 22 (1987) 151.

92. See R. A. Cohen, "The Privilege of Reason and Play," *Tijdschrift voor Filosofie* 45 (1983) 242; and H. Johnstone, "Toward a Philosophy of Sleep," *Philosophy and Phenomenological Research* 34 (1973) 73.

93. Karen Hanson, *The Self Imagined: Philosophical Reflections on the Social Character of Psyche* (New York: Routledge and Kegan Paul, 1987).

94. This is why H. Jonas calls the ability to hold a whole before us a general faculty of "vision" analogous to the special faculty of sight.

95. "Being an attendant" involves respect, as do several forms of attending: noticing, caring, being interested. See A.R.White, "Attention," in his *The Philosophy of Mind* (Random House, 1967).

96. This is U.T.Place's "restated disposition theory" of attention at p. 220 of his "The Concept of Heed" (1954) in *Essays in Philosophical Psychology*, ed.Gustafson (Doubleday, 1964). Place then (p. 221) aligns this with the obtaining and the holding of the object of human consciousness as the object of attention. Consciousness, in turn, is his key feature in the traditional concept of self. See also G.E. Myers, *Self* (Pegasus, 1969).

97. It has been noted, however, that for example the classification "mestiso" makes the person either "brown" or "white" depending as the person is poor or rich.

98. Mary-Lou Grad, "Play as an Ethical Paradigm for Sexual Intercourse," *in Essays in Morality and Ethics*, ed. James Gaffney (New York: Paulist Press, 1980), 162.

99. Marc Bekoff, "The Evolution of Animal Play, Emotions, and Social Morality: On Science, Theology, Spirituality, Personhood, and Love," *Zygon* 36 (2001), 615.

100. Christopher Cherry, "Games and the World," *Philosophy* 51 (1976) 57; and "Games and Language," *Mind* 84 (1975) 528.

101. Martin Davies, "Another Way of Being: Leisure and the Possibility of Privacy on [Rilke's 'Der Leser']," in *The Philosophy of Leisure*, ed. Winnifrith, 104; Graeme Hunter, "Can You Read? Philosophical Reflections on Labour, Leisure and Literacy," *Eidos* 10 (1991) 47: Maria-Rosa Palazon-M., "La literature como juego," *Analogia filosofica* 11 (1997), 109.

102. James W. Keating, *Competition and Playful Activities* (Washington DC: University Press of America, 1979); Nicholas Dixon, "Open Sportsmanship and 'Running Up the Score' ," *Journal of the Philosophy of Sport* 19 (1992) 1; Tom Winnifrith, "Playing the Game: Morality versus Leisure," in *The Philosophy of Leisure*, ed. Tom Winnifrith (New York: St. Martin's Press, 1989), 149; Simon Eassom, "Sport as Moral Educator: Reason and Habit on the School Playing Field," ibid., 129.

103. Transcendent dimensions are suggested by: Ruth Caspar, "Play Springs Eternal," *New Scholasticism* 52 (1978) 187, and "The 'Neglected Argument' Revisited: From C. S. Pierce to Peter Berger," *Thomist* 44 (1980) 94; Richard M. Zaner, "Sport and the Moral Order," *Journal of the Philosophy of Sport*," 6 (1979) 7; Edmond Radar, "A Geneology: Play, Folklore, and Art," *Diogenes* (1978) 78.

· A P P E N D I X 1 ·

PAIDEIA, SCHOLE, PAIDIA
THEN AND NOW

Paideia, the citizen's education, is extensively tied up with liberal studies in most of Aristotle's discussion in book eight of the *Politics*. But this tie-up intellectualizes the leisure at their root in the first few chapters of the book.

While my undergraduates in leisure studies always need to be drawn up from their sole focus upon sport, perhaps my philosophy colleagues need relief to de-intellectualize *paideia* back down to *schole*. There are dimensions of Aristotle's comments which are remedial to contemporary streams of leisure theory. This appendix will recapitulate his comments, then apply them to three types of contemporary theory.

His first chapter justifies the reason why politics is not meddling when it takes an interest in the formation of its citizens. This is because any constitution will not be workable unless citizens' characters, their virtues, are compatible with it.

His second chapter opens what should be taught. Without doubt, useful things should be taught. But not all useful things: useful things which "vulgarize" the citizen should not. To vulgarize is to make one less fit for the practice of virtue, the city's concern. Any occupation, art or science can vulgarize. An occupation will, if it is paid employment; that degrades the mind by absorbing it. An art will, if it deforms the body; the Spartans did that, by their excruciating and savage routines. And a science will, if it is pursued to its perfection of detail.

Our bywords about workaholic compulsives, steroid stars, and nerdy scholars, show that we experience the three instances he speaks of, even if paradoxes appear that do not trouble him. Why learn anything at all that is useful, if we can't earn a living at it? How is it virtuous to be never the master but ever a dabbler? Is it not inherent in science to drive us to its ultimate details, one way toward its principles and another toward its applications?

These three are more localized problems, however, than his fourth limitation on useful education. That the very same activity is first excluded from the teachable useful, and then is re-included merely by a change in its object, touches our Aristotle with an anachronistic subjectivity, whereby the subject constitutes whatever identity the object has. Excluded if done for others, a study is included if done for one's self, friends or virtue. Perhaps this can best be grasped as the learner's selection of the latter's ends from among the complex of goals which attach objectively to a learnable study.

What follows comes naturally to our modern eye. "If he's excluded all employments, then of course all that left to talk about is leisure." To his eye, however, this is because leisure is the principle of all other activities.[1] Leisure is central not as the residue from busyness but as its purpose and thus its meaning. Leisure is core to both the non-useful and the useful learning in *paideia*, even in the contracted "useful" which is properly taught.

Play is not excluded from leisure studies, as the four vulgarities are from useful studies; but care is taken not to equate them. Usually translated amusement, his *paidia* is closer to what we call recreation. That is, this activity is not the purpose of life, but instead contributes to something that is not our purpose. Work or toil is debilitating; no one would do it for its own sake. If anything, work is done for leisure. And, in turn, recreation is done in view of work, since it restores one from-and-for work. Unwinding is what gives pleasure; we all experience that.

Leisure, on the other hand, involves pleasure with reference to nothing else. Pleasure comes from leisure's being already at its end, in both modern senses: leisure has no goal but itself; and it drives forward to nothing else. It is a state, not a process, in our speech; it is practice, not production; governed by prudence, not by art, in his speech. It is hard to keep from identifying it with happiness, instead of simply associating them as he does.

It is equally hard to keep from affirming that studies at leisure consist of music, in the comprehensive Hellenic sense or the commonplace one Aristotle discusses through the end of the *Politics*. But this has not kept philosophers, psychologists and sociologists from coopting leisure to the practice of their own discipline as its heart, or at least its sole adequate statement.

Contemporary leisure theories range from completely objectifying leisure to completely subjectifying it, neither of which was among the errors available to a pre-Cartesian philosopher. At the objective end is the so-called "classical" theory of leisure, most famous in Pieper and DeGrazia, and updated by Green.[2] To rest in whatever is eternal is the fulness of leisure. Short of God-given mysticism, leisure becomes speculative philosophy. Other activities share leisureliness to the degree they approximate philosophy.

Dispensing with gravitation around deity and the eternal, its more Eleatic tack is made by Fink in the wake of Husserl, Heidegger, Gadamer, and by Rorty in Pierce's and Dewey's, not far from the death-wager in Suit's version of Aesop's story of grasshopper and ant.[3] Leisure is the comprehensive category of life because it is the world which plays us, not vice-versa. The lifeworld of Fink and the conversation of Rorty are bounded, but by nothing, and so not necessitated by the whole, which the part can never appropriate and confirm.

What is noticeable is that Aristotle, for all his emphasis elsewhere upon undying reality and for all his invocation as the patron of the "classical" view, never ties up leisure to pure act, to the spheres which imitate it, or to our reproduction which strives for them. One hint of his unwillingness to philosophize leisure, is his indecision whether the happy life is the speculative or the political, or whether happiness—so close to leisure in its pleasures, as has been seen—relates to the changeless or the changing. At the very least, whatever need he saw for eternity was satisfied in his *Ethics* by the autotelism of doing rather than of making, with no need to invoke the virtue of scientific necessity in order to purchase enough footing for leisure.

The temporal category dear to the classical theory is "diurnal" time. This is the time of large and recurring natural units, to avoid frantic disintegration of actions into the separate fragments which things have, especially machines, more especially clocks. Its eternity drives Pieper and DeGrazia; the unavailability of this value to us today drives Green to jettison classical leisure from the paideia he'd have liked to set up.

Even without it, the following is available. The merit of Huizinga's work, contemporary to Pieper's and unmarginalized by its apt criticisms in Callois' and Ehrmann's developments,[4] is to locate in play the features which provide sufficient local eternity to satisfy the needs of classical leisure theory. Playtime is distinguished from other times. It is set apart, and its temporal units have meaning only from the inside; the sets of tennis, the innings of baseball, have nothing to do with the passage of minutes and seconds. Even the timed periods of other major sports are bent by timeouts, incompletions, delays, penalties defined in their rules and nowhere else. The rules themselves, the costuming, the venues, the identifying of players and non-players hive off a world that is self-contained. Its experience is not so much the one of derivative pleasure for which Aristotle rejected paidia or play, as it is the completeness of the event. Classical leisure can be as fully realized in these pedestrian and democratic forms of sports, of games, and of narratives, as in the exacting and excluding forms of speculative philosophy.

A second contemporary theory of leisure takes and turns this objective formation into its opposite. Csikszentmihalyi and colleagues affect the social psychologists' factual objectivity while driven by the critical theorists' moral imperatives.[5] Less the self-containment of Huizinga's play than its rule-boundedness, is what these theorists take up. They locate experiences similar to reports of "discovering something new," "exploring a strange place," or "solving a problem." These activities have no external payoffs, but people pursue them anyway. The activities are "autotelic," they contain their own goals. Thus far their objectivity.

In parsing out what makes these activities autotelic, he finds that there is a definite sense of control within them. The activities are ones whose challenges are suited to the participant's capabilities, whose procedures are not ambiguous but are spelled out in rules, and whose feedback is clear and quick enough for the participant to know how well he has succeeded. These make up "flow" experiences. Joining in these activities brings satisfaction, which he distinguishes from pleasure; pleasure is attached to fulfilling basic needs, to consumption, to consumer substitutes for autotelic activities.

Each person has one's own level of capability; and so the opportunities which each decides to challenge those skills against, and the rules upon which feedback will occur, differ for each. That is to say, it is not the activities which are autotelic, but the agents. They seek each his own idiosyncratic end. No comprehensive norms stand by to check the uprightness of this leisure. Only its being autotelic is its norm; and that is different for each.

Csicszentmihalyi tries to save his doctrine from this psychological subjectivity by stressing that social construction of reality is always at work. But this sits as mere moralizing atop what is fundamentally a scientific solipsism. Small matter that, verbally, Csiczentmihalyi opposes flow experience to leisure; this is only because of his taking leisure in the sense of consumer activity, freetime from work, time free to use up for one's own pleasures.

Has Aristotle anything to help out with here? First, it is clear that what is autotelic for him is the activity, not the agent. Leisure is what is an end in itself; the agent does not seek differently than leisure or the state of happiness for his end.

Next, pleasure is not simply set apart from the satisfaction of leisure; pleasure accompanies it, although pleasure is not its goal (if ever it can be a goal).
The pleasure is a sign that taking leisure is as natural as consuming for the political animal. For leisure he need construct no abstruse post-kantian satisfaction
uncorrupted by pleasure.

Finally, "the pleasure of the best person is the best, and comes from the best
sources" (1138a9). Does this reduce the subjectivity of satisfactions, or reinforce
it? The best person is the most virtuous; virtues are attuned by mediating the circumstances each person meets, "the right thing at the right time;" the circumstances each meets and their meaning which each mediates are peculiar to
each one's culture and society; so being the best man is relative to these local
meanings. Does this only replace individual relativity with social relativity? That
will be discussed next; but, here, the point is that it appears do at least that.

A third contemporary refererence point upon leisure philosophy is the communitarian.[6] While not as visibly represented in leisure monographs, it coordinates leisure studies to the eighties' political philosophy of communitarianism,
and its cultural precipitate in political correctness.[7]

The communitarian insight is that people's relationships form their identity equally as much as do their individualities. At an extreme, relation completely forms their reality. The liberal error was to think that relata precede
relations; the communitarian corrective error is to say that relations precede
relata. While the former makes it impossible to ascribe significance to relations,
communitarian thought makes it difficult to describe how any new relations
could ever be formed, much less how a person could form them by himself.

The application of communitarian philosophy to leisure emerges in the insistence that any leisurely activity be in the service of community. Therapeutic
recreation, adaptive sports, remedial reading, interventionist travel, music-studio-
drama therapy: these become the sole upright manners to perform leisure; for
"when one is [deprived], all are [deprived]," using the form but not the content
of rights theory. Leisure is set toward an extrinsic end, the betterment of others; but in the communitarian framework, this is not external since the others
are identified with me.

The moral claustrophobia this imposes upon the *eleutheros* who is Aristotle's
man-at-leisure can be remedied by returning to the "best man" once again, to
finish the description of his pleasures. It is not only in view of the virtues peculiar to one's own society that someone's pleasures are best; for that society itself
may be judged as only more or as less a reservoir of virtue. Aristotle, in fact,
never ceases judging his and others' societies severely; nor is his judgment

nothing but ethnocentric, although it is surely that, too. For the virtues he demands are not those which perfect being Hellene, but which perfect being human. In his eye, Hellenic society (often) succeeds best at that; but other societies are contemptible not because they are not human, but because they fail humans. Their societies have degraded, "vulgarized," some feature or another of what it is to be human—body, or mind; courage, or articulateness, etc.

The paragon of leisure is connected; but he is also autotelic. This person is articulate, but in play as well as in science, craft, work and politics. This paragon, therefore, is not beyond the reach of any person. While the details of the paideia towards it remain to be fleshed out, as they did for Aristotle, nonetheless preserving these insights from one revealer of our humanness should block a few of the blind alleys in designing the paideia for leisure.

Notes

1   This takes, with all translators, the *auté* of 1337b33 to refer to *scholazein*, not the more plausible *mousiké* or *phusis*; as the reference at 1338a11 to *scholé*, not the more likely *hédoné*.

2   See Josef Pieper, *Leisure; The Basis of Culture* (New York NY: Random House, 1970); and Thomas F Green, *Work, Leisure and the American Schools* (New York NY: Random House, 1970).

3   By Bernard Suits, *The Grasshopper: Games, Life and Utopia* (University of Toronto, 1978).

4   See discussion in text at Ch. 7, section "Play and Seriousness," of Johann Huizinga, *Homo Ludens; A Study of the Play Element in Culture*. (Boston: Beacon, 1950).

5   See Mikail Csikszentmihalyi, *Beyond Boredom and Anxiety; The Experience of Play in Work and Games* (San Francisco CA: Jossey Bass, 1975); and, with Robert Kubey, in *Television and the Quality of Life; How Viewing Shapes Everyday Experience* (Lawrence KS: Erlbaum, 1990).

6   One such discussion is by Sheila Mason and Randy B. Swedburg in "Education for Leisure: Moving Toward Community," Denver CO, Second International Symposium on Leisure and Ethics, 11 Apr. 1994.

7   Correspondences could be perceived, if one wished, between intellectualist or metaphysical leisure, and the resurgent liberalism of the forties; between freetime leisure, and the scientistic economism in service to the industrial ethos of the fifties; between "flow" leisure, and the sixties' and seventies' refusal of consumerism by the negativities in critical theory. In the libertarian nineties, thinking about leisure-through-downsizing was made invisible by such devices as Canada's renaming unemployment insurance as "employment insurance."

· A P P E N D I X   2 ·

IMMORTAL PHILOSOPHY: WHAT DOES A PHILOSOPHER DO FOREVER AFTER?

Immortality puts a radical spin onto the future of philosophy. It would have been enough, to query how to keep doing philosophy for the next few years, after 'boomers retire from teaching it, cybersurveillance sets controls on its scope, and nursing homes replace universities as its preferred venue. But the unending future is far more challenging, for a philosopher who considers himself immortal.

Can we continue doing philosophy forever? Do we even want to? Should we want to? Or, on the contrary, can philosophy give an answer to what it asks, and then stop? Or stop without that? Would we find its eternal recurrence revolting, and should we consider its continuance only a bad habit, an addiction that death will help us to break?

Problematic

A nihilist approach is to assume that philosophy's questions are ill-posed, unanswerable, and so cannot be halted, the only question being how to stop doing philosophy. A humanist way is to consider its questions well-posed, but answerable only because each answer is humanity's growth to a level of spirit where one poses it anew about that level.

The only way to say the questions are not only well-posed and answerable, but are also everlasting, is to move outside both perspectives. For Aristotle, to keep wonder going even when its questions are answered (983a18) requires entities which can be contemplated (1072b24); these call to human history from outside, not inside it. Archimedes' impossible fulcrum is required. But the believer in Christian immortality says there is a fulcrum: the entry of God by revelation as incarnation, as genesis and as judgment.

Repositioning the future of philosophy by asking "Is there philosophy in heaven?" does not disqualify the question as non-philosophical. First the question attaches to the real features of a real human institution, philosophy. Next, it sets this over against a plausible state of human being, one which is not self-contradictory but is complementary to human nature.

Further, the question is not irrelevant to the current practice of philosophy. Let us postulate counterfactually that philosophy is a practice in which we believers just pretend that we don't know the answers, when we really do; we hobble our revealed knowledge for the sake of talking with *goyim* and *hoi poloi*. If that were so, the best that could be said of philosophy is that it is a charitable act. But if philosophy has more enduring worth than a public relations exercise, then both its current practice and its everlasting practice benefit each other, by giving an advanced footing to spring off from when the time is ripe.

Lastly, there are secular counterparts wherein similar problematic questions about philosophy need to be put: what place if any is there for philosophy in an achieved "classless society," in the "society of explorers," in the "community of discourse"?

The problematic common to these "heavens," too, is that the deficiencies of mankind which elicit philosophy are remedied there. Whether they are deficiencies, whether they are what elicit philosophy, and whether they are remedied remains to be determined. Leaving believers in those other apocalypses to handle their own business, the content of revealed heaven involves three principal features: the beatific vision; the glorified body; and the new heaven and earth.[1] These relate to the ongoing philosophical objects—God, man, and world—about each of which the ongoing philosophical inquiries are posed: What can we know? What ought we do? What may we hope?

The beatific vision is loosely identified with "seeing God as he is." That it is not a cognitive event in contrast to an appetitive one is shown by its involving the remaining "supernatural" virtue of love, or unbreakable attachment to divine community. Next, the glorified or resurrected body, besides having divine adoption, is laden with the "praeternatural" gifts, now restored, of impassibility, inerrancy and incorruptibility, that is, freedom from harm, error and sin. About the new heaven and new earth, finally, no dominant tradition exists, their characterization ranging from our very own planet but restored as a city of God; through the different material environment of planetary and anti-matter speculations; to some non-material home, despite a hard time making that consistent with glorified bodiliness.

Into this universe, philosophy must be set. The beatific vision asks after the place of foundational epistemology and ontology there, while the glorified body and earth allow scope for speculative questions on the faculties of human being for philosophy, and for practical questions on the place of normative philosophy.

Tasks of Philosophy: Truth

Founding

What is it that the beatific vision presents? The loose description earlier, "to know God as he is," is inadequate since that remains impossible to any but God; on the other hand, he is already known as he is, namely as love through revelation, and with attributes or "names" through the dialectic of the threefold way. Instead, the enhanced knowledge of God must have to do with recognizing the source of meaning and truth. Whether God is taken as exemplar of essences which reflect him platonically, or peripatetically as goal for the final causes of particular things, still knowing God is to know better what things are. It seems that we cannot, then, be wrong about them since we know what they really are, because we know the foundation for our knowledge of them.

But are foundations for our knowing what we it is that we are looking for in philosophy anyway? Perhaps modern philosophy did, since when facing universal doubt no knowledge or truth seemed possible without incorrigible foundations. But our pre- and post-modern philosophical question is how the truth indisputably present in our judgments is present when it is, and how it can be absent. It is not the usual answer to say that God enlightens us; and so an even more penetrating beatific enlightenment is beside the point, so far as we mean to bring philosophy to its culmination.

Overall, the explanation for the truth in singular judgments is not provided by identifying another singular different from the one judged, even an eminently singular God. Explanation must not only be located, but must be connected. Fine, that God is source and exemplar of the beings we know. But that does not explain why we know them, rather than knowing him; for really knowing him while thinking we know them would be a recipe not for truth, but for fundamental error. The "third man" problem is not relieved by making it into a "third God" problem.

The only explanation for truth that is satisfactory has to emerge from the characterization of the knower and the known. Knowing something different from either of them is no help. In seeking why a proposition is true, we are looking for principles, not for more entities. Knowing better an entity which is "principle" only in the originating sense and not in the constitutive sense, does not supply anything about the knower or the known. This branch of the problem of truth is posed by the facts that, while thinking we know, we can remain in error; but that is not ignorance. If we were ignorant and blocked, the addition of another third entity to burst the bottleneck might be just what we needed; but that is not the problem, and so this is not the solution.

Appearing

Otherwise, the structure of truth would change. As things are now, we are in truth when realities appear to us. Not only is there real entity, and we who know it; but there is also its appearing to us. What we know is reality; and we know it appearing. Reality appears; in knowing it appearing, we know reality. It is a reality with potential for many sets of appearances; in knowing any one set, we do not know the reality fully, but neither do we know the reality we do know any the less, or less truly. Reality is hidden, but not in the sense of being obscured by appearances, but rather in the sense of not being exhausted by them at any one time. Reality reveals itself, but not all at once. If reality and appearances coincided, this would mean that there was no further potentiality to show itself, that this present appearance exhausted it, and so annihilated it. Its reality would become pure appearance, no longer appearance of anything.

So knowing reality as hidden is no more a deficiency of ourselves than the hiddenness was an alienation of reality from appearances; instead it is the very structure of being. This is a hiddenness which beatific vision does not alter.

Judging

No vision of the divine source of reality alters it even if the failure of appearance to exhaust the reality lies on the side of the knower, not only the known. And if one source of error is our precipitate finalizing of some appearances as all that this reality is, no release from this error is to be found in beatific vision, either. The remedy remains the philosophical one it always did, of recognizing this structure of being, followed by the scientific remedy of connecting its appearances more fully.

This precipatation, however, is not the sole block to truth In addition to character faults, are character differences. Perspectives upon reality which one person may take up, may be unavailable to another. It is possible to delay judgment of reality until the knower has taken up some of the other perspectives upon the known as they open up for him. But no amount of delay will open for him the other knower's perspective. No more than bodiliness—standing as a way to check truth rather than as an impedance to it—does individual character stand in the way. For not only our self-interest and indulgence, the unhappiness and defensiveness, the revenge and insolence lie open to remedy; so also does our most rooted "idol," the inclination to seek more truth and coherence than is available. This is cured by the clear sense of finitude, of knowing you are only human.

Of that, socratic discipline gives no less evidence than does heavenly experience. Under socratic discipline, no one will answer when he has no answer; no one will cease looking, either, when lacking an answer, since both responses imply he knows it all. Its professional analogue is to make philosophy the be-all of truth. But while avoiding error in this way, he will still not have truth, the truth of others' perspectives. And, again, beatific vision is no remedy for this; only philosophy begins to be.

Means of Philosophy: Reason

Let us move from the tasks of philosophy to its methods. Whatever else philosophy purports to be, it is rational. It is one exercise of rationality, an exercise of discursive reason. While not alone in this, philosophy is a movement from the known to the unknown, to making the unknown known. This is its pattern whether by deduction of conclusions from principles, or by the movement back and forth of reflective equilibrium, or by generating hypotheses with which to check the inconsistencies of a grand vision. Knowledge does not rest in vision alone. This is partly because not everything is known. And that does not change under conditions of beatific vision. If God is not everything, because he created it different from him, then we do not know everything in knowing him. We remain capable of knowing everything, in the sense either of universality, or of our knowing ahead into nothingness; but we were already capable of that, even if we did not know him, although only because he created this.

Another reason for the persistence of discursive reason, including philosophy, is that evidence for truth is needed. Why evidence, when we know truth? Isn't evidence or proof simply a second best until we know simply? The presumption in that claim is that direct vision or presence, intuitive knowing, is immune to falsity. If intuition is not merely a synonym for truth—and it cannot be because intuition is no more incessantly active than is discursive knowing, but is also intermittent—then truth is a feature which perfects intuitive knowing just as it does rational knowing. Perhaps intuition cannot be false; but even if it cannot—and who will say it cannot, without some reason?—its truth must be shown, since the vision itself does not show that.

A third aspect of this issue occurs from considering whether rational, discursive, mediate knowledge has any value in itself, rather than a merely instrumental value for knowing truth, such that it can be dismissed once reality is known truly. No truth except truths of fact can be known without the details; we must define them, compare and contrast them. This is all part of their proof. The proof, then, is inseparable from the conclusion it proves. A different mode of proof may well have proven a different truth.

Overall, knowledge is one value, and regards realities; truth is a different value, and regards knowledge. The knowledge of one reality, and the certain truth of that knowledge, ensures no truth in the knowledge of other realities; only rationality allows its transfer. Just as the perceptual knowledge of material singulars—the closest we come to intuitive knowledge, despite its theory-laden character—may be true but needs to have its truth confirmed by rational investigation, so does intuitive knowledge of spiritual singulars. Even if our knowledge is told to us by spiritual beings, still (with all due respect) what do they know? Of spiritual reality, their intuition too needs proof; and of material reality, we humans are the authorities.

If this is the status of philosophical knowing in heaven, then it cannot be assimilated into some other form of discursive knowing. Science and art, leaving aside any discussion of their own heavenly provenance, may seem capable of doing the work of philosophy if all doubts about truth have been resolved. If there is no problem with truth, any knowing may seem to be concerned only with matters of fact, especially when our ability to go-and-look is no longer hampered; or the only remaining concern may seem to be one of style or expression, rather than of truth. But each of these alternatives has been eliminated by the restoration of philosophy to concern with matters of principle, which neither science nor art pretends to do.

Works of Philosophy: Speculative

Existence

Even for a philosophy of existence in which God is subsistent act, it is not his own *esse* which acts as the copula of true propositions, nor animates the essence of singular beings. They must be known in their own right, then as now, the presence of subsistent actuality only adding confidence. The categories of being, the aprioriciities of knowing and the predicables of saying, all remain to be discerned, justified and used as they do in our present ontologies.

And so do the reasons for doing ontology. We do not do it now to earn either our heavenly or our daily bread, *pace* Philo and Foucault. We do not perform metaphysics either to defend our weak psyches or to whistle away our fears of the cold world, *pace* Lucretius and Lazerowitz. We do them now for the joy of coming alongside the house of being; and we will do it then when no tests and no threats remain, when we truly live where existence dwells.

Bodiliness

What work there is for philosophical reflection on space and time surely remains, for its objects of study do. Glorified body is not one whose basic bodiliness is eliminated. Having part outside of part is the feature of a being which does not have each of the moments in its existence identified with every other, with its whole, and vice-versa. But the manner in which human beings relate to one another—which is everywhere taken as the entitling condition for heavenly residence—is intrinsically bodily. Standing sole as each one species is not our mode of being; we stand singular within one species, which involves us in relationships of respect for each being's singular integrity, as well as being joined together by that respect. In this relation, bodily spatiality is not dispensable, but is both the link and the separation of persons, as well as their sign. This demands the reflection of philosophy no less than it presently does.

Temporality

The temporality of human being remains, also, in a heavenly state. Personal time as a measure of change still has place in a life devoted to growth in love and knowledge of its inexhaustible object. And a future anticipated as the possibility of growth has as its counterpart a history recalled as the source of merit. Deeds and their effects are not forgotten but, in fact, are manifested in the present reality of their bearers. While only the visions in hagiography confirm this for now, it is fitting for a matured person not to show its beauty only by hiding its scars on some callow portrait in the attic.

Freedom

The maturing of choice into unchanging commitment provides the source of new reflection on what human freedom is. The standard line is that achieving freedom of determination (freedom-for) is not the loss but the fulfilment of freedom of choice (freedom-to), which is only the means to the former. The particulars of this as well as the novel quandries for space and perception, time and history await the experience of the events. The reason for presently seeking clarity persists, however: not simply the curiosity about what we fail to understand, but the absence of any greater evidence than we now already have.

Works of Philosophy: Normative

If character is fixed in its drive toward good, even if not fixed in some single terminal stage of growth, this might seem to dismiss the whole range of normative philosophy. More straightforwardly, if everyone is good, what need is there for ethics or for jurisprudence? The question implies that normative disciplines are concerned with choosing between good and evil, a concern that is absent once the possibility to choose evil is gone.

Ethics

But this is the case, even now. We may still be confused about what is evil, even if not inclined to it once identified. And we may be unclear about the many different goods on which we must act, their priority, timeliness and proportion, even if we are directly relating to the source of good. But this is part of the work of ethics even in our current state; some would say that is its only role, giving ethics no role at all in distinguishing right from wrong. But at least that is a role which persists.

Jurisprudence

Even more is this true for social choice, in jurisprudence. The need to select *which* good way to act remains, even when there is no occasion for ensuring that good is chosen and rewarded, not evil. Once again, most of even current law is concerned with these matters. Criminalizing wrongful acts or *mala in se* takes up but a small portion of the criminal law, itself but a morsel of public law alongside administrative and constitutional law. Public law in turn is minute compared to the innumerable decisions under civil law on how to do which of the many possible good things.

Why have to decide these things at all? Because we will still be social beings, indeed perfectly so, and will be acting together; we will not be acting in a demographic totality of singular relations each toward God alone. As well, rather than paralysis by interactions of mutual deference—"after you, Buridan!"—or a submersion of the timid as in our current decision processes, action then will be fully confident and assertive, whatever its objects. It will require procedures for breaking honest disagreements about the good to follow. While attributions of malice, venality or cowardice will be out of place, that does not solve the disagreement. While it would be delicate to speak of a democratic "rule of law," it would be equally blithe to speak of an authoritative "kingship" over decisions, despite the pastoral, feudal and mercantile images in which tradition has been spoken. Normative philosophy appears to be no more out of place in heaven than does speculative philosophy.

Of course, one might conclude from this that, if heaven is the most advantageous milieu for performing philosophy, then we'd best wait, and not waste time now on its frustrating exercises. But the opposite is the conclusion to be drawn: If a valid exercise then, a fortiori now; for the research then, however endless, can begin better advanced on the basis of work done now

But whether that is the right scenario or not, this study of philosophy's long-term future is not idle and sectarian speculation, for it has impact on how and even whether we bother giving philosophy any short- and mid-term future. Occupational prudence requires that we describe this paper to our colleagues as only a "jeu d'esprit." Still, the study need not blush before other contemporary heuristics—Turing machines and Nozick transformers, Pareto superiorities and Parfit transporters—from which extensive, dour and respected philosophical sobrieties have been educed. It even has an advantage that they do not: that at least some sensible people think it is not impossible, is not an empty fantasy; that it is likely, even inevitable to traverse; and that at least some already have gone there.

Note

[1] This is set out in the context of Roman Catholic belief. It varies; even among Western revealed religions, Islam has a dramatically different metaphysical basis for characterizing heaven due to the dominance of *sha* over even *shari'a*; Judaism retains the splits in characterizing heaven that separated the saducean and pharisaic parties in its 37th century; and some Christian views vary widely, others not at all.